(34) £5.50

CW01635389

HAWICK & DISTRICT

From Old Photographs

ALASTAIR M. REDPATH

AMBERLEY

This book is dedicated to everyone who helped to make it a reality, with particular gratitude to my long-suffering partner Jaime-Lynn Moffat.

Front Cover
Sculptor William F. Beattie addresses dignitaries and a crowd of several thousand people, as the 1514 Memorial is unveiled on 4 June 1914.

Back Cover
Arguably Hawick's most architecturally splendid street, North Bridge Street as it looked in 1907.

First published 2015

Amberley Publishing
The Hill, Stroud
Gloucestershire, GL5 4EP

www.amberley-books.com

British Library Cataloguing in Publication Data.

A catalogue record for this book is available from the British Library.

ISBN 978 1 4456 4752 4 (print)
ISBN 978 1 4456 4753 1 (ebook)

Typesetting and Origination by Amberley Publishing.
Printed in the UK.

Introduction

Hawick is a town of great natural beauty set within the Border region of Scotland. Nestled among rolling hills sculpted by the last great ice age, it sits at the confluence of the River Teviot and Slitrig Water. The undulating terrain has over time given up its secrets, revealing a cluster of ancient hill forts and scattered Roman connections. The Romans created an advance post at Trimontium, near Melrose, and a signal station on nearby Ruberslaw, but never ventured beyond a temporary camp at Eastcote, two miles east of the town. It is widely believed that the current settlement was founded in the twelfth century, when the Anglo-Norman Lovel family was granted lands by King David I. Their primary residence came to be at Castle Cary in Somerset, but they established a 'motte and bailey' castle in Hawick – a fortification with a palisaded wooden keep on a raised earthwork, surrounded by an enclosed courtyard, protective ditch and a small settlement of houses and farm buildings. Indeed, a popular theory as to the origin of the name 'Hawick' is that it derives from the Old English words '*haga*' – enclosure and '*wic*' – dwelling. The Chronicle of Melrose later details the dedication of the Church of the Holy Mary in 1214, from which St Mary's kirk can claim an 800 year lineage today.

The medieval village was often overshadowed by its near neighbours, great Border Abbey towns like Melrose, until a royal charter created Hawick a Burgh of Barony in 1511. This allowed the settlement to grow and hold weekly markets. The Town Charter of 1537, afforded by Sir James Douglas (7th Baron of Hawick), noted that the settlement had grown in size, comprising 110 houses, a manor house, church and mill. These rights were confirmed in another royal charter of 1540 (by the infant Mary, Queen of Scots), with the Burgh's municipal privileges surviving relatively intact until the eighteenth century.

A period of great unrest followed in the time of the Stewart kings in Scotland and the Tudor dynasty in England. Situated in the heart of the 'debatable lands', Hawick often paid a heavy price during the time of the Border Reivers, being razed to the ground on more than one occasion. The ranks of the reivers consisted of both Scottish and English families, and they raided the entire border country without regard to their victims' nationality, paying heed only to their own skewed codes of honour. Numerous stone fortifications were built to protect the surrounding land and its people, including Drumlanrig's Tower – the vaulted portion of which is the town's oldest building. Hawick's cultural epoch can arguably be traced back to 1514, when the settlement's young men or 'Callants' were called to arms to defeat a marauding band of English invaders. The Battle of Hornshole is today celebrated through the annual Hawick Common Riding, which, combined with the ancient tradition of 'riding the marches', adds to the town's unique and rich heritage.

The size and shape of Hawick did not change radically until the Industrial Revolution, when the town was at the forefront of a boom period of growth and innovation. The four gates or 'ports' were closed at night to prevent the spread of disease and protect the town from invasion. North Port (at Walter's Wynd), East Port (opposite Baker Street), South Port (at Cross Wynd) and the West Port (at the foot of the Loan) clearly marked the limited extent of the town, with very little building beyond the High Street, Howegate and Sandbed. It was only in the 1750s, following the Turnpike Road Act, that these gates were removed and the land beyond the town was opened for expansion.

Stocking frames were introduced by local magistrate John Hardie in 1771, while many ideas and practices were adopted to develop a burgeoning knitwear industry. This eventually became the backbone of the local economy and attracted many immigrant workers from across Britain and Ireland. From a population of just 2,798 in 1801, Hawick grew to become a large town of over 19,500 people by 1891. A merger with the neighbouring Wilton Parish in 1861, long an independent settlement in its own right, also contributed to this growth. The period 1850–1900 brought with it large-scale building projects. From textile mills to roads, bridges, schools, hospitals, churches and sports grounds – Hawick expanded to almost double in size. A railway to Edinburgh (1849) and Carlisle (1862) further connected the town to the outside world. It was during this time that most of Hawick's cultural and sporting institutions were also established.

The twentieth century brought with it a new training ground for the British Army at Stobs and the continued growth of the local knitwear industry. Indeed, for many years Hawick was a byword for high fashion. Many locals answered the call in both World Wars, though over a thousand did not return home. These brave men and women are remembered through a multitude of fine war memorials and a roll of honour at Wilton Lodge Museum. During the 1950s Hawick experienced another period of rapid expansion, with new housing schemes at Burnfoot, Silverbuthall and Stirches. In 1969, the town was deprived of a key transport link with the closure of the Waverley Route, effects of which are still being felt today. Though a period of decline came in the 1980s and 1990s, with the loss of hundreds of jobs from the town's traditional employers, the new decade has brought much optimism for the future of Hawick. An important milestone in the town's history was marked in 2014, the 500th anniversary of the Battle of Hornshole and the Quincentenary Common Riding.

For a place of its size, Hawick has been home to an extraordinary wealth of talented photographers. From the earliest photographs of Hawick in the late 1850s, up to the current digital age, the 'grey auld toon' has been the subject of many fine snapshots – each capturing a unique moment in local history. This book aims to provide an insight into the past by uncovering history through old photographs. Though not intended as an all-encompassing encyclopaedia, it is hoped this title can provide new knowledge and evoke memories for the reader.

Alastair M. Redpath

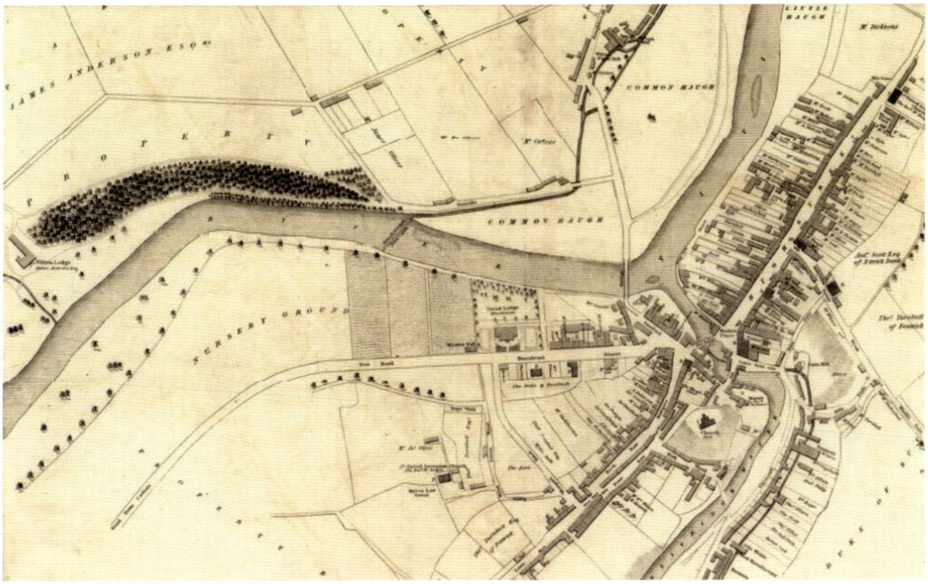

1824 Survey of Hawick

John Wood's survey of Hawick in 1824 provides the reader with an idea of the town's layout, prior to the Industrial Revolution and the age of photography. He noted that 'Hawick and its environs are the admiration of every stranger'.

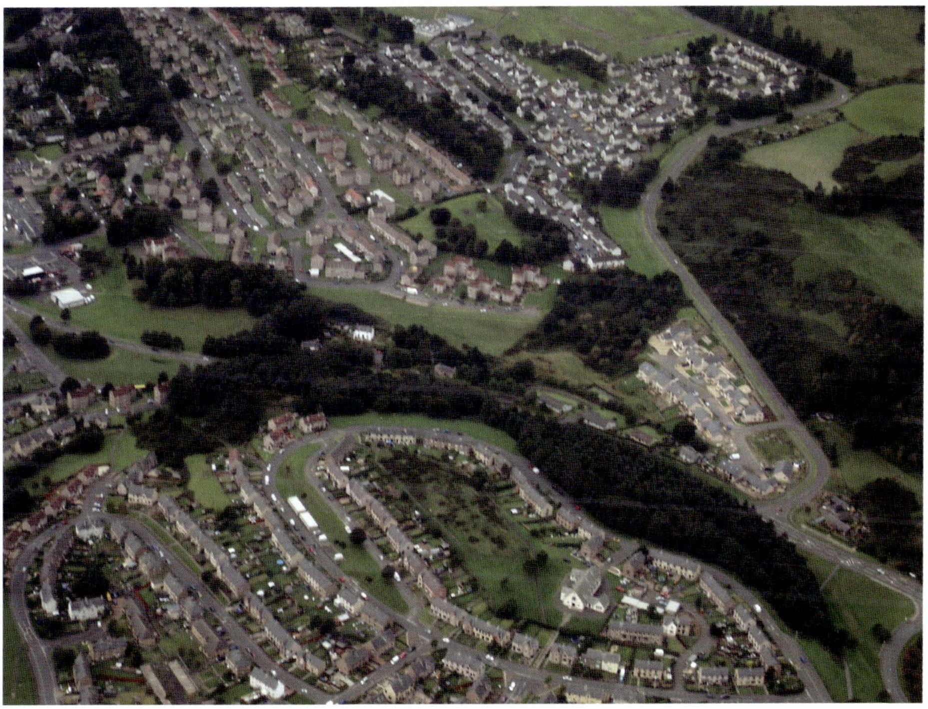

Hawick Expansion Following the Second World War

This aerial shot from 2009 shows how Hawick expanded following the Second World War. New social housing was erected to the north of the Teviot, at Silverbuthall, Burnfoot and Stirches.

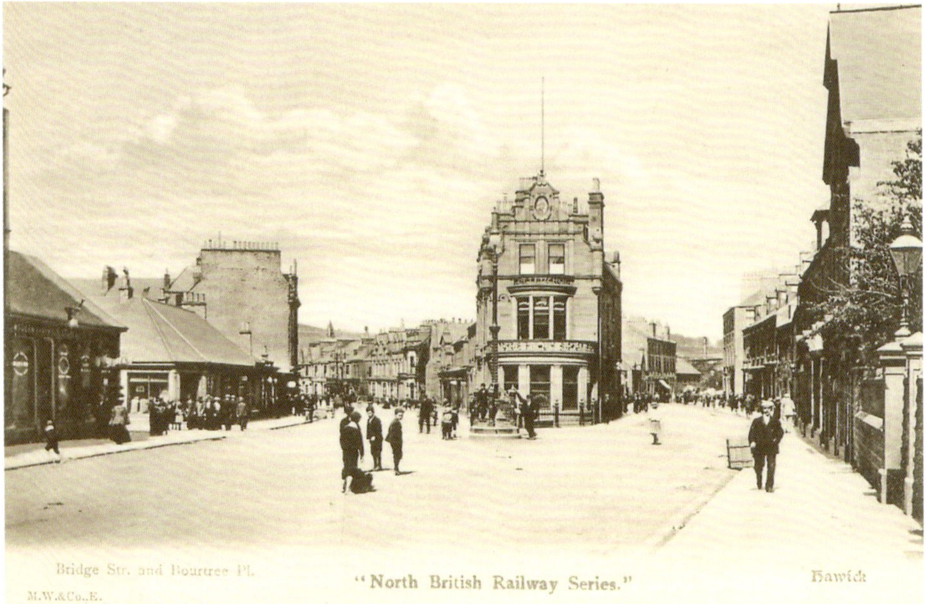

Central Square afore ‘The Horse’ in 1903

Named after the nearby Central Hotel, the name was first recorded in 1852 and used until the unveiling of the 1514 Memorial, in 1914. The distinctive Coffin End building was demolished in 1893 and replaced by one housing Prudential Home Insurance.

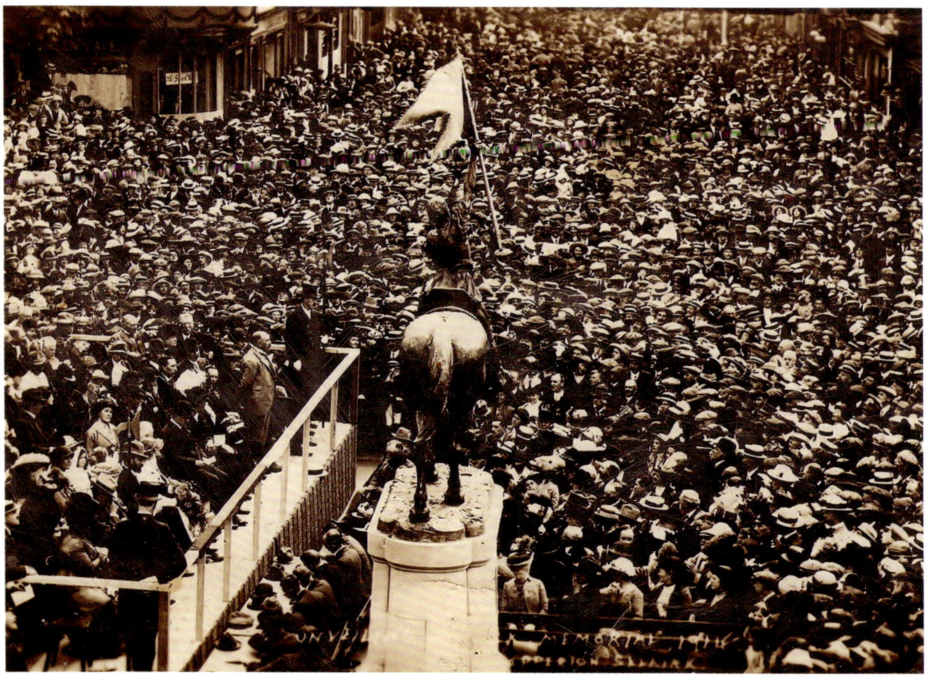

The Unveiling of the 1514 Memorial on 4 June 1914

This monument was designed to commemorate the 400th anniversary of the Battle of Hornshole and was financed wholly by public subscription. It is arguably Hawick’s most famous landmark.

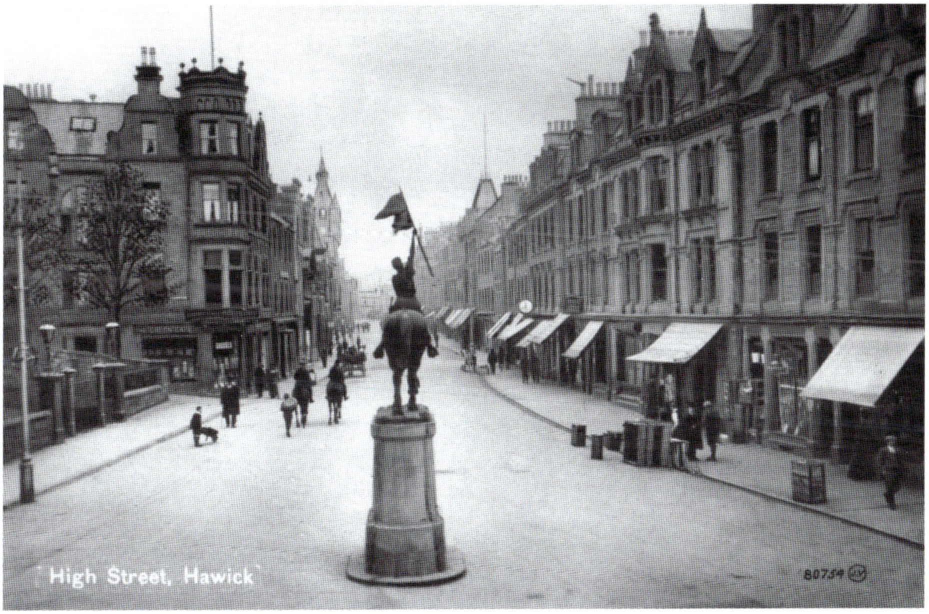

The 1514 Memorial at the Head of the High Street in the 1890s

It was moved in 2003 as part of a £500,000 traffic relief scheme. A time capsule was discovered, with its contents displayed in local jeweller Hamish Smith's shop window.

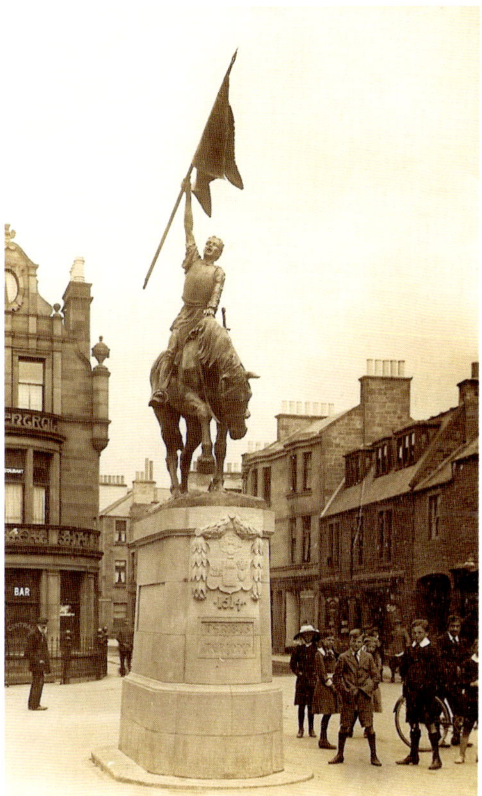

The 1514 Memorial in the Late 1910s

Known as the 'hei gate' or 'common gate' until the late eighteenth century, the High Street once formed a large portion of the medieval Burgh of Hawick.

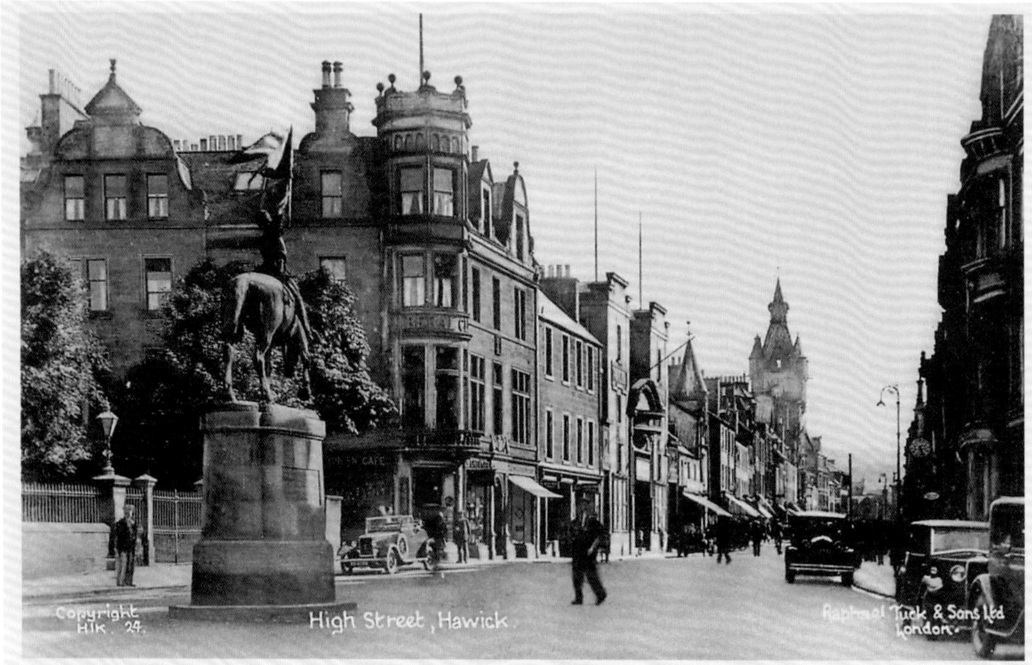

The Green Cafe, 1956

In this view from 1956, you can see the much missed Green Café (established in 1838) and the 'Piv' (theatre, later a cinema, opened in 1915 and demolished in 1964).

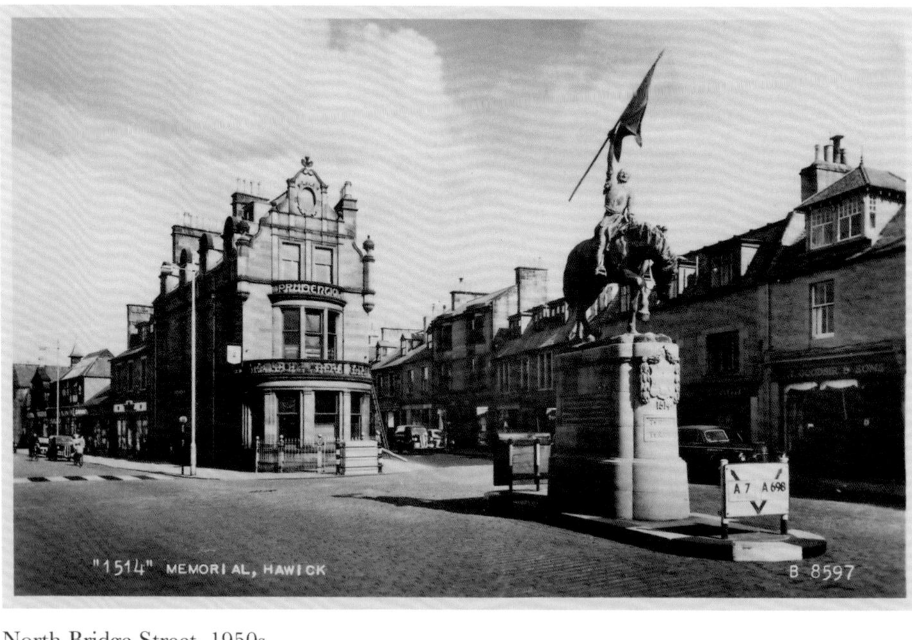

North Bridge Street, 1950s

1 North Bridge Street was designed by J. P. Alison, and built in 1894 on the site of the Washington Hotel (*c.* 1857–93). The balcony balustrade originally read 'The Central', but was modified to 'Prudential' when the insurance company took over the building in 1919.

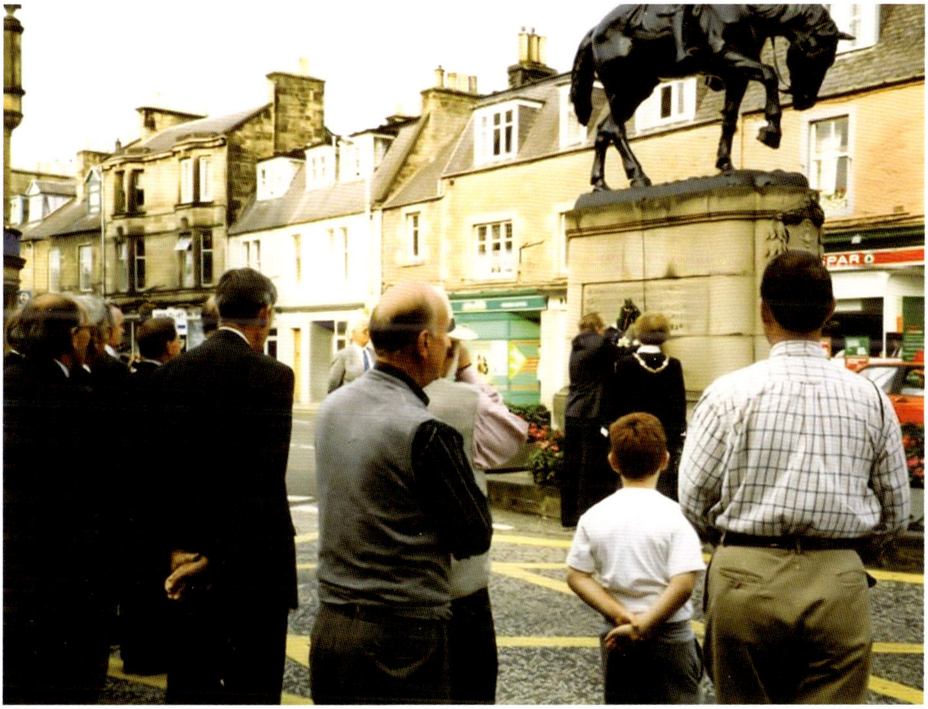

The Callants' Club Laying a Commemorative Wreath at the Horse Memorial in 1988
A circular letter was sent out in 1903 by ten local men, keen to preserve the traditions of Hawick and its people, against the perceived threat of incomers to Stobs Camp.

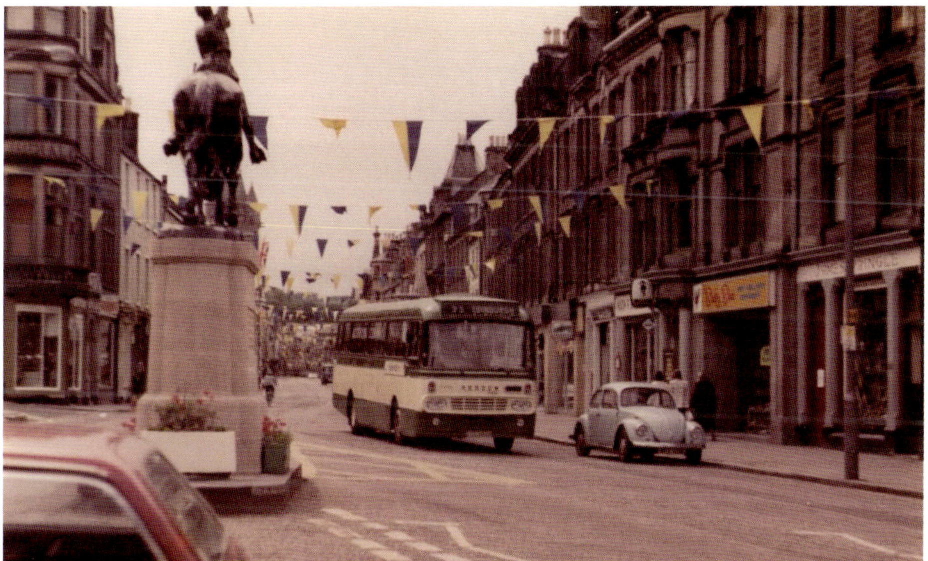

Eastern Scottish Buses, 1979
The distinctive fleet of Eastern Scottish buses were once a common sight in Hawick. This 95 service to Edinburgh was captured around 1979, during the Common Riding.

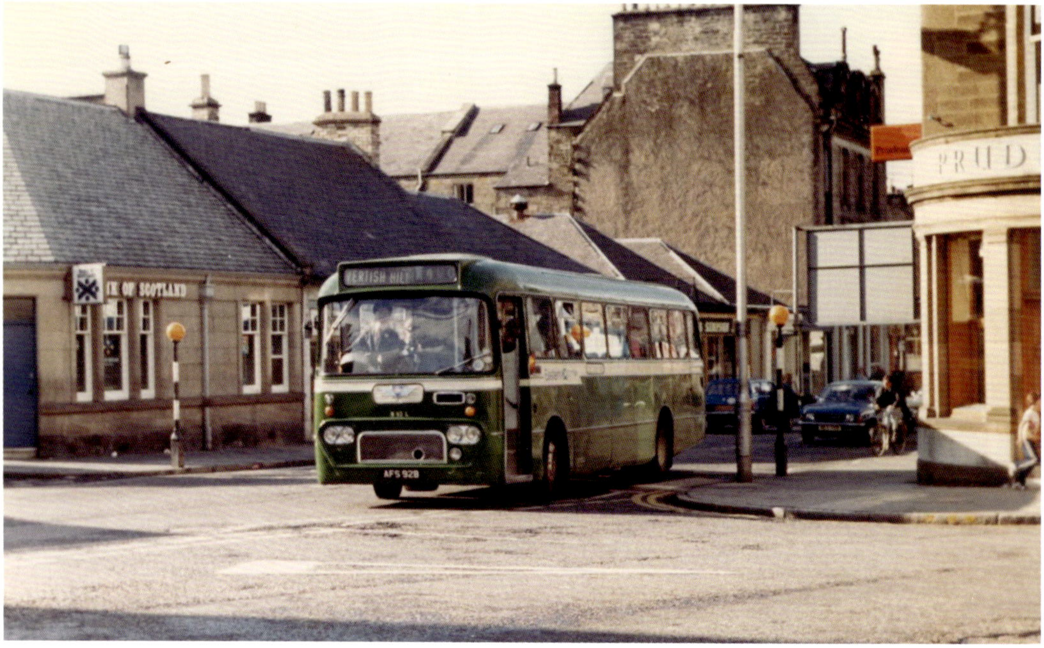

Eastern Scottish Service to the Vertish

Another Eastern Scottish service, this time to the Vertish. In the background you can just make out Deans & Simpsons, a business founded by William Simpson around 1870, and carried on by his sons.

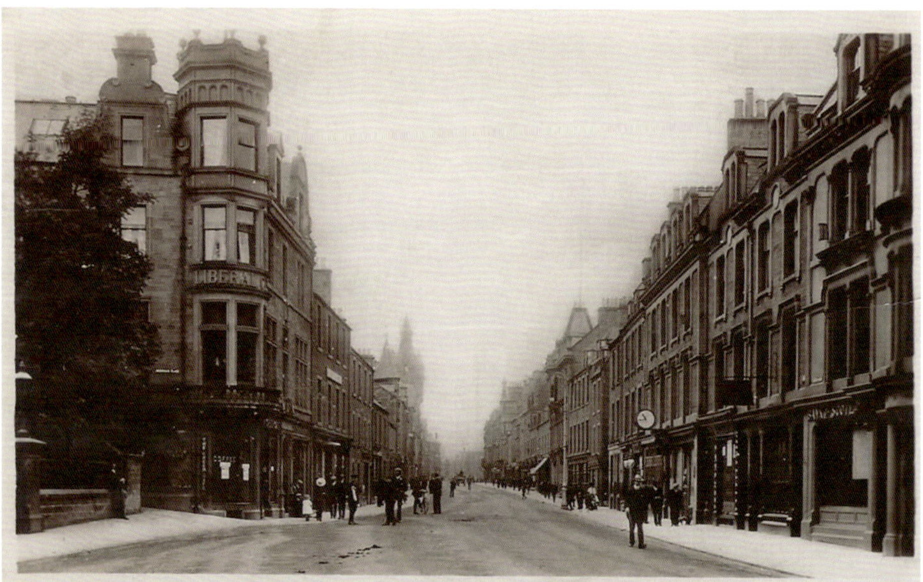

Liberal Club, Early 1900s

The iconic Liberal Club replaced George Milligan's cabinet shop and wood yard in the early 1900s, at a cost of £6,000. Designed by J. P. Alison, the club had a peak membership of 773 people in 1914.

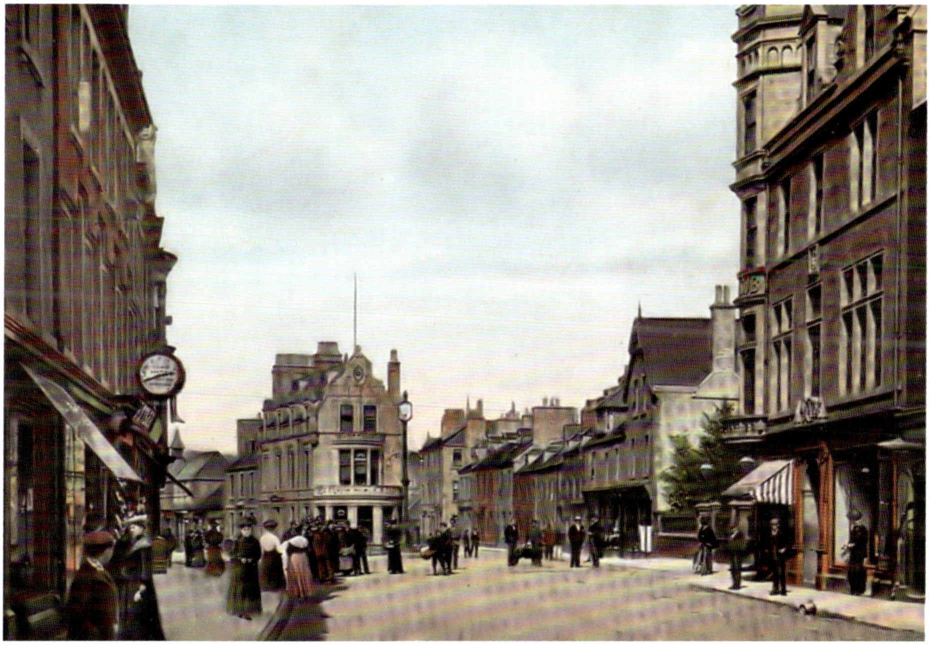

Trinity Gardens and the Top End of the High Street in 1907

The gardens replaced the old East Bank kirk, erected in 1780 as the meeting house of the East End Burgher Congregation.

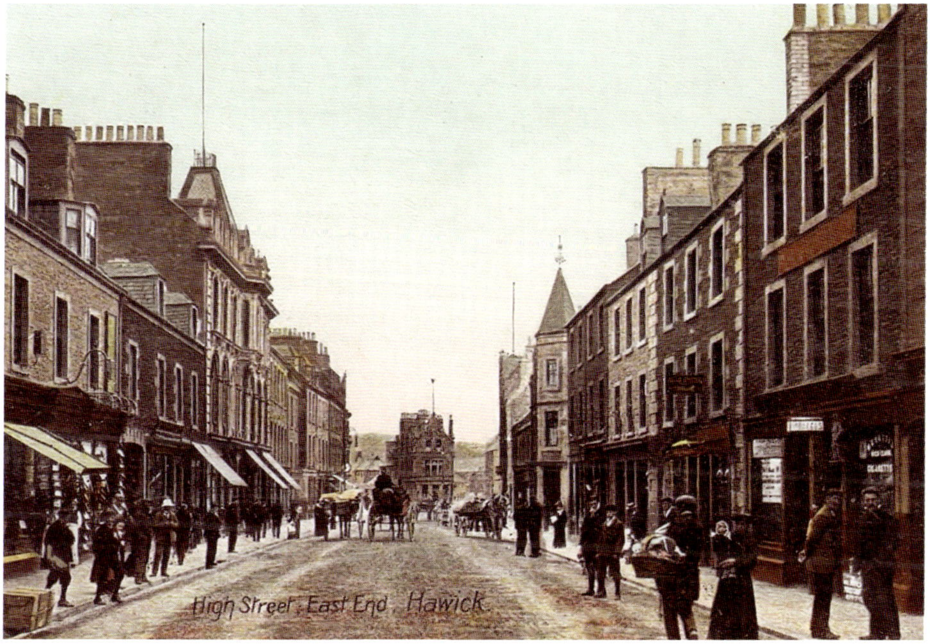

Another Edwardian Snapshot of the High Street

To the left lies Hawick Co-operative, founded by the Hawick Chartist Association in 1838. The buildings eventually stretched all the way from No. 65 to No. 71, with the main branch closing in 1987.

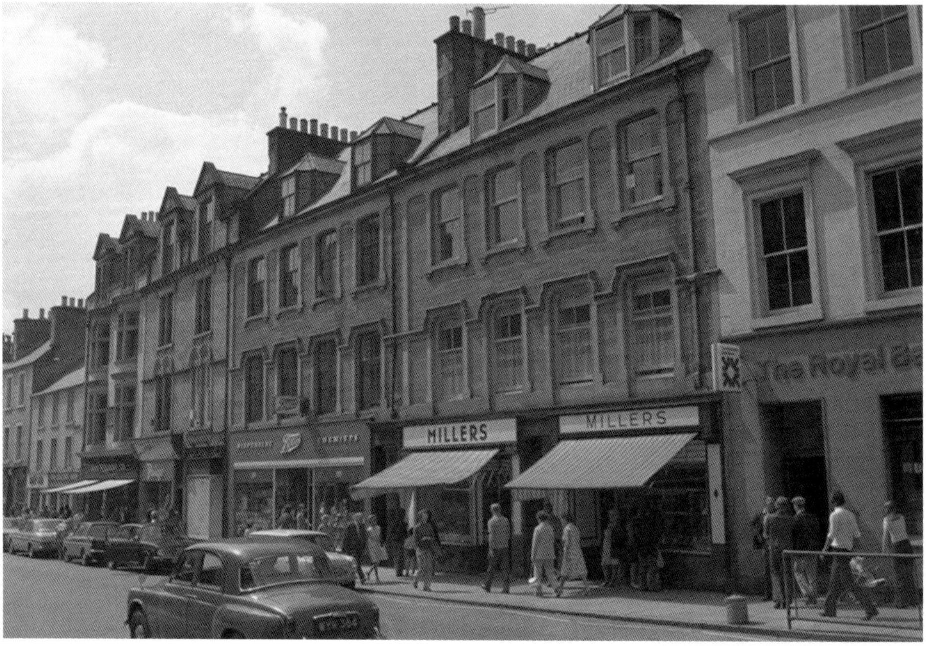

The High Street, 1975

Here the image looks across the High Street in 1975, at Nos 23–29. In that year South Bright Street, Hawick Railway Station, the Teviot Viaduct and Saint Margaret's kirk were all demolished.

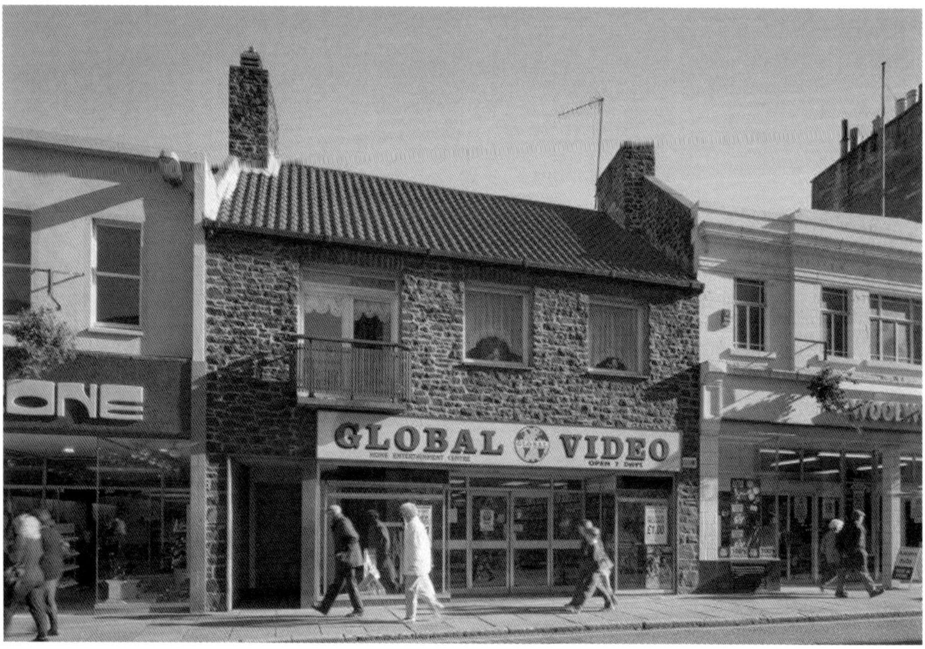

The South Side of the Street in 1995

50 High Street has a freestone cornice salvaged from Stobs Castle at the beginning of the nineteenth century. West Teviotdale Farmers' Book Association ran a library here in the latter half of the same century.

John Turnbull at the Family's 51 High Street Store in the 1950s
He served a design apprenticeship with Wilson & Glenny before taking over the business founded by his great-grandfather in 1855. He later served as a town councillor and founded the Turnbull Clan Association in 1977.

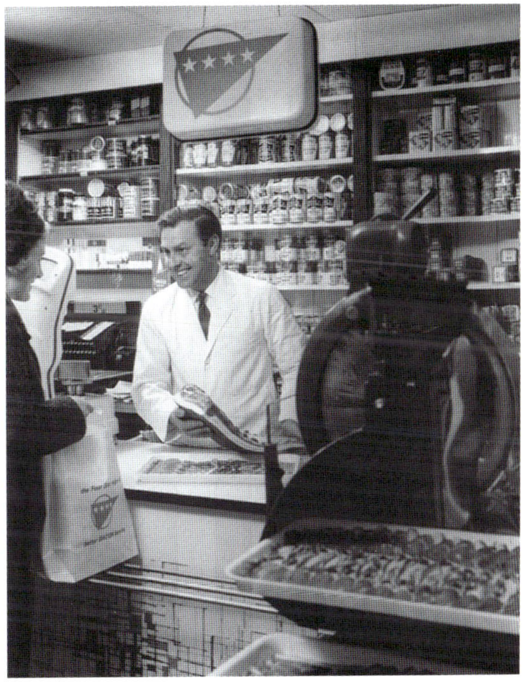

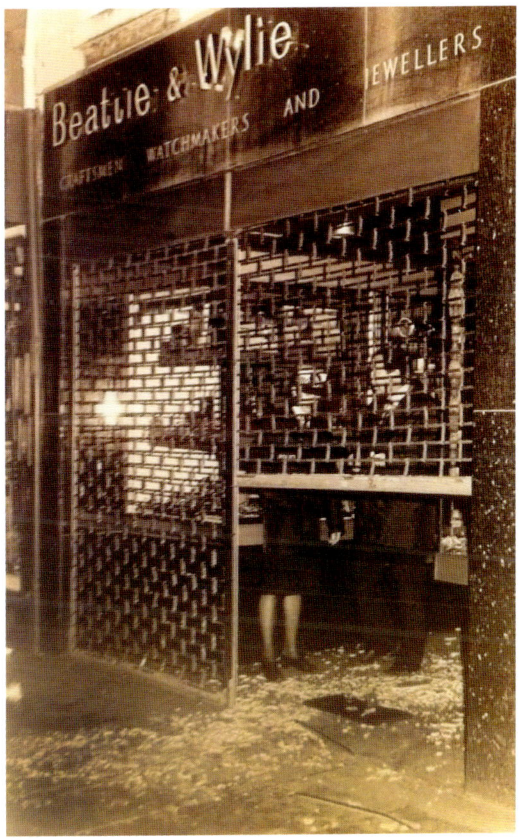

Beattie & Wylie's, Mid-1980s
Beattie & Wylie's shop on the High Street, which was broken into in the mid-1980s. Here you can see the immediate aftermath.

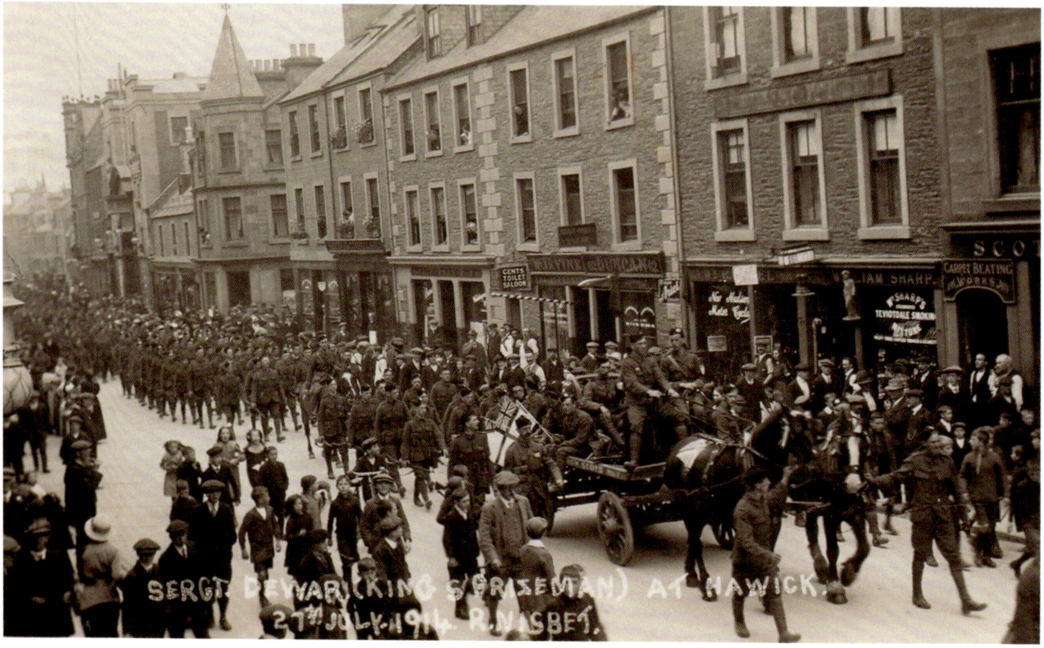

Sergeant J. L. Dewar, of the 4th Royal Scots, Is Paraded Through the Town on 27 July 1914
He won a competition in London to be crowned the King's Marksman. The ulterior motive of the competition was to encourage enlistment in the war effort.

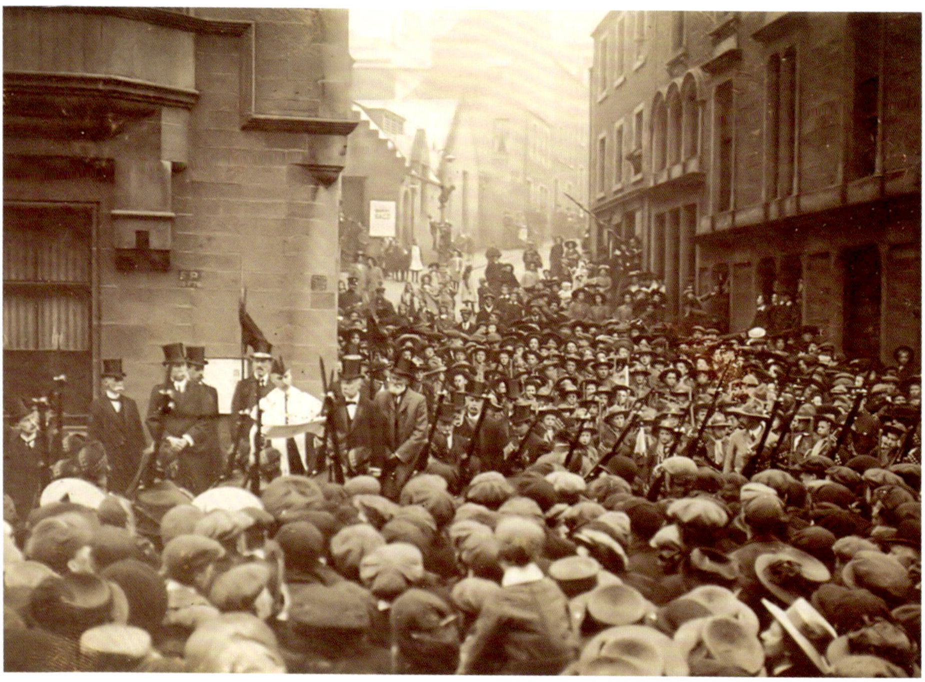

The Proclamation of King George V, 7 May 1910
Teries gather at the Town Hall to hear the Proclamation of King George V, on 7 May 1910. After the death of Edward VII the night before, a statement was read aloud to the waiting crowd.

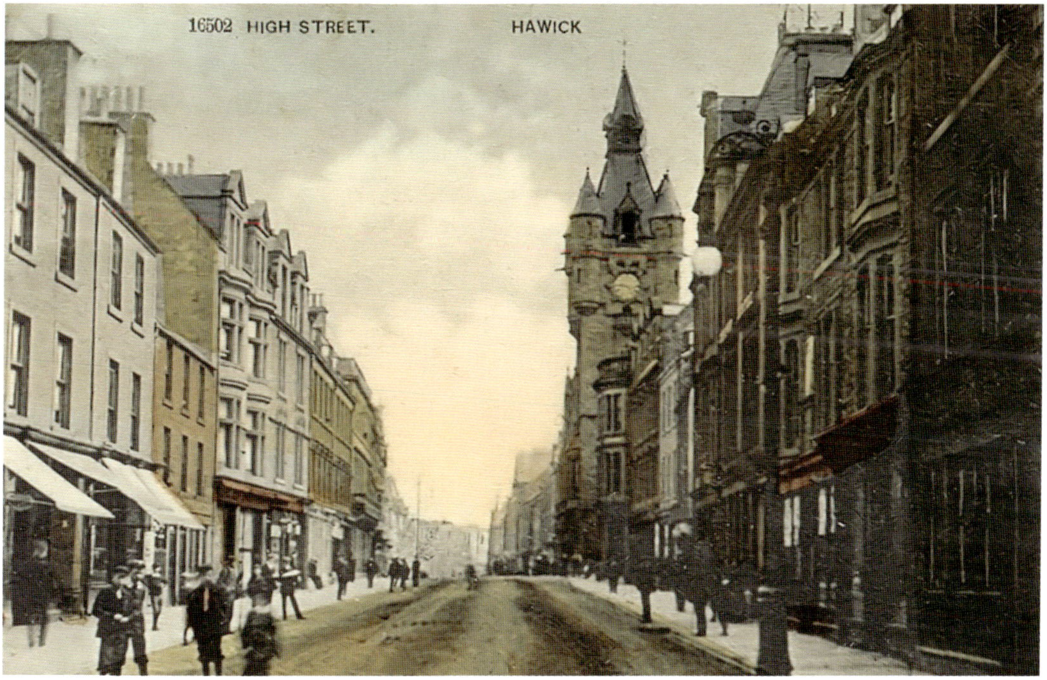

The Toon Ha'

Hawick's most prominent landmark is the Toon Ha'. The old municipal Tollbooth was superceded by Hawick Town House in *c.* 1781, which in turn was replaced by 1886 with the Franco-Scottish Town Hall you see today.

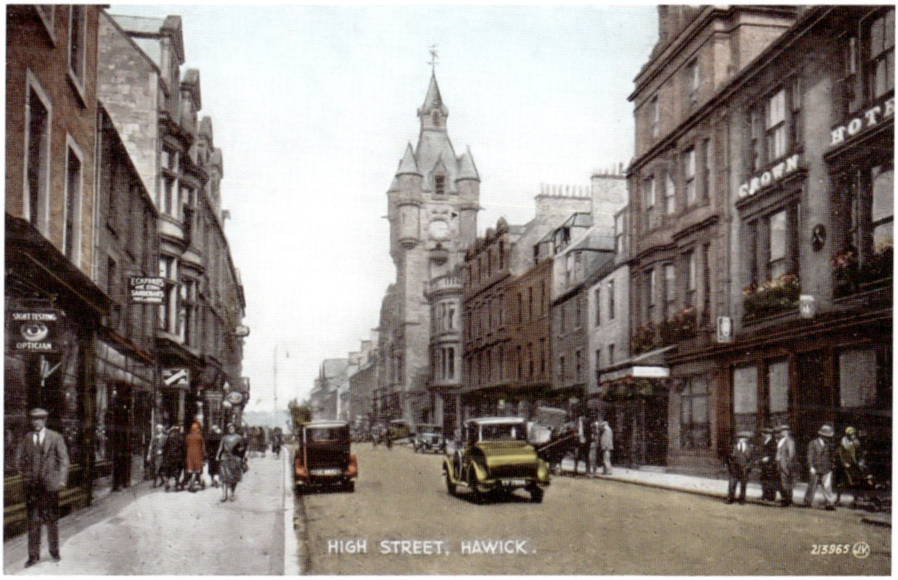

A 1920s View of the Crown Hotel

Opened in the early nineteenth century by the Grieve family, The Crown closed in the late 1980s following a fire and was converted to offices in 1993.

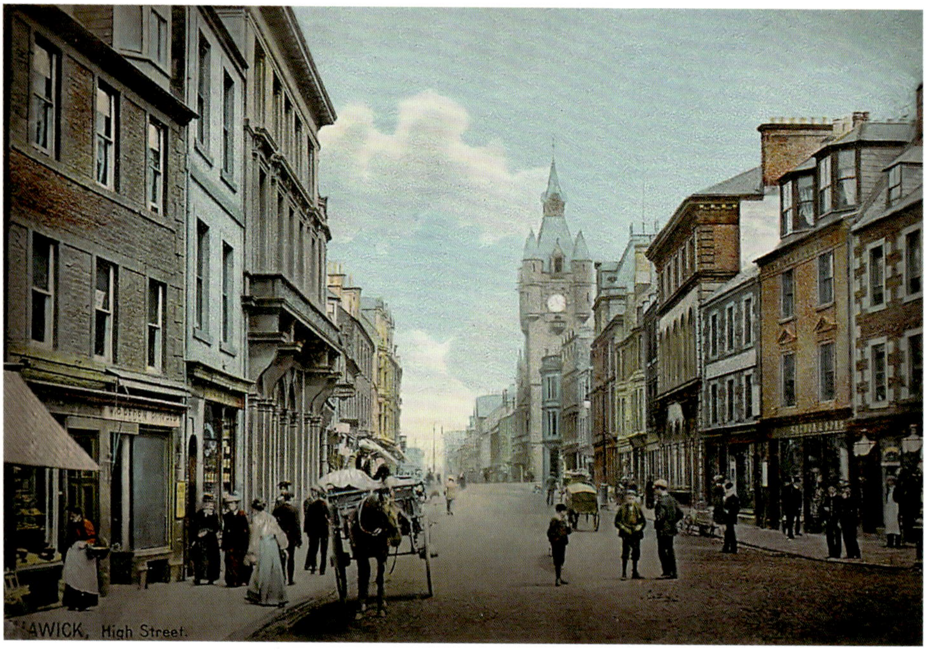

An Edwardian View of the High Street, with the Distinctive British Linen Bank on the Left
Built in 1862 on the site of the Ruecastle Tenement, the Hawick branch has been a Bank of Scotland since 1971.

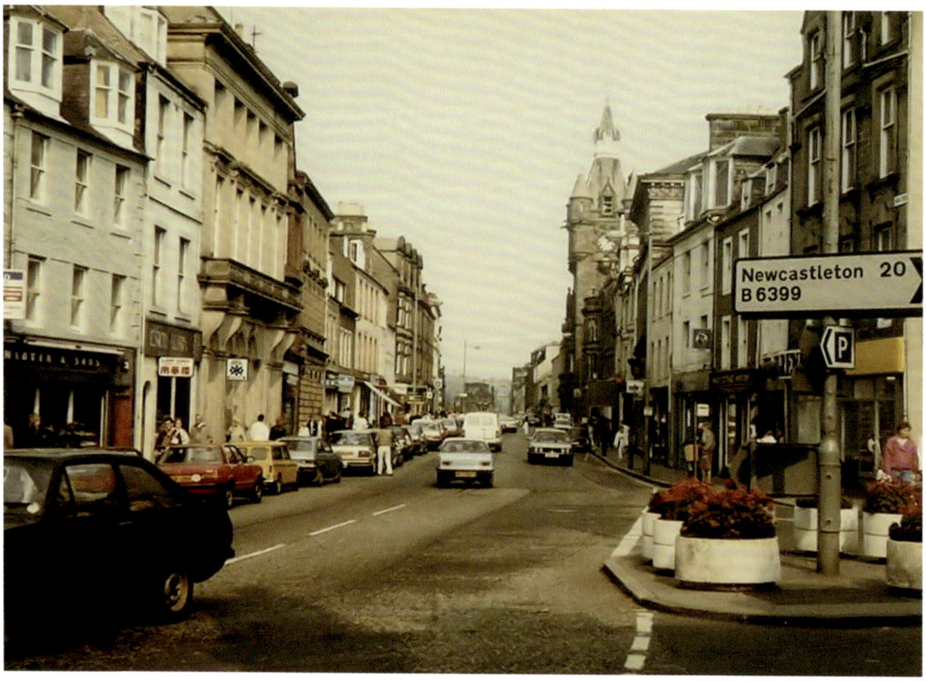

A Look Back to 1986 and Two-Way Traffic on the High Street
In 2008, a new one-way trial was introduced, with traffic flowing north to south, which was made permanent the following year.

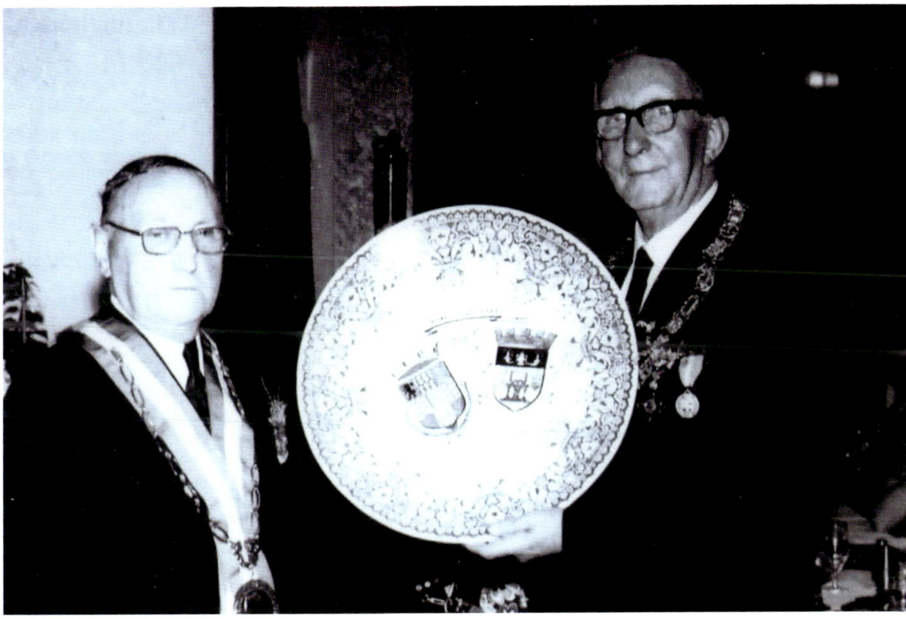

The Twinning Ceremony of Bailleul and Hawick
Joseph M. Legrand, Mayor of Bailleul, and David Atkinson, Provost of Hawick, conclude the twinning ceremony between the two towns in 1973. The French town remains a strong ally to Hawick and its people.

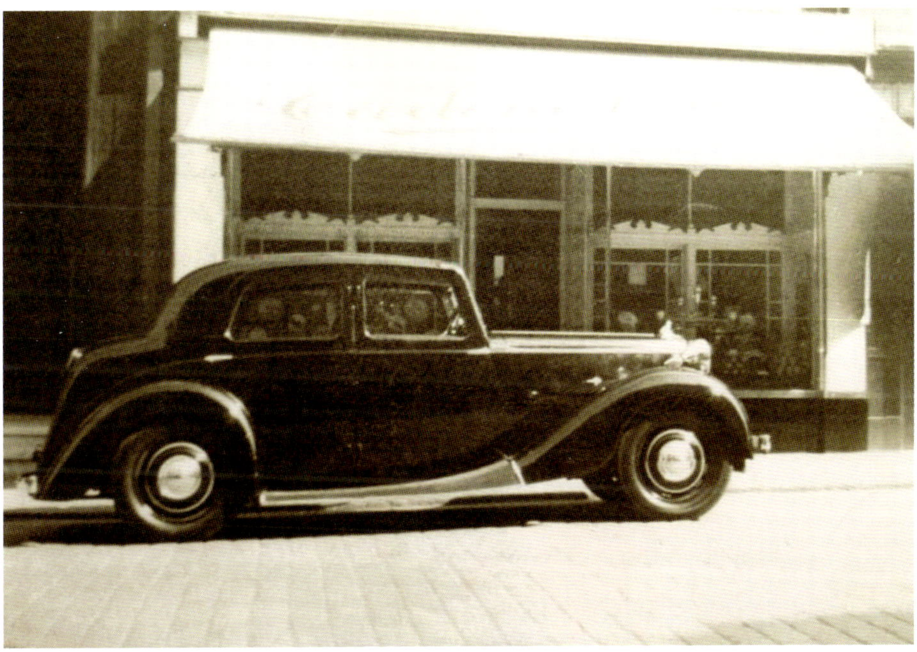

The Cadora Café in the Mid-1950s
This was an extensive coffee shop and restaurant on the south side of the High Street, run by Guido Taddei. The family also owned premises at Oliver Place and North Bridge Street, the latter a famous bingo hall.

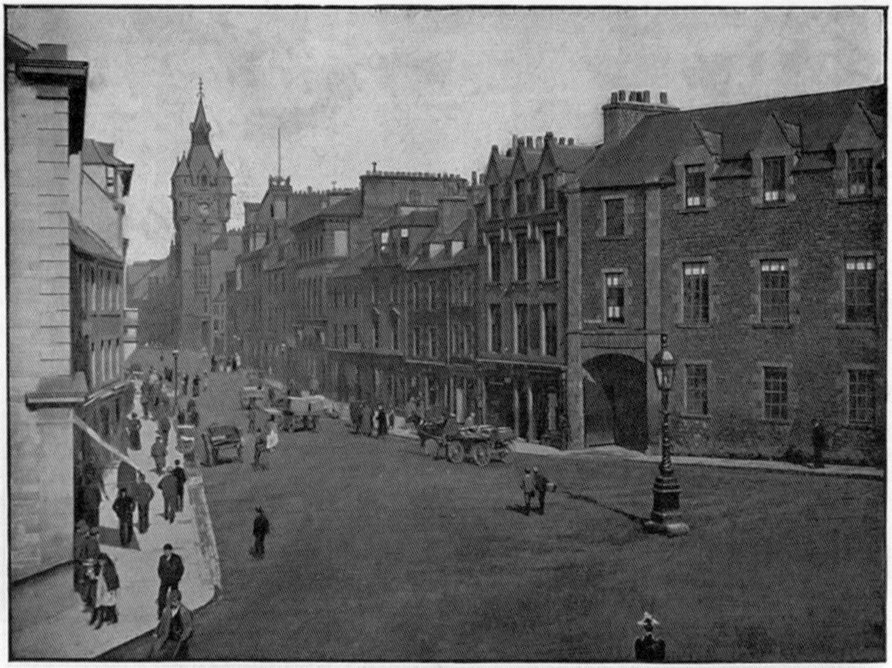

Tower Knowe as Captured in the 1890s, by Prominent Hawick Photographer J. E. D. Murray
The slight rise of the street (or knowe) outside Drumlanrig's Tower was lowered that same decade. J. E. D. Murray was a man of many talents who penned songs, poems and plays, and helped to shape the modern Common Riding.

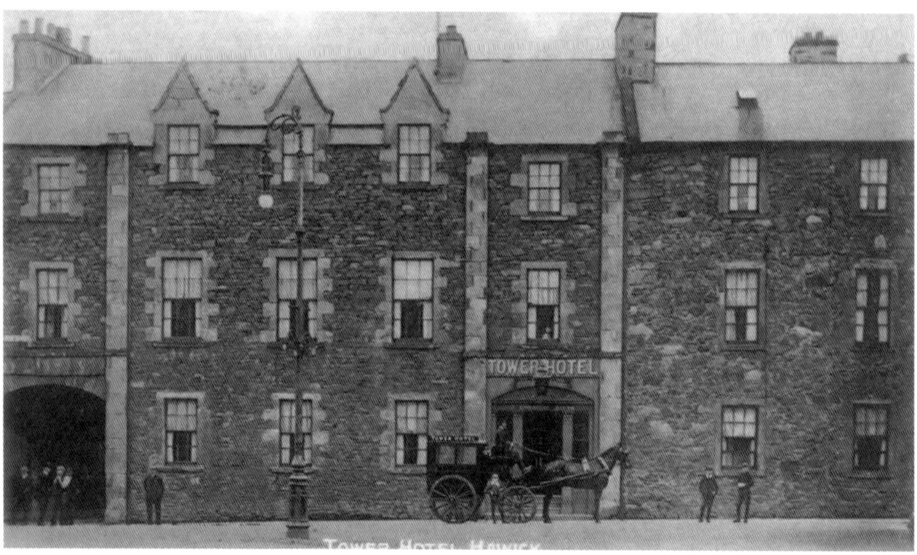

The Tower Hotel as It Looked in the 1880s
The vaulted room to the rear of Drumlanrig's Tower is Hawick's oldest surviving building (early 1550s). Duchess Anne Scott later extended and altered the building to become a town house.

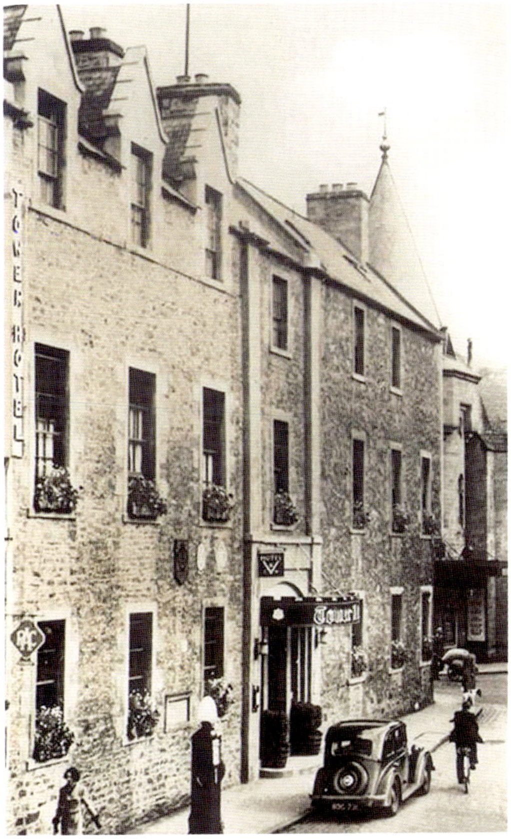

Another Snap, This Time from the 1930s

In 1769, the tower was renovated to become a coaching inn. It survived through various owners, closing in 1981. A large-scale investment and refurbishment allowed the tower to re-open as a museum in the late 1990s.

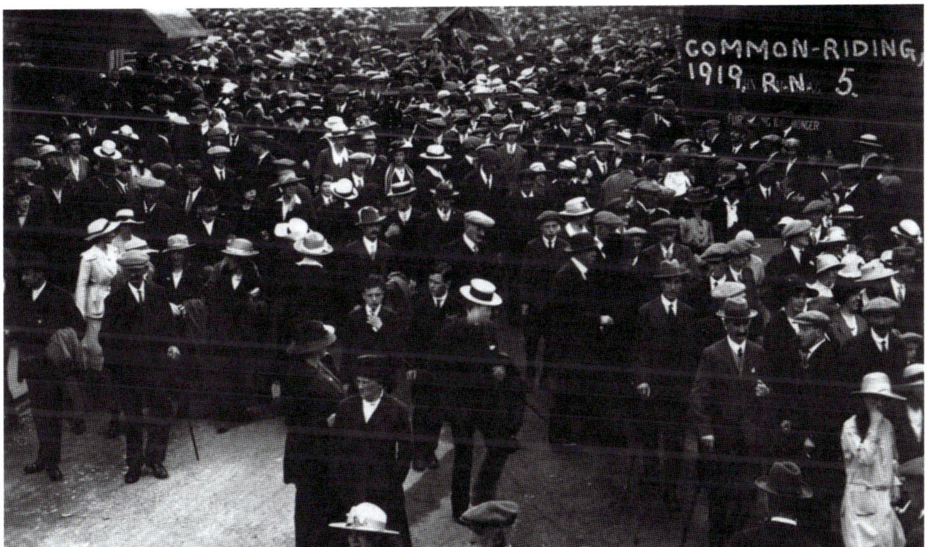

Led by Cornet Tom Winning, the Crowd Make Their Way Past 'Airmstrangs' in 1919

John Armstrong was an ironmonger at No. 4 Tower Knowe, until the building was partly demolished to widen the street and extend the premises of the Commercial Bank in 1935.

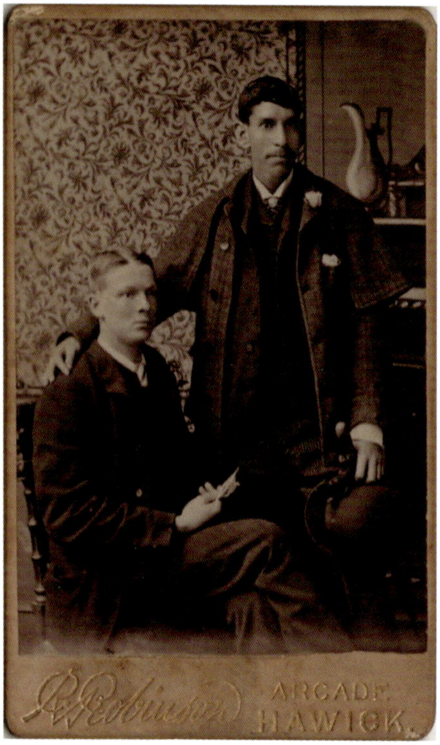

G. Allen Robinson's Studios in the Late 1870s
Two well-dressed gentlemen pose for a 'carte de visite' style photograph, taken in the late 1870s at G. Allen Robinson's studios. According to the National Archives he was based at four locations across the town until 1910, including the Exchange Arcade.

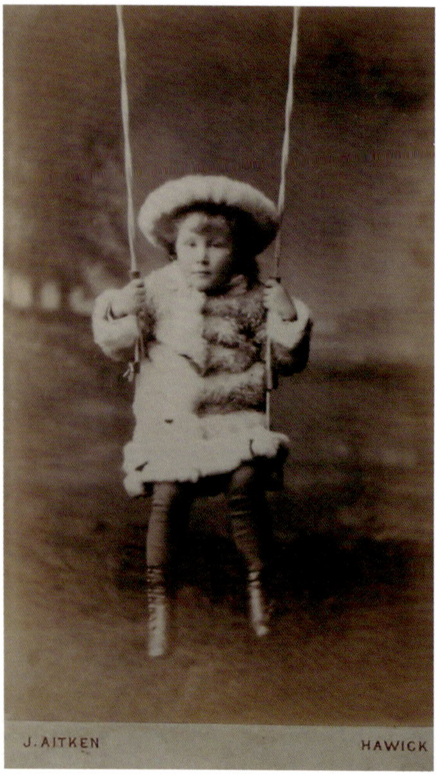

The Exchange Arcade
A sullen looking customer of J. Aitken's photography saloon, also based at the Exchange Arcade. Aitken used small images which were enlarged to life-size portraits and finished in oils and watercolours.

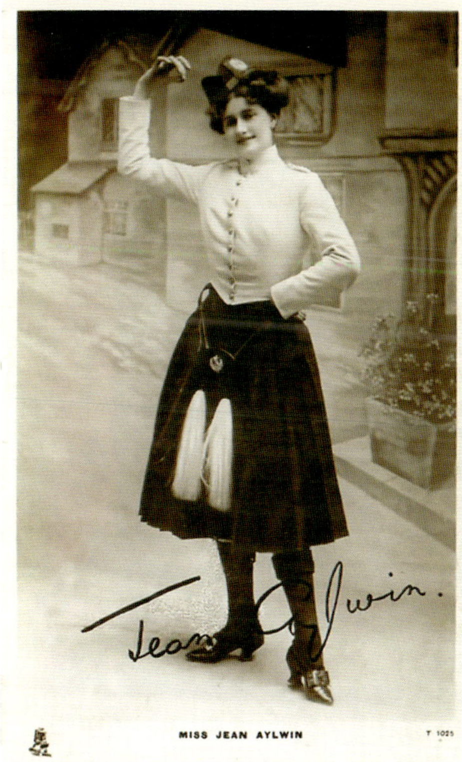

Hawick's Forgotten Film Star, Jean Aylwin
Described as the 'Lady Harry Lauder', she featured in a variety of musical comedies, popular plays and silent movies. Although a divorce scandal threatened her career, she went on to become an early radio broadcaster with the BBC.

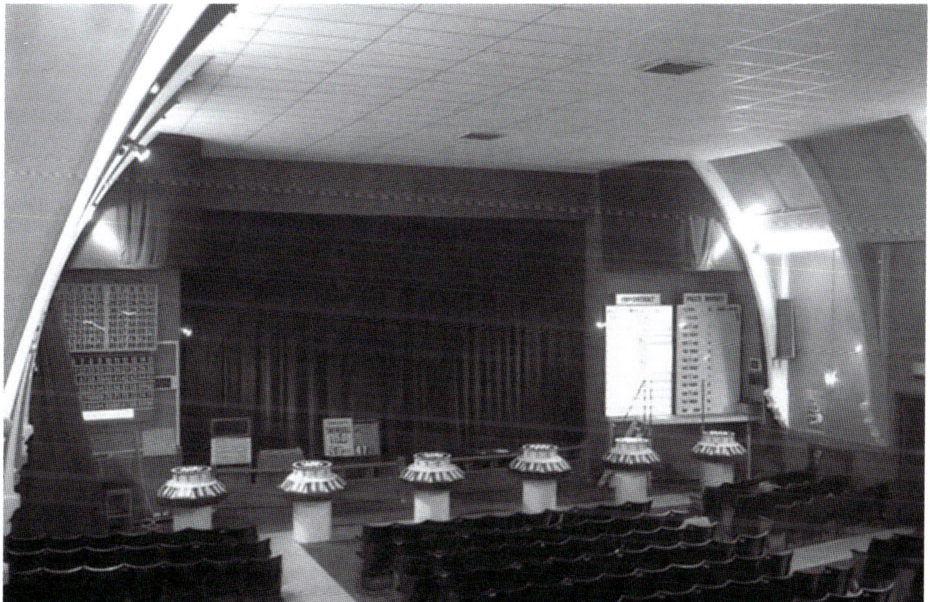

The Interior of the Former Bingo Hall at the Exchange Buildings in 1985
The game moved from local social clubs into the mainstream by the mid-1960s, with Taddei's among the first to offer a dedicated venue in the early 1970s.

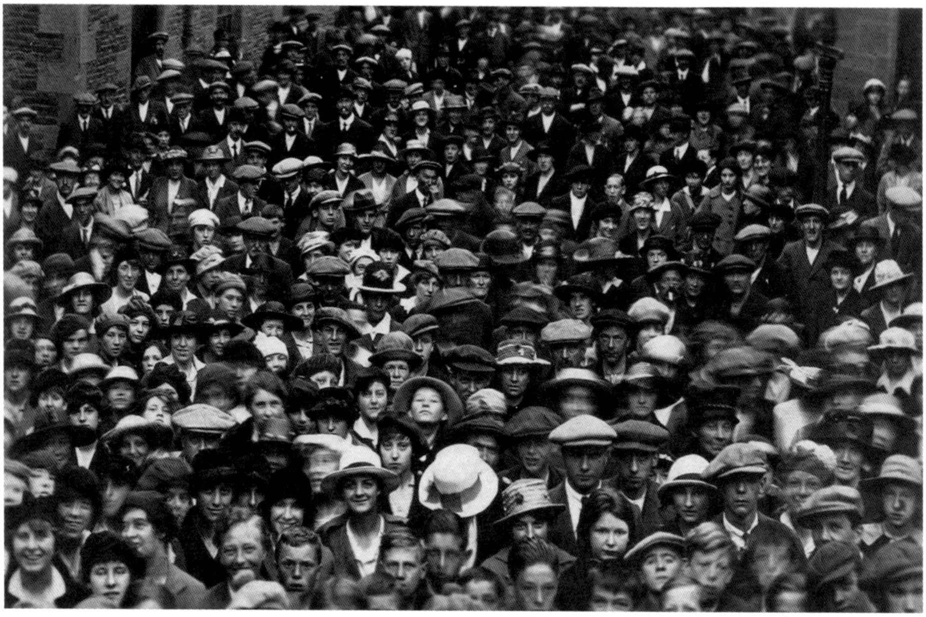

The Crowd Prepare for the Annual Snuffin' Ceremony, 1911
The original horn mull is still in use. Kirkstile is built partly on a bridge over the Slitrig Water, created to replace the Auld Brig in 1852.

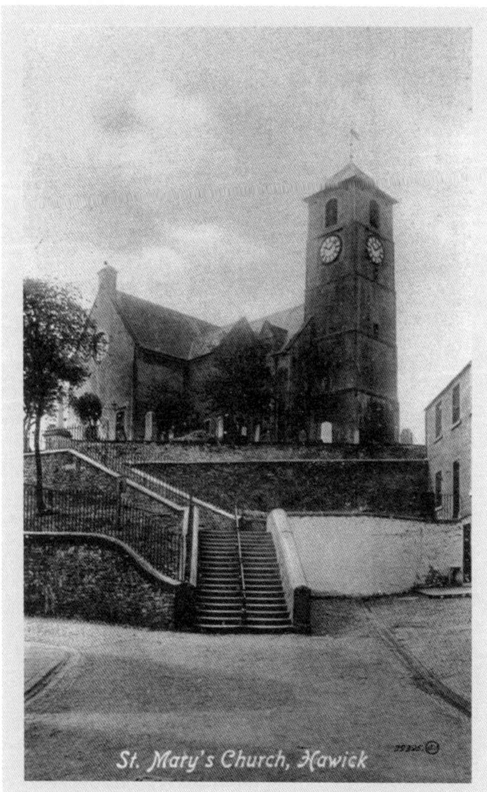

A Black-and-White Photograph of St Mary's Kirk From 1903
Widely considered to be the oldest occupied site in Hawick, it was first recorded as a place of worship in 1183. Severely damaged by fire in 1880, the church was substantially renovated.

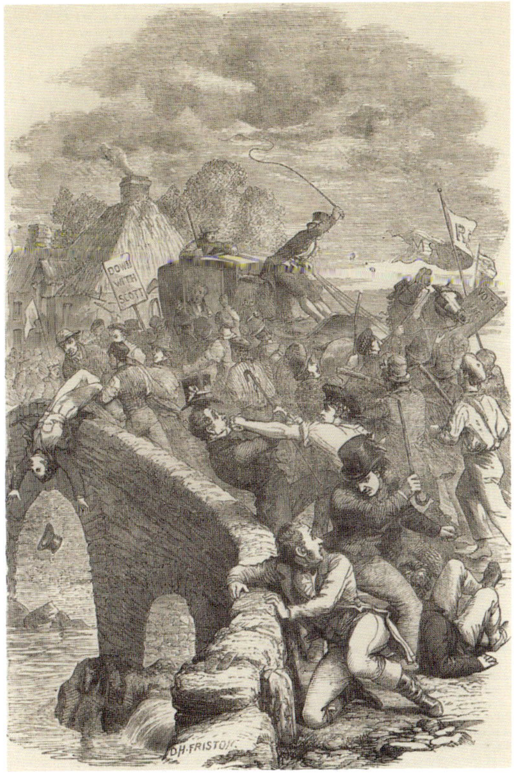

David Friston's Sketch of the Infamous 1837 Tully Riots on the Auld Brig
The General Election that year saw mobbing and rioting, assaults, and the belated election of a local MP and farmer, David Tully who was later allegedly dunked in the Teviot, hence the name.

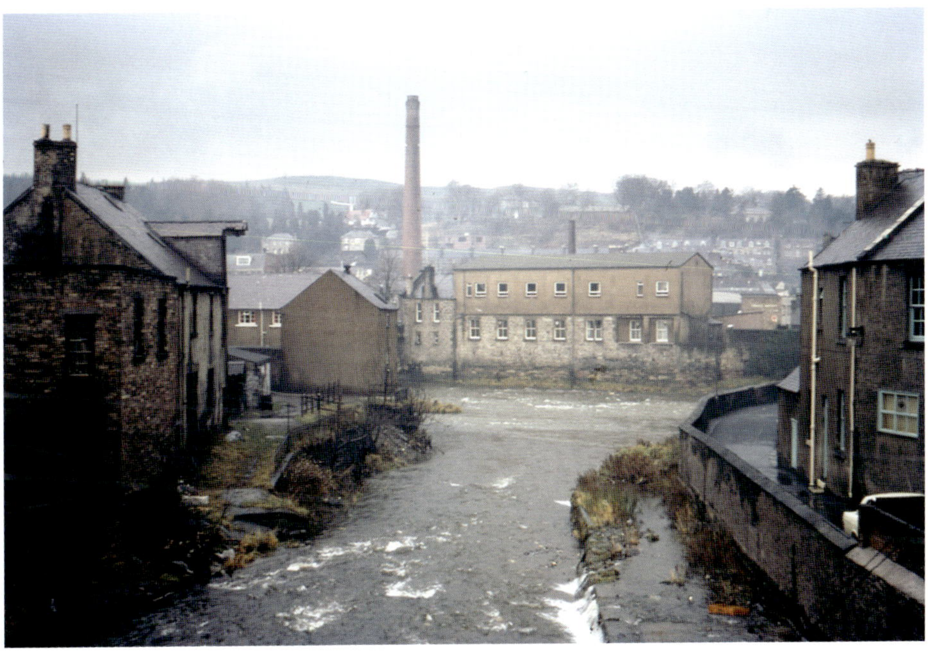

A Smashing Colour Photograph of the Plum in 1970
Also known as 'Pate's Plum' after the nearby Paterson's joinery yard, this is the confluence of the River Teviot and Slitrig Water.

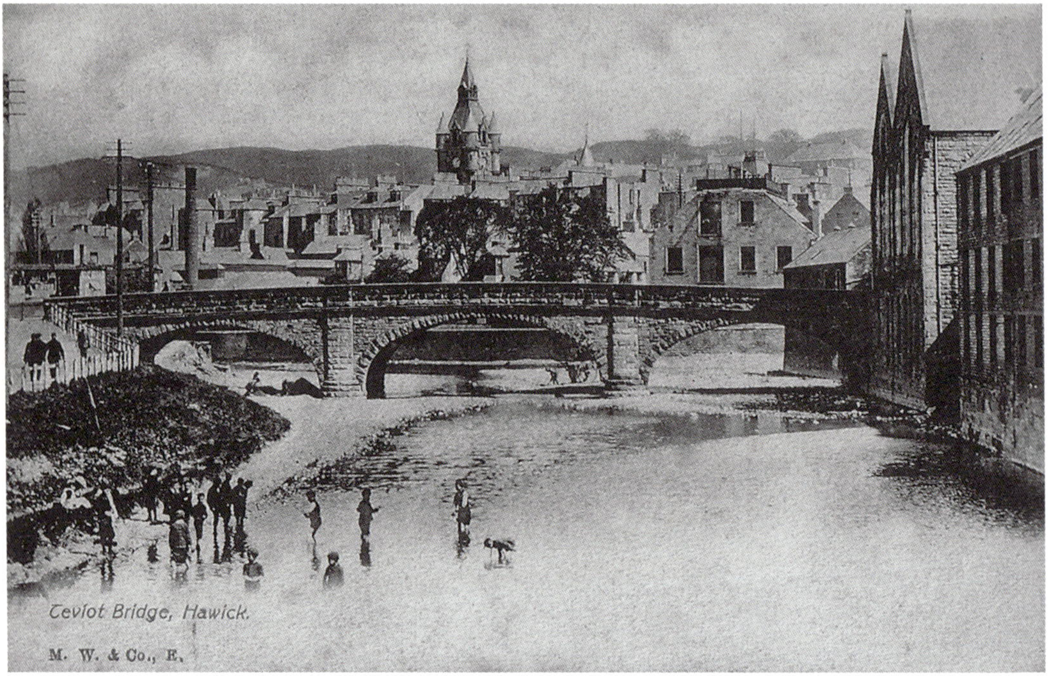

The Teviot Bridge in the Early Twentieth Century

A ferry boat or 'coble' was used to cross the river when it was not fordable, prior to construction of the original bridge in 1741. The current stone bridge opened in 1865.

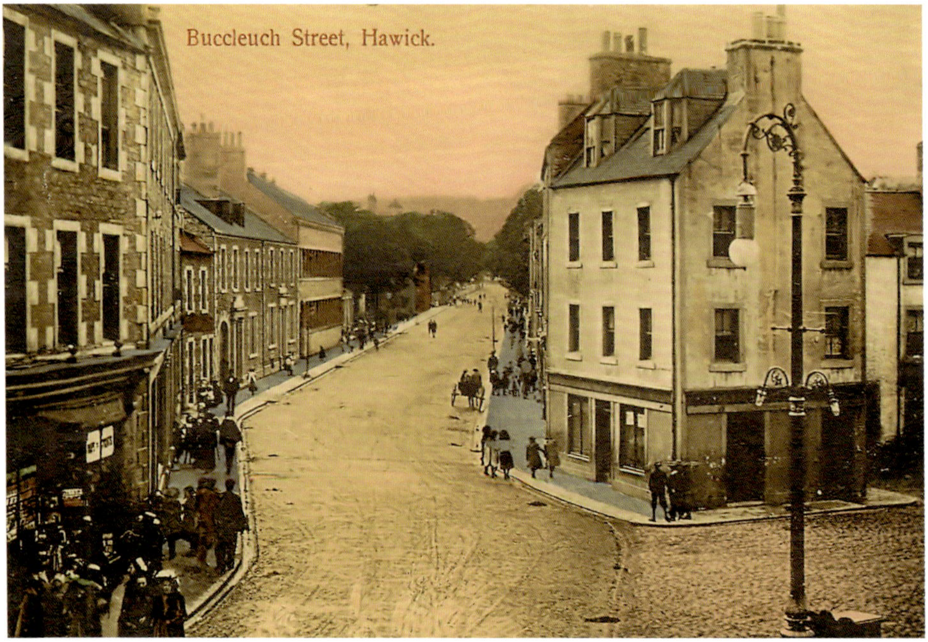

Looking along Hawick's New Road (Buccleuch Street) in 1912

Here you can see the famous local businesses of Pesco's (Peter Scott Knitwear) and W. & J. Kennedy, booksellers, bookbinders, publishers and stationers at No. 2 Sandbed.

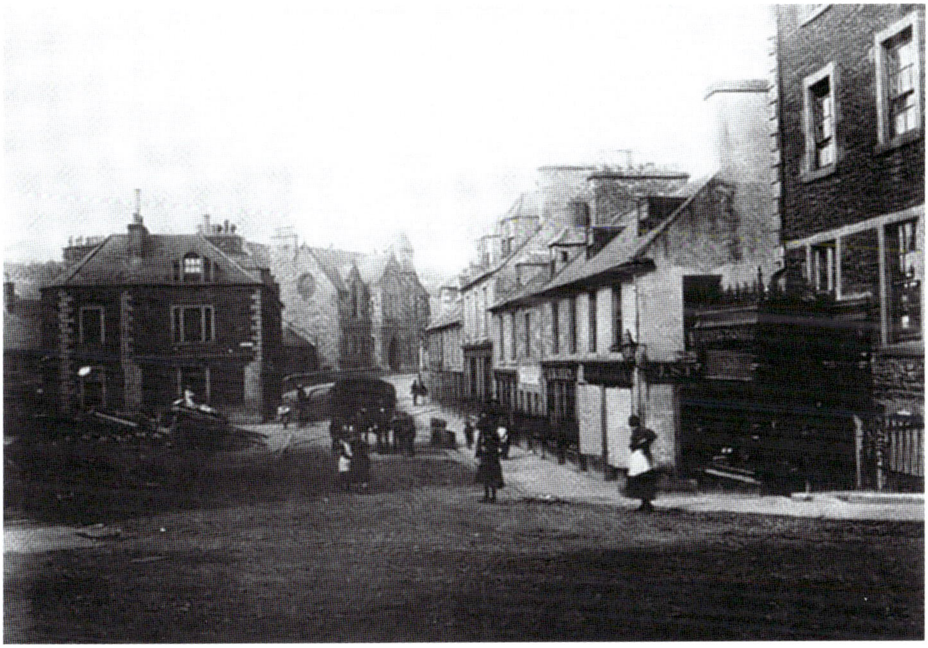

A View of the Sandbed from 1887

This name derives from the sandy deposits which were present long before the land was built upon. It was once an enclosed space that hosted the town market.

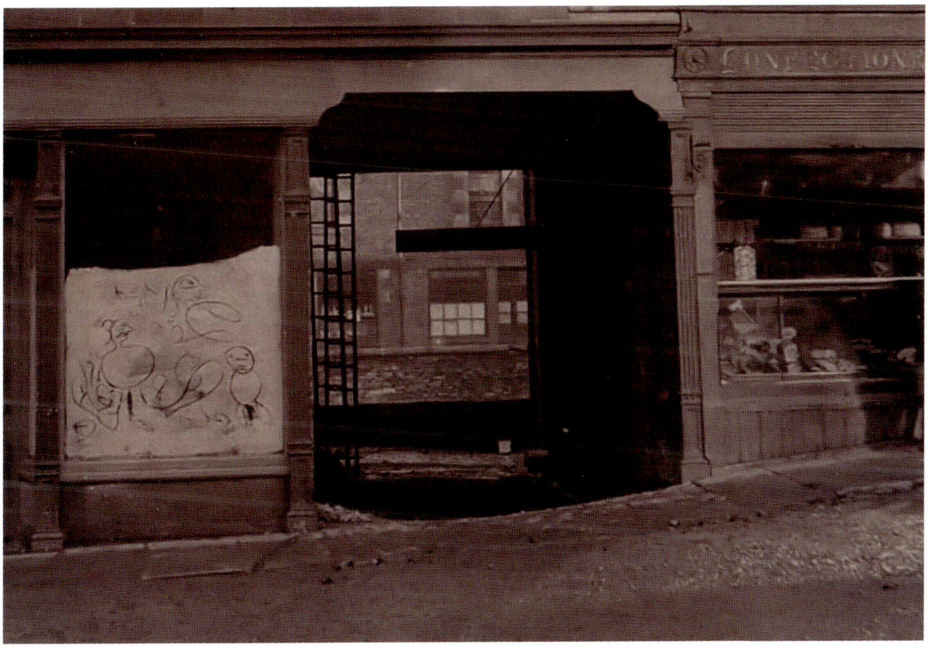

Looking Through the Old Close at the Sandbed, Pre-1900

Thomson's, the newsagent and confectioner's shop, is to the right. The building of the first Teviot Bridge in 1741, and the opening of the New Road in 1815, both altered the layout of this street. Houses between the Howegate and Orrock Place were demolished to provide greater access.

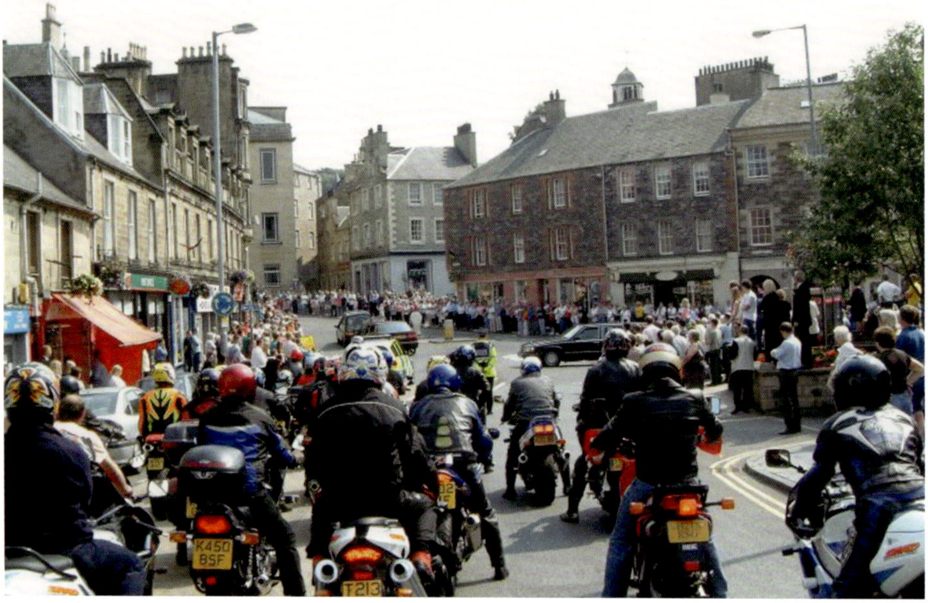

Steve Hislop's Funeral Cortege Passes the Sandbed in 2003
'Hizzy' won the Manx TT eleven times, the British 250 cc Championship and the British Superbike championship twice. Tragically, he died when piloting his own helicopter in July 2003.

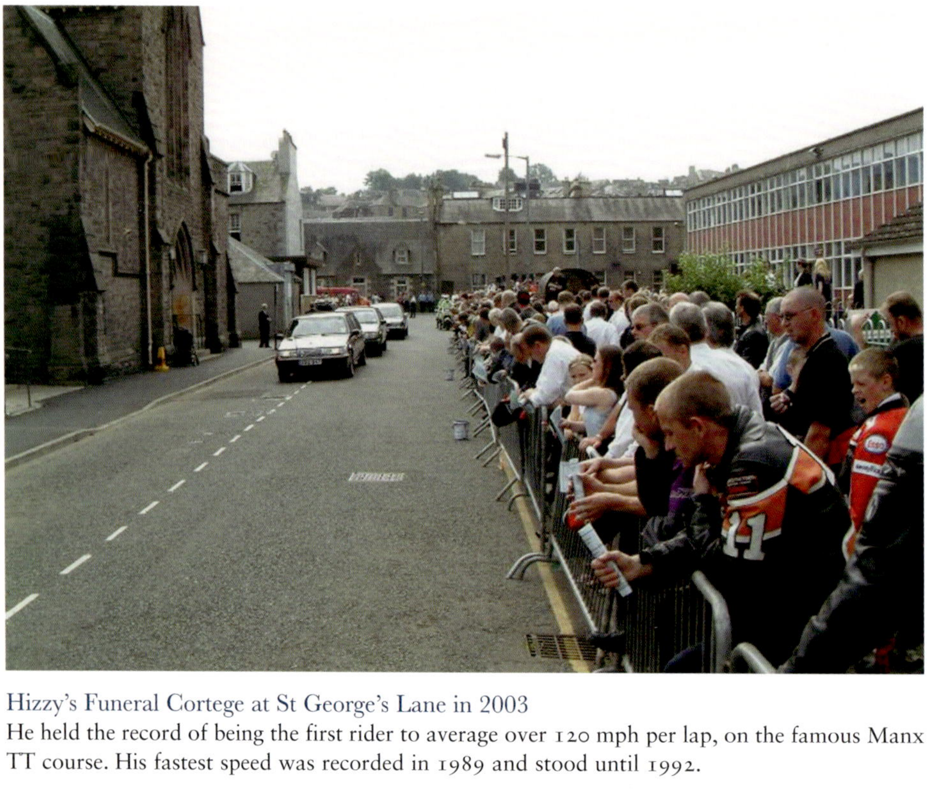

Hizzy's Funeral Cortege at St George's Lane in 2003
He held the record of being the first rider to average over 120 mph per lap, on the famous Manx TT course. His fastest speed was recorded in 1989 and stood until 1992.

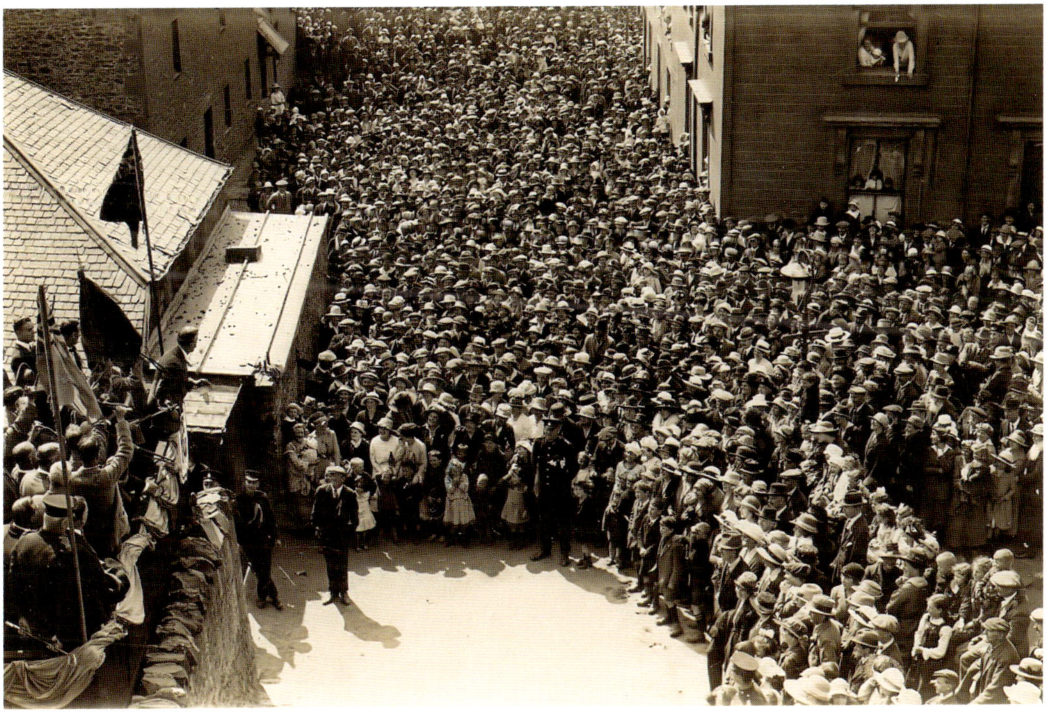

Singing Songs at Mill Path, During a Common Riding from the 1930s

Traditionally songs were sung on Tibbie, the Fiddler's roof, until 1859. The ceremony moved across the road in the 1960s following its destruction.

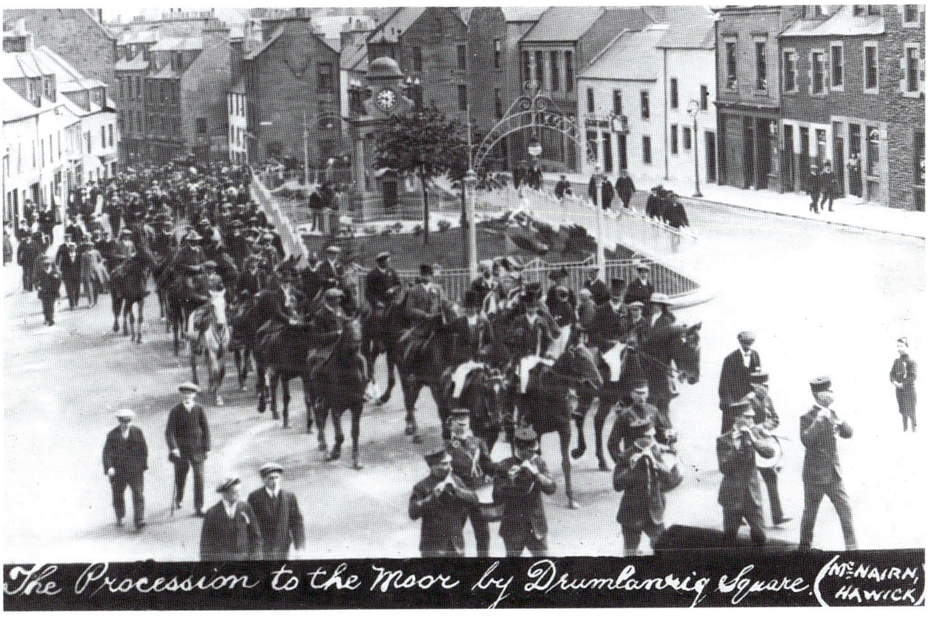

The Procession to the Mair Passes by Drumlanrig Square, During the 1911 Common Riding

Drumlanrig Square is named after the seventh Baron of Drumlanrig, Sir James Douglas, who granted the Hawick Charter of 1537.

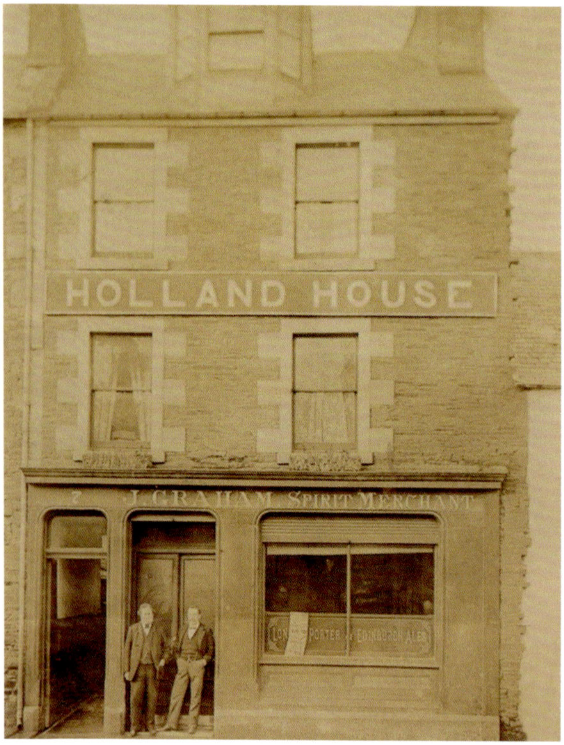

Holland House at the Turn of the Twentieth Century

This public house began as Graham's Hostelry in 1869, on Back Raw, and was the location of the inaugural meeting of the Hawick Burns Club in 1878.

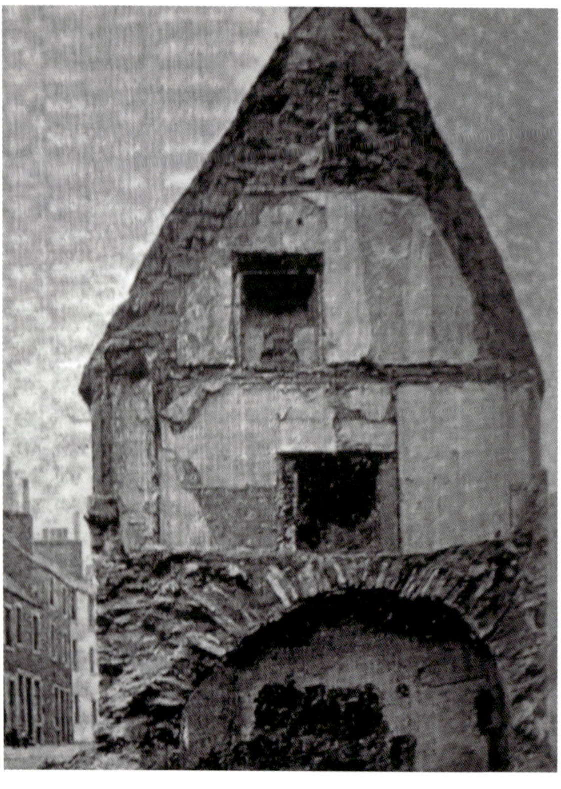

A Print From 1884, Showing the Demolition of Auld Mid Raw

Funds raised by public subscription allowed the Burgh Council to buy the slum buildings from their various owners and each was demolished by the end of the decade.

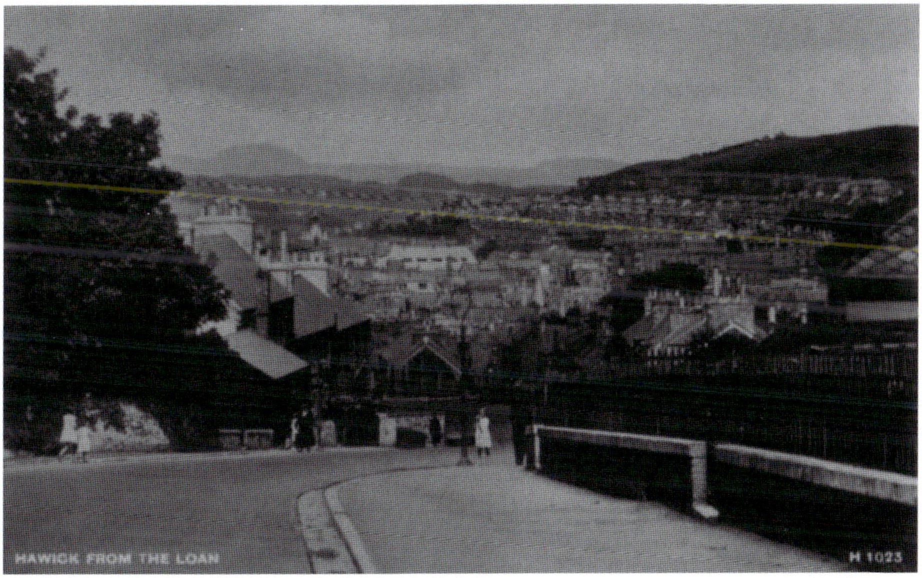

An Early Twentieth-Century View from the Loan

Once a country lane to the pastures on the Common, it was first feued in 1792. It was also once the main road to Carlisle, until the New Road was built in 1815.

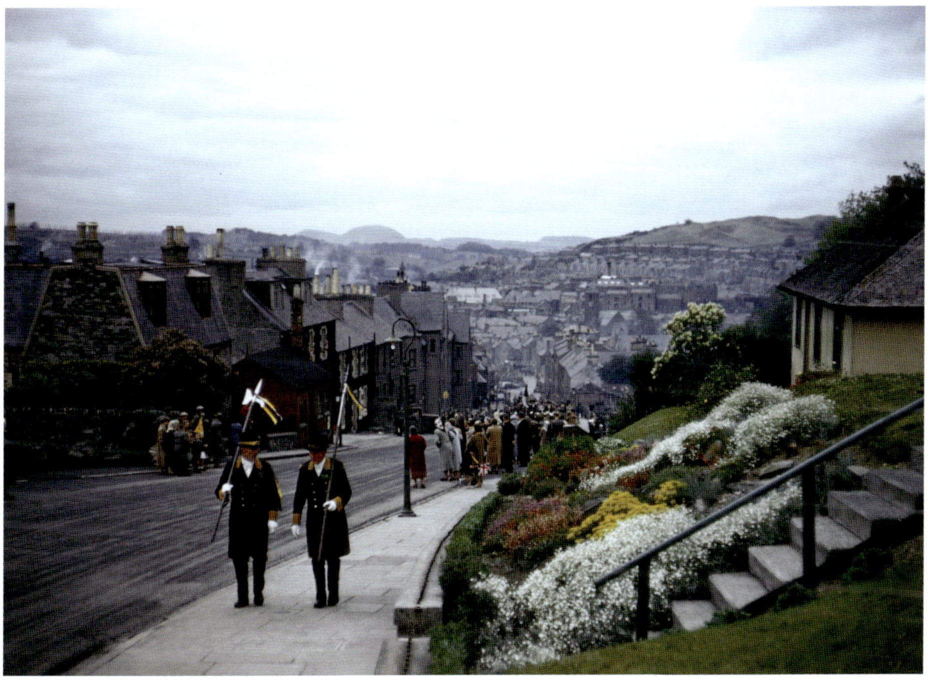

Two Halberdiers Await the Cornet at the Loan, Late 1950s

A fantastic colour photograph of two Halberdiers deep in conversation, as crowds await the Cornet at the Loan in the late 1950s. The Steel House on the right is a reminder of the old prefabs constructed on the Loan following the Second World War.

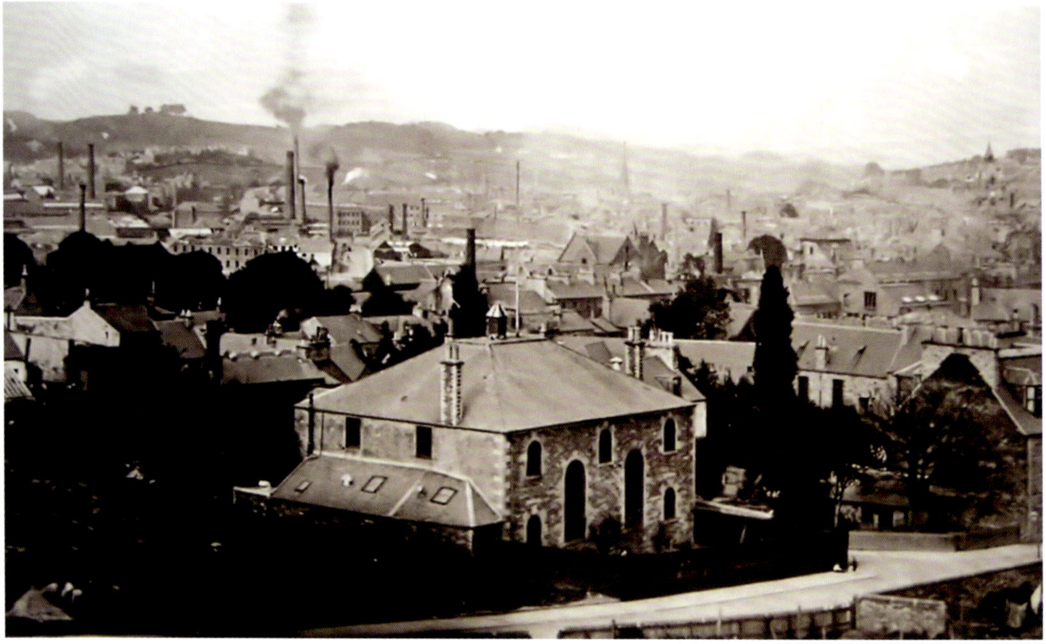

Looking Across Hawick From Green Terrace Early Last Century
This street is named after Myreslawgreen – a green marshy hill. This area was originally used for grazing sheep and cattle, and for many years the Green Kirk (foreground) was the only building here.

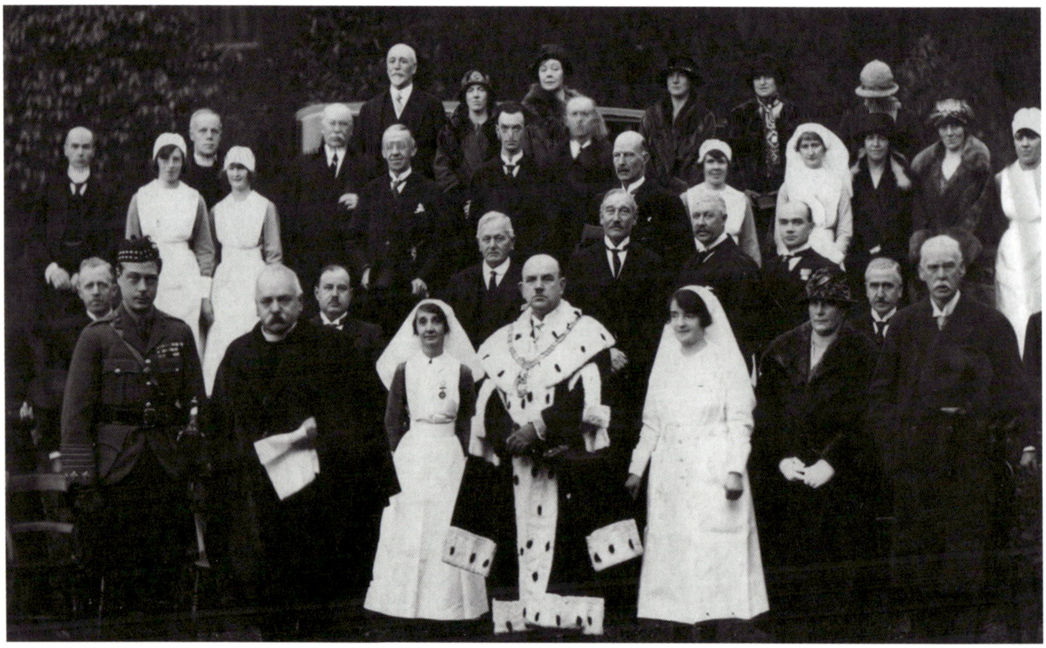

The Opening of the Esmond Elliot Memorial Ward, the Old Cottage Hospital
HRH the Prince of Wales opens the Esmond Elliot Memorial Ward at the old cottage hospital in the early 1940s. Opened in 1885, the facility closed its doors in 2005 with the opening of a new community hospital on Victoria Road.

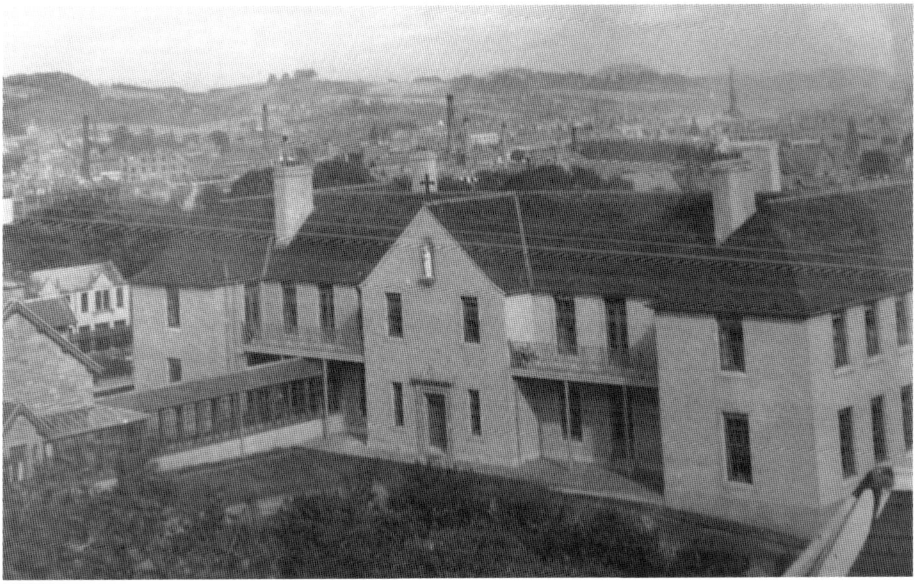

St Margaret's Home, as Seen in the 1940s
Built in 1909, this was the first convent of its kind in Scotland. It became a 'home for incurables' in the 1920s. Since the nuns left in 1987, it has been run as a private care home.

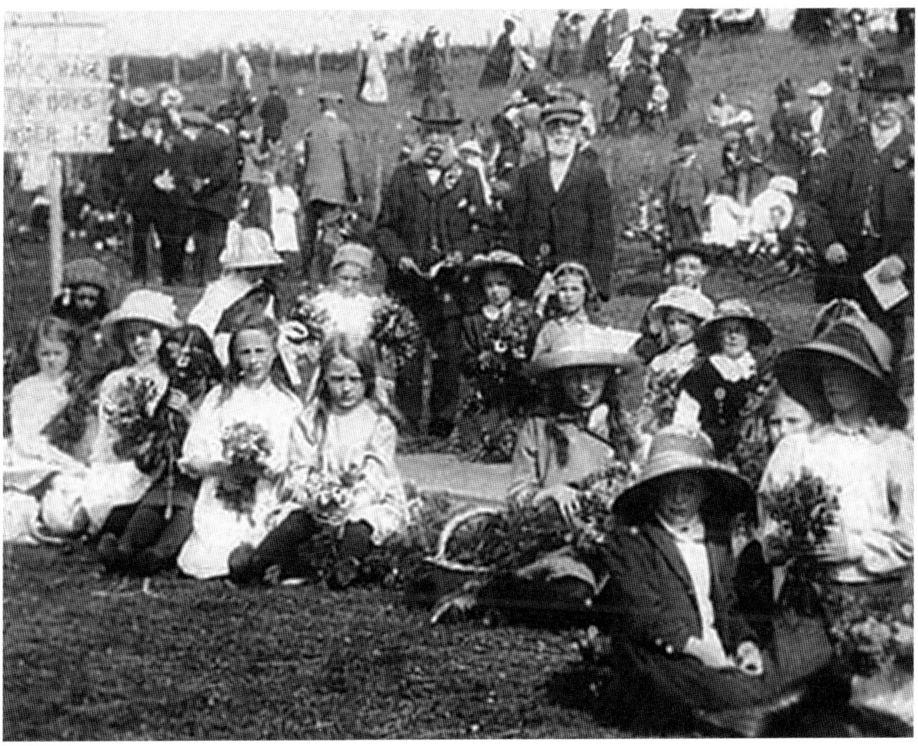

Spectators Take in the Vertish Hill Sports Day in 1909
Among the day's events were the egg and spoon race, a skipping demonstration, Highland dancing, and an undefined obstacle race. This popular event has been held annually since 1881.

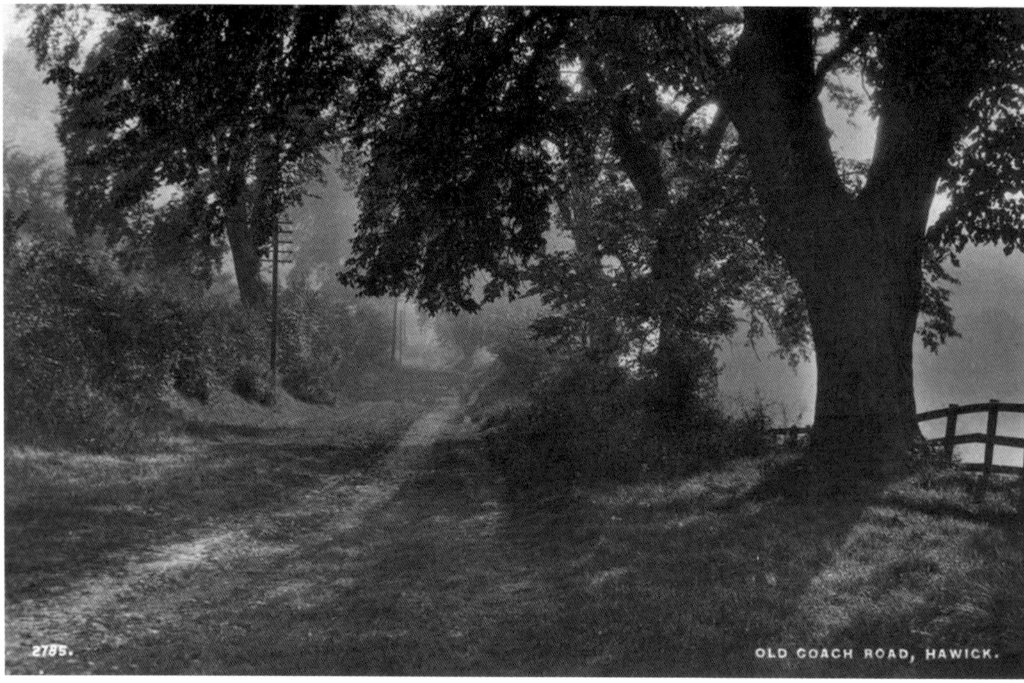

An Early Twentieth-Century View of the 'Lumback' or Langbaulk Road
The name derives from a long 'baulk' or strip of land that had been left unploughed. This thoroughfare once formed part of the main road to Carlisle from around 1762, and remains a public right of way.

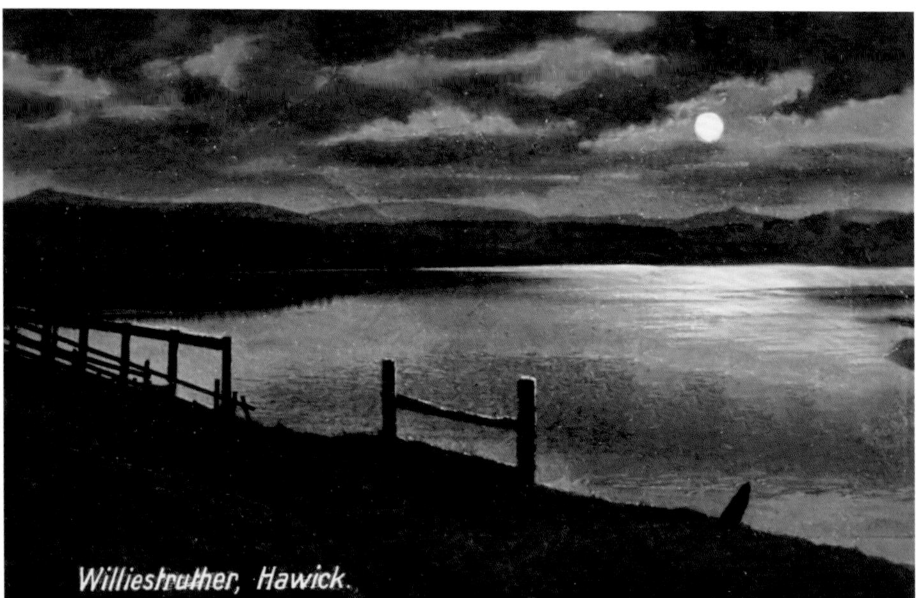

An Old Picture of Williestruther Loch by Moonlight
The loch covers about 17 acres and is well stocked for fishing. Its level was raised by damming in the early nineteenth century, to supply mills along the Slitrig Water during dry spells.

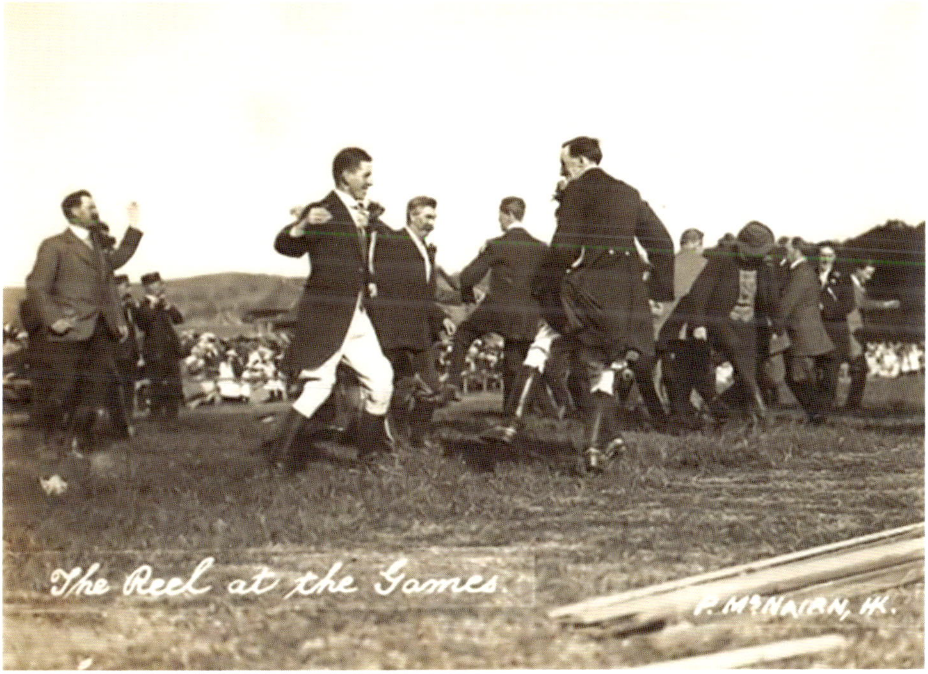

Dancing the Reel During the 1911 Common Riding

The Mair is a part of Hawick Common, containing Saint Leonard's Racecourse. This is the location of the main social event of the Common Riding on the Friday and Saturday afternoons.

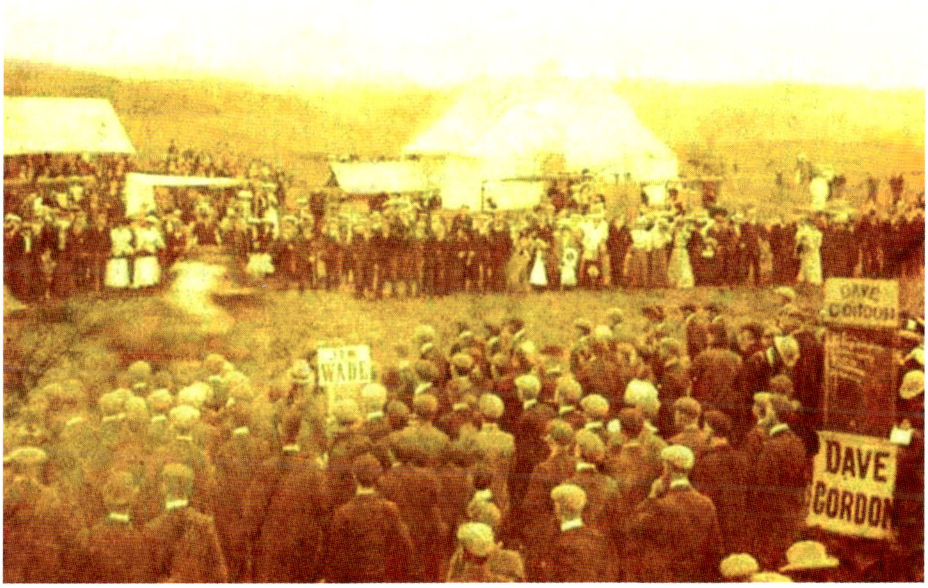

Saint Leonard's Racecourse, Early 1900s

This light-damaged photograph from the early 1900s shows a packed crowd for Common Riding races at the Mair. Saint Leonard's Racecourse opened in 1854, and is one of the highest courses in Britain.

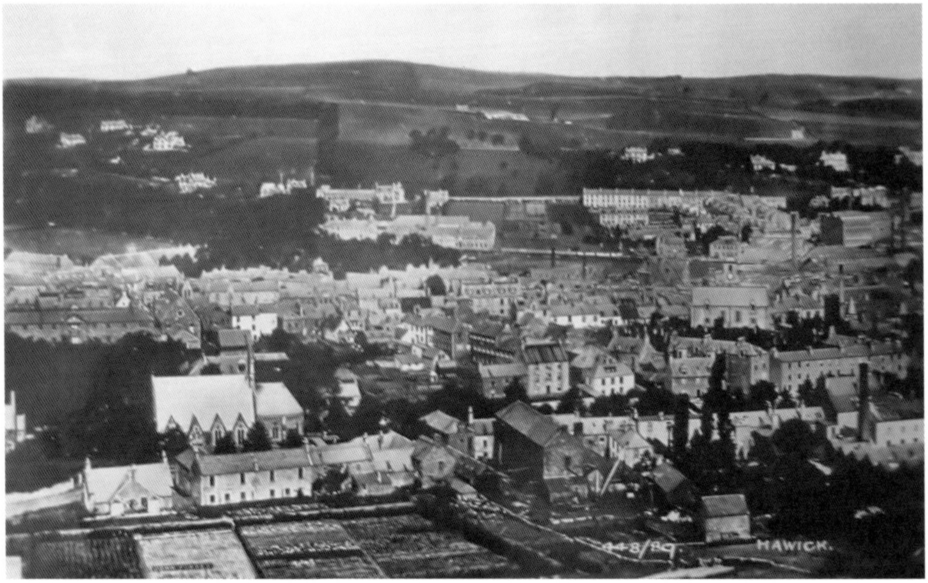

A View of Hawick From Stonefield, Early Last Century

To the left lies St Cuthbert's kirk, erected on land donated by the 5th Duke of Buccleuch, in 1857. Funded by an annual endowment from his estate, this was designed by renowned architect George Gilbert Scott.

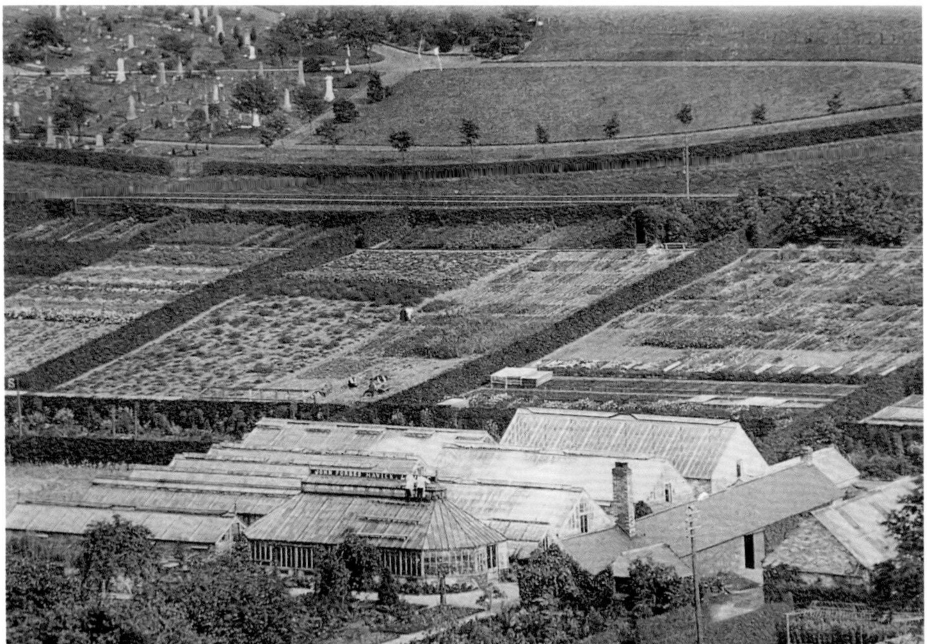

Forbes' Buccleuch Nurseries, 1907

A scanned image of Forbes' Buccleuch Nurseries from 1907 (the same year the company was granted a Royal Warrant). This was a former commercial plant nursery begun in 1879. A pioneer and regular attendee at the Chelsea Flower Show, sadly the business closed in 1968.

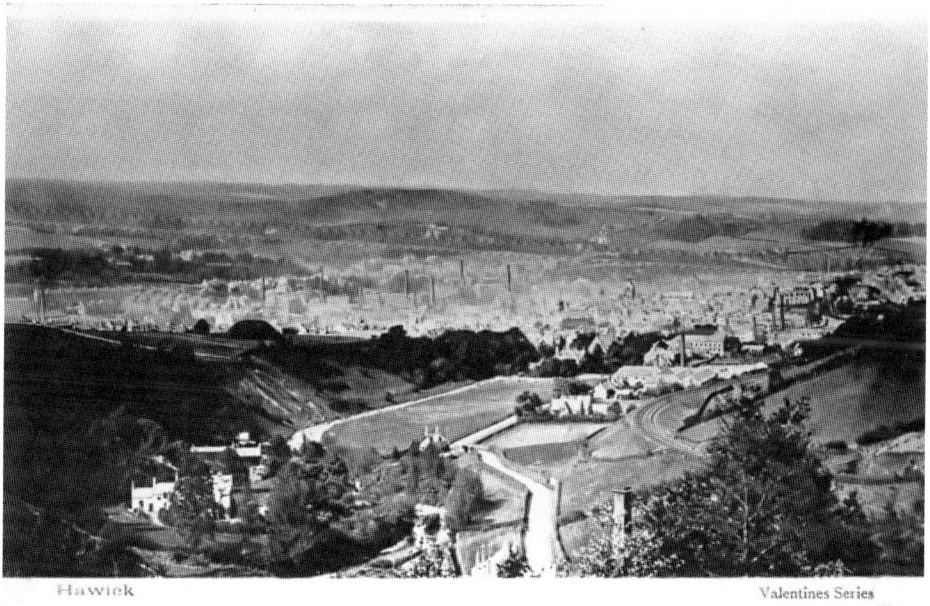

A View of Hawick From the Duke's Wood in 1903
This area is named after its historical links to the Duke of Buccleuch, who still owns tracts of land here. It is a designated Site of Special Scientific Interest and a Scottish Wildlife Trust reserve.

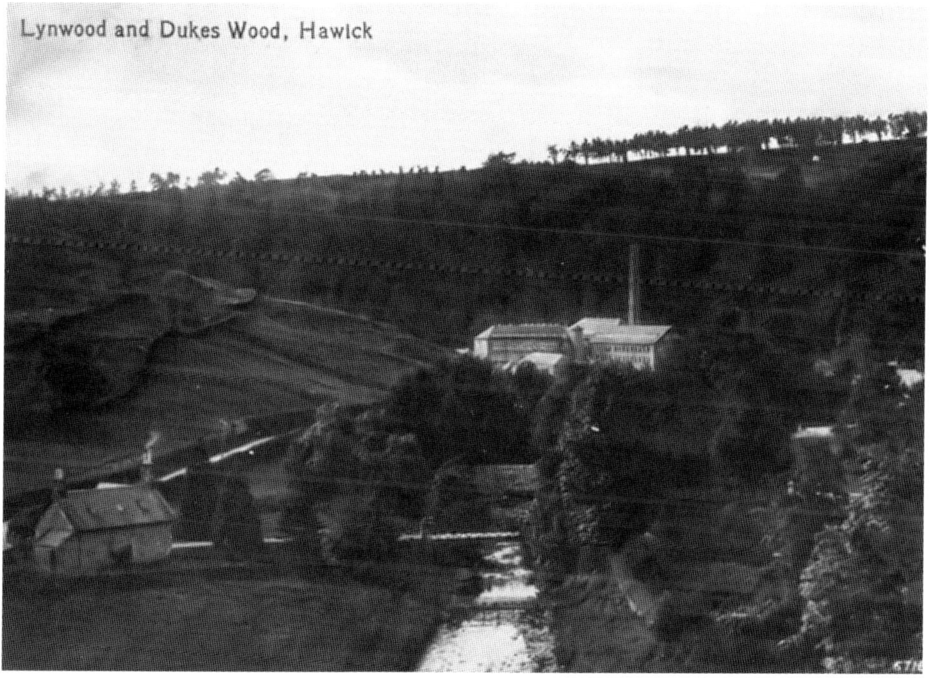

A Beautiful View of Lynnwood From 1910
Central to this image is the former carding mill of John Nixon & Sons, built in 1803. The mill closed in 1909 and the site was cleared completely by 1921 (later to become Lynnwood housing estate).

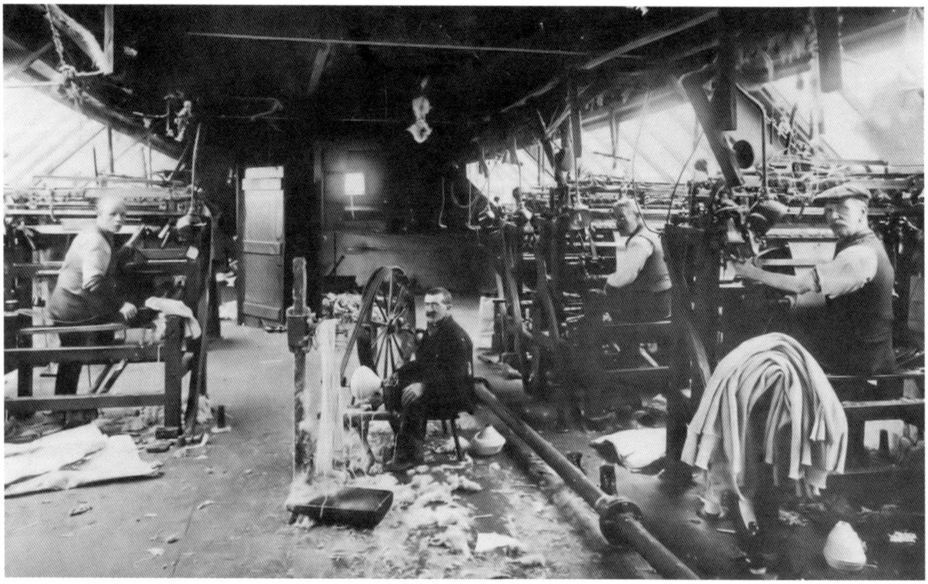

Workers on the Shop Floor of Lyle & Scott's Stonefield Mill in the 1910s
William Lyle and Walter Scott founded a knitwear company with £800 of borrowed capital in 1874. Today it remains a highly fashionable brand, with a number of outlets in London.

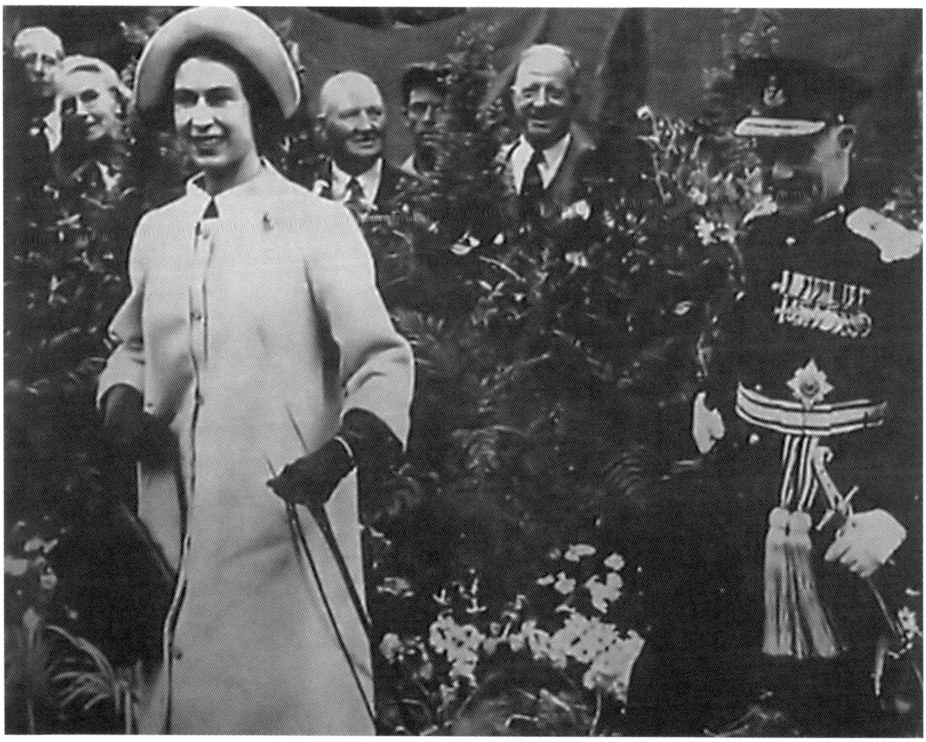

Queen Elizabeth II Visits Lyle & Scott's Stonefield Mill in 1962
The factory buildings were built on the site of Brewery Haugh recreation ground; it was here that Hawick YM played their first ever game – a 14-0 defeat to Gala Red Triangle.

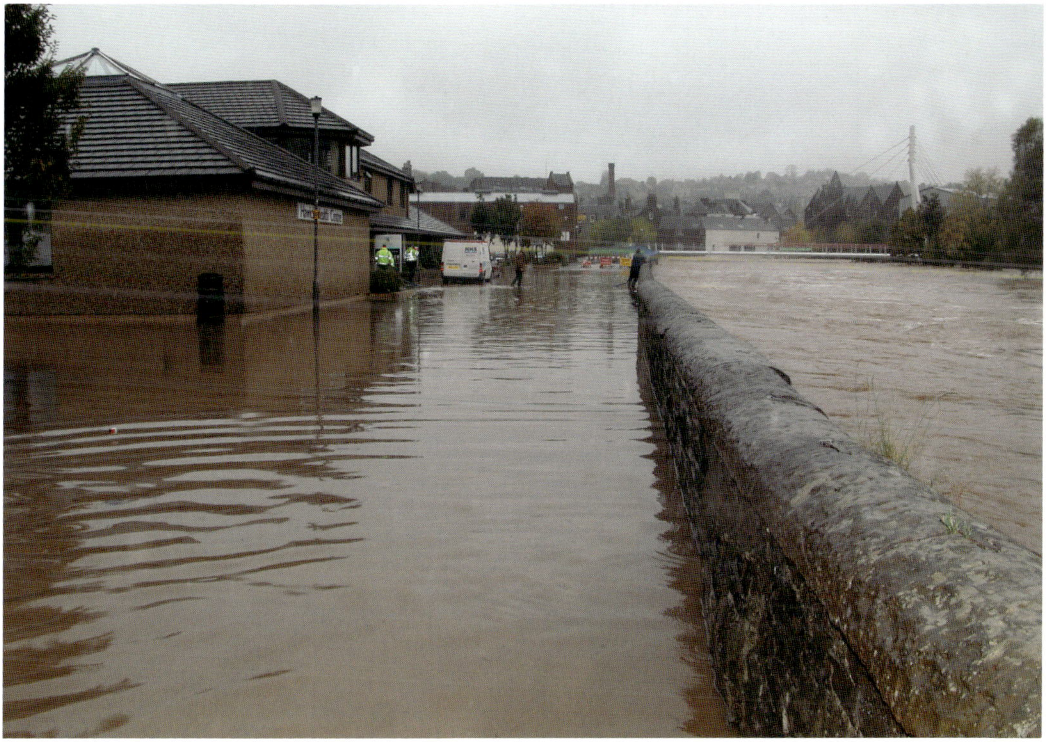

Above: Teviot Crescent Overwhelmed by Flood Water in 2005
The site to the left was once Pringle's Rodono Mill, which closed in 1976 due to rising production costs. Teviot Medical Practice was built here in 1989.

Right: The Wee Haugh after Water Levels Subsided in October 2005
Hawick has a long history of floods, with the levels of 2005 the worst in recorded history. It affected hundreds of properties and caused millions of pounds' worth of damage.

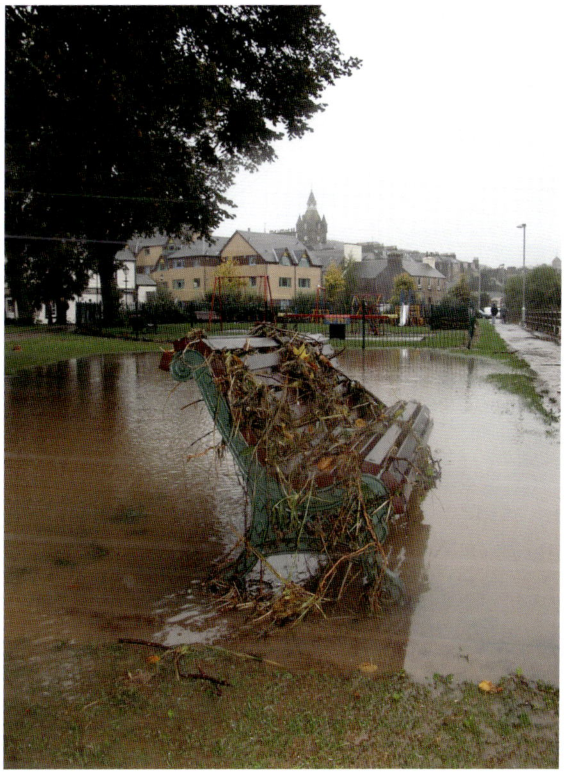

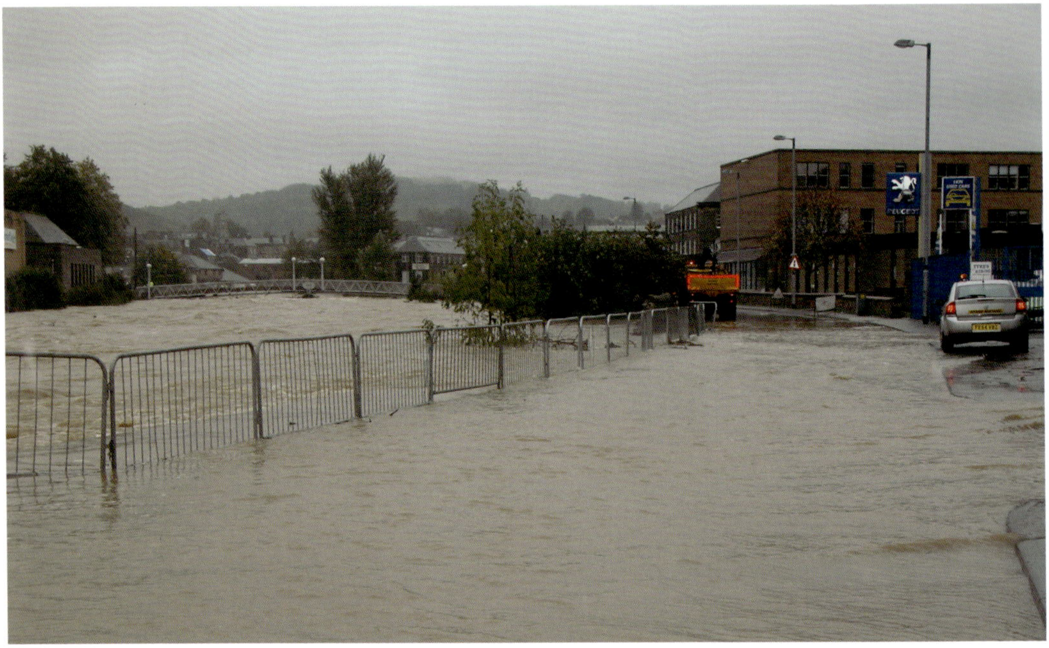

A Scene that Has to Be Seen to Be Believed

Water levels reached to as high as the top end of Commercial Road in 2005. The street was so named in 1884, having being referred to previously as Teviotside Road.

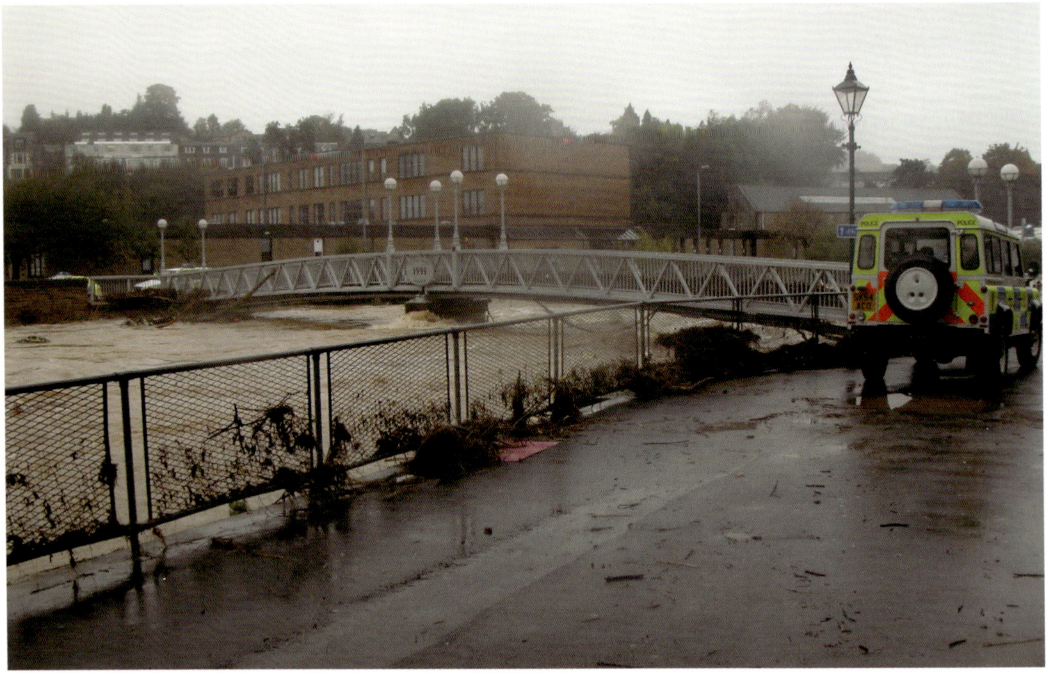

The Teviot Almost Touching the Victoria Footbridge in 2005

The bridge from 1939 was replaced in 1991 (as noted by the sign). The position of the original foundations can today be seen just a few yards upstream.

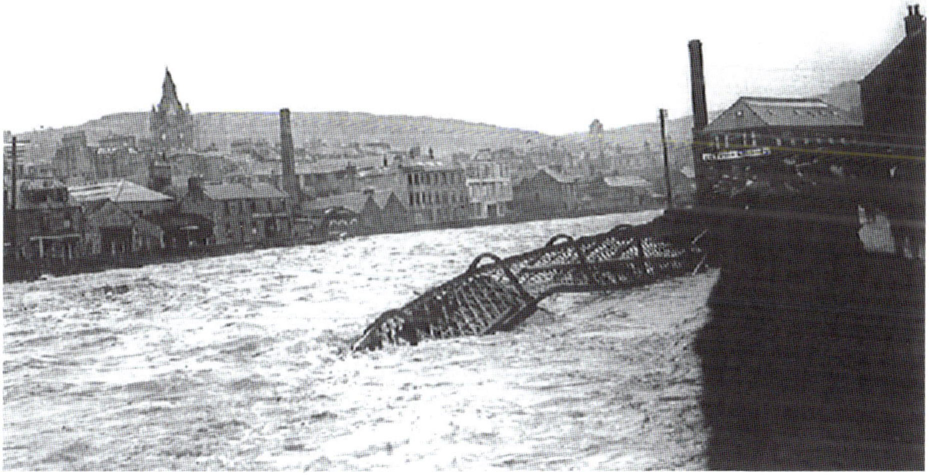

The Collapse of the Victoria Footbridge, 1938
The flood of November 1938 washed away the original Victoria footbridge, as well as the Mansfield crossing further upstream. The first bridge to span this point featured a wooden trellis design and was built in 1851. This was replaced by a cast iron replica in 1873.

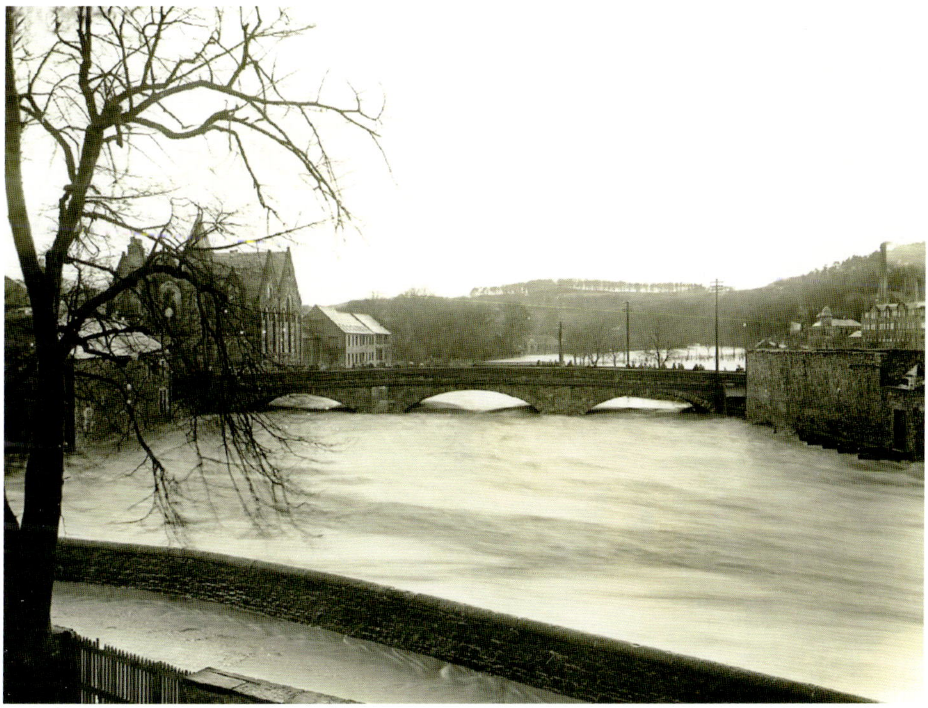

The Extent of the Great Flood of December 1924
Orrock kirk (left of the bridge) was built in 1874 and ceased to be a religious meeting place in 1951. The halls now play host to fitness classes and events.

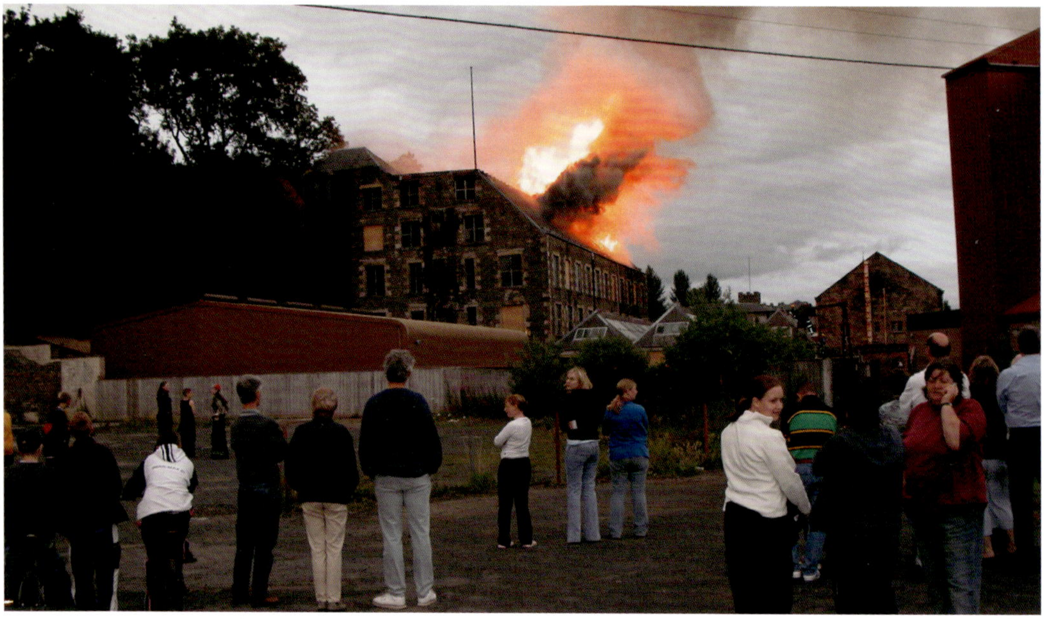

The Dangerfield Mill Fire, 2003

Onlookers watch the historic Dangerfield Mill go up in flames, on Common Riding Friday in 2003. Two fires in less than a month destroyed all but the wool sorting shed. The spinning mill had been the only surviving example in Britain, with the original machinery still in place.

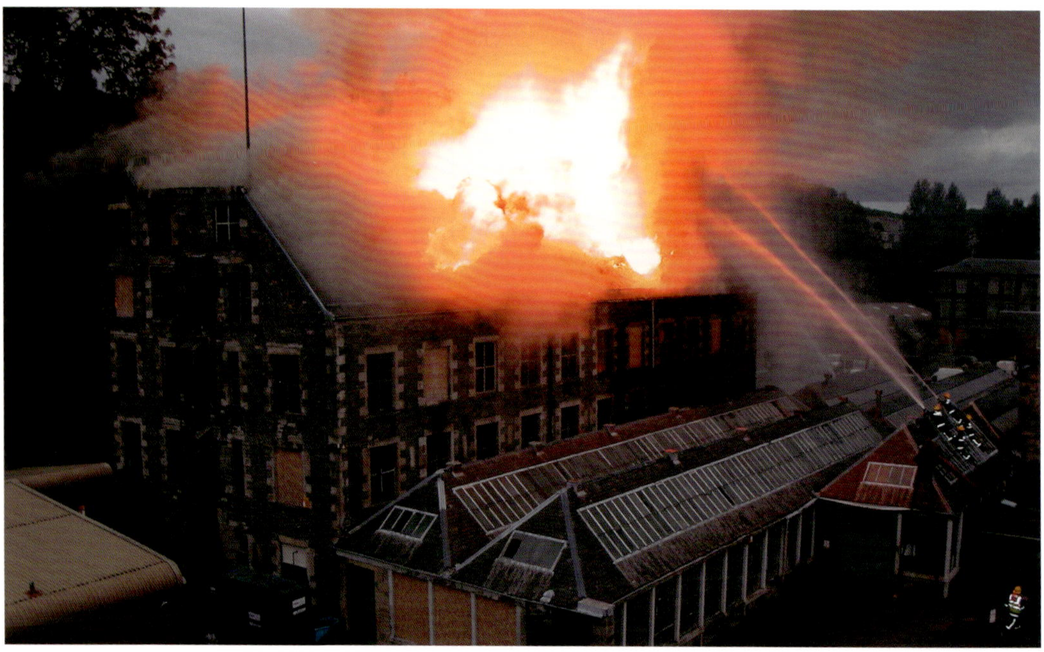

The Battle to Save Dangerfield Mill, 2003

Another dramatic snapshot of the battle to save Dangerfield Mill, founded as a hosiery works in 1806. The fire destroyed most of the firm's records, including pattern books and the letter establishing the word 'tweed'.

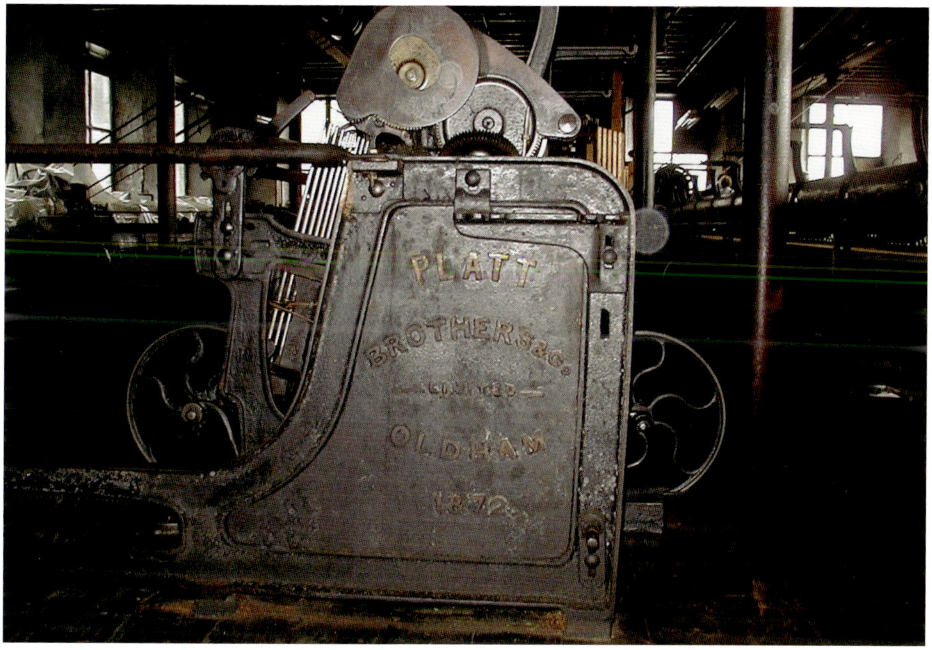

Dangerfield Mill Interior, 2002

The interior of Dangerfield Mill in 2002, with equipment from Platt Brothers of Oldham, originally installed in 1872. The Dangerfield name refers to the haugh which defined the boundary of the Common at its north-west end, the site of an old archery range.

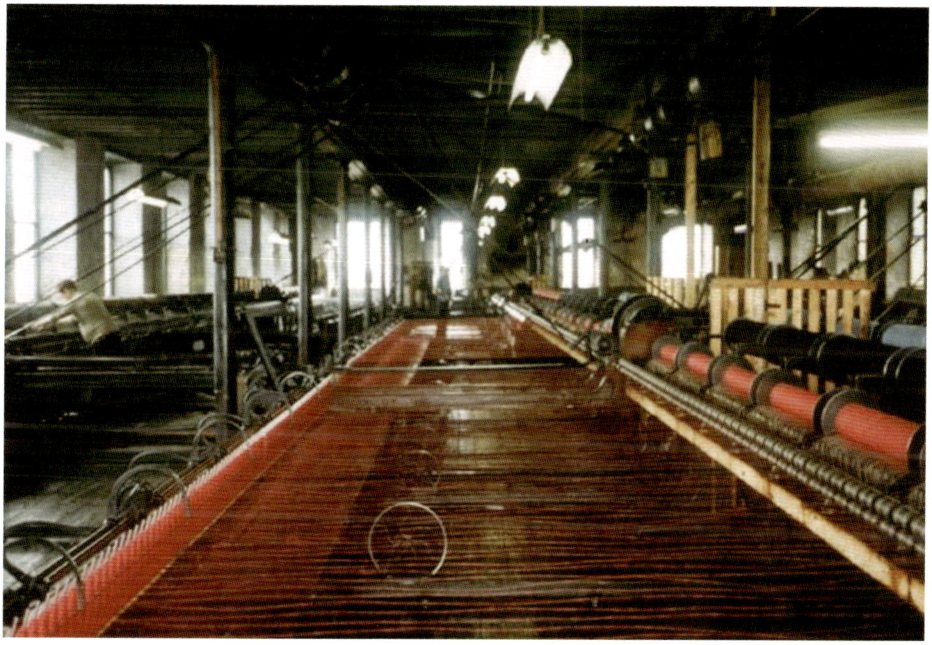

The Interior of Dangerfield's Sorting Shed in the Late 1980s

Despite the closure of the mill in the early 1990s, the shed was still in use as late as 1998 for cashmere manufacture. The site was levelled to make way for a Sainsbury's supermarket.

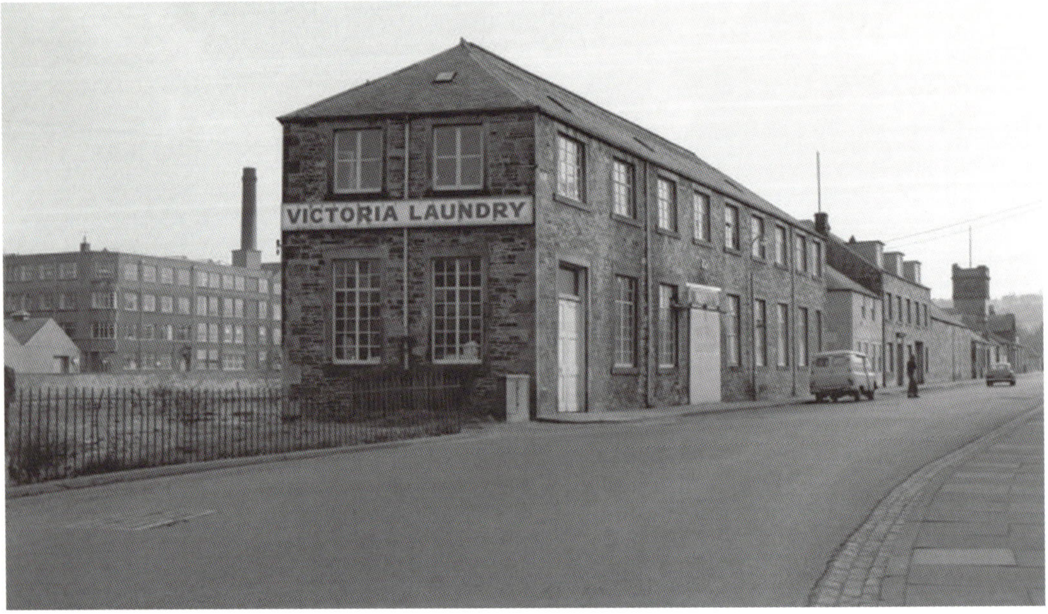

Outside the Old Victoria Laundry on Commercial Road in 1974

Originally opened as the Victoria Baths during the 1890s, it was developed into a laundry in 1912, when the nearby Corporation Swimming Baths were gifted to the town. It closed in October 1989.

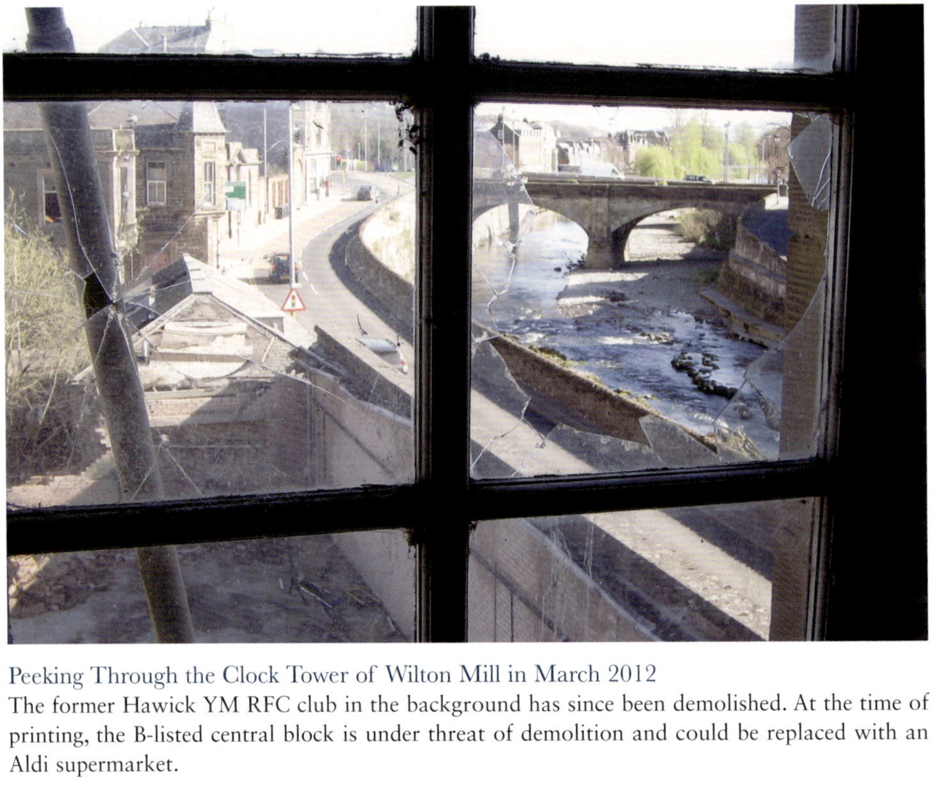

Peeking Through the Clock Tower of Wilton Mill in March 2012

The former Hawick YM RFC club in the background has since been demolished. At the time of printing, the B-listed central block is under threat of demolition and could be replaced with an Aldi supermarket.

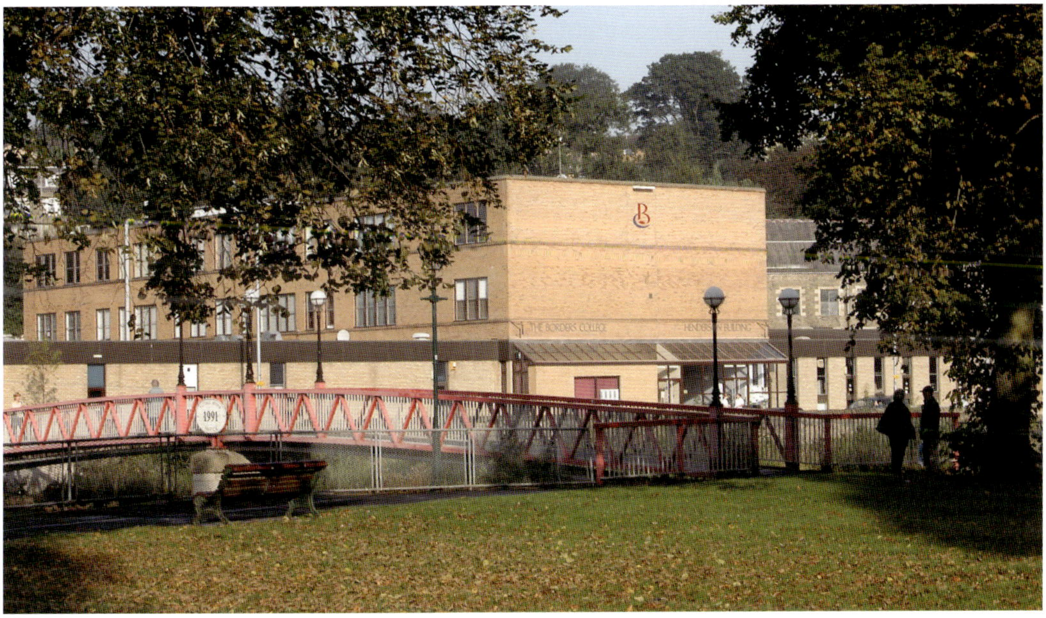

The Henderson Building on Commercial Road, Seen Prior to Demolition
Henderson Technical College was built in 1926 on Buccleuch Road, through the benevolence of Thomas Henderson. The new building was opened in 1971 on Commercial Road and closed in 2009 to make way for a supermarket.

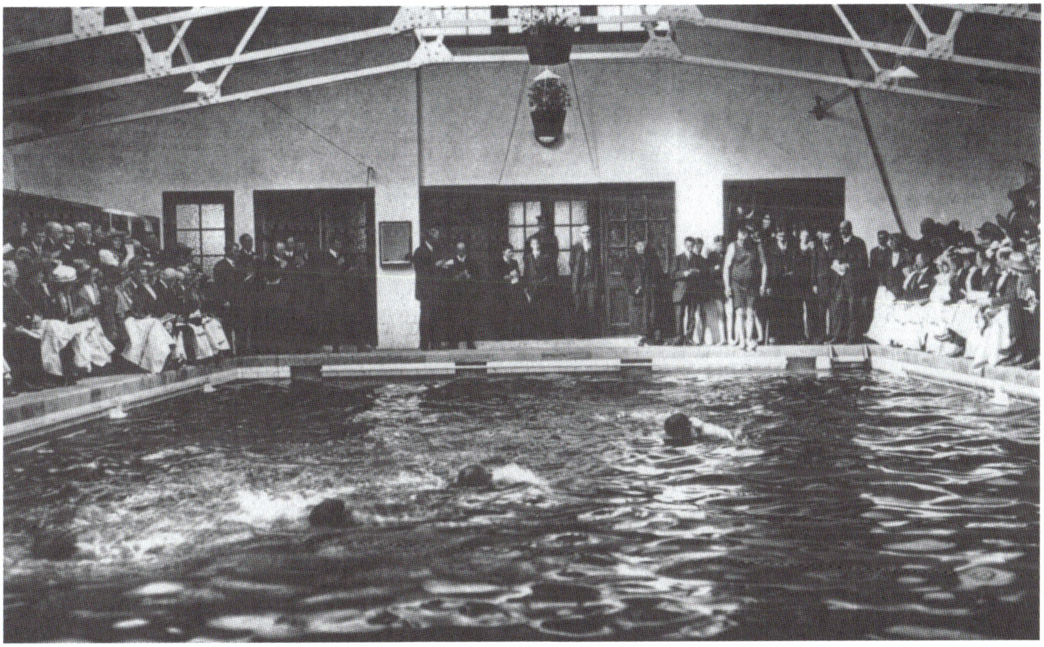

The Official Opening of the Corporation Swimming Baths in 1913
The building was gifted to the town by James Glenny, Charles John Wilson and George Murray Wilson. Though the pool underwent refurbishment in 1980, a new leisure centre was opened at nearby Mansfield in 1982.

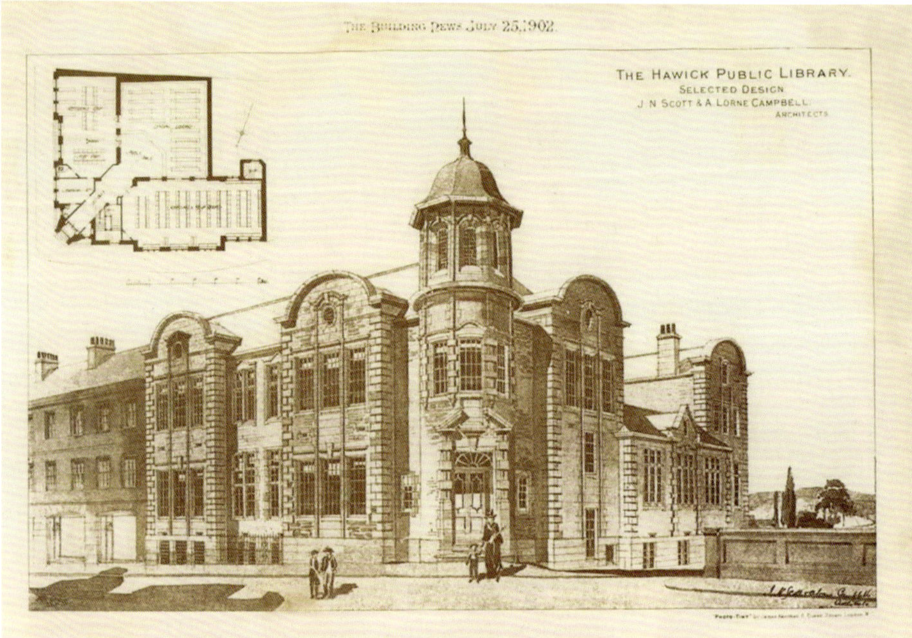

Hawick Public Library

A print of Hawick Public Library, from an edition of *The Building News*, 25 July 1902. Hawick Public Library was founded in 1878 and began in rooms at the former Corn Exchange. The current building was opened by Andrew Carnegie in 1904.

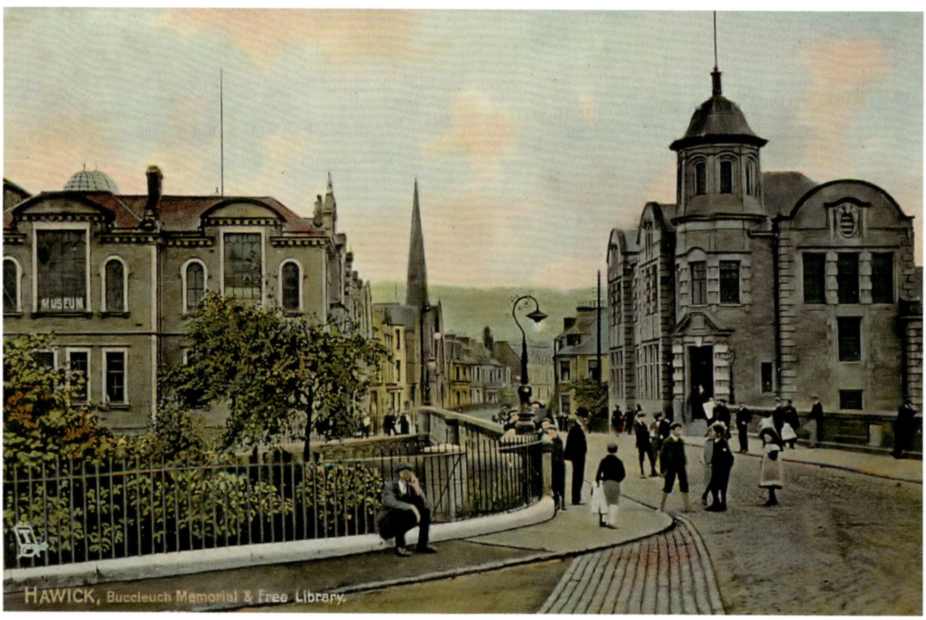

Three Historic Buildings

Three historic buildings – the Buccleuch Memorial, St Andrew's kirk and the Carnegie Free Library – as seen in 1907. The Buccleuch was built by public subscription in 1887, to honour the 'Good Duke Walter'. Demolished in 1973, the site is now occupied by Waverley Housing.

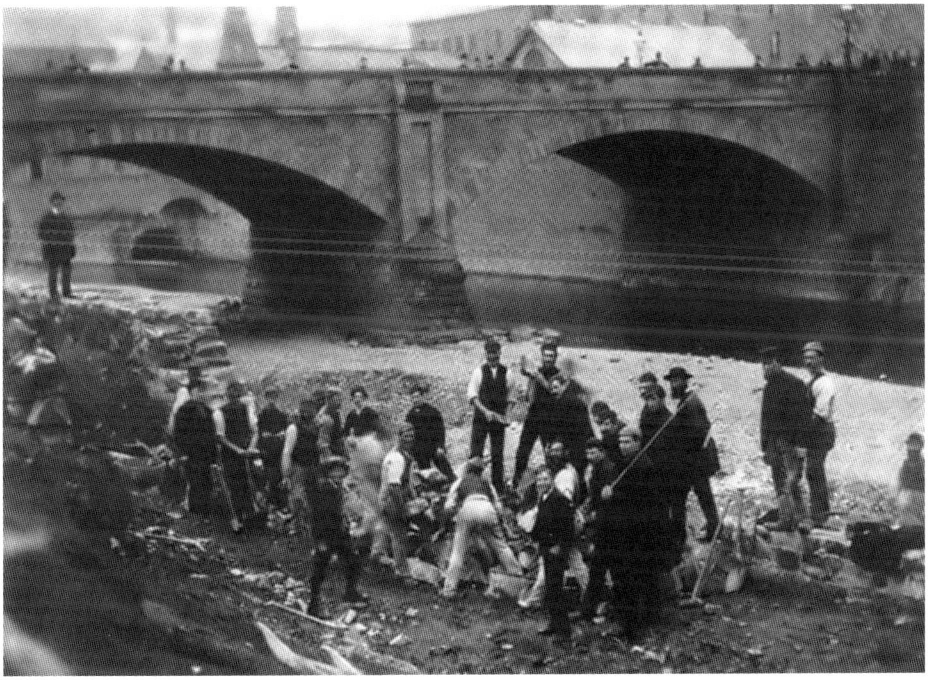

Landscaping the Banks of the Teviot in 1890
Behind the workers lies the North Bridge. Built in 1832, the bridge no longer carries road traffic, having been superceded by the nearby Waverley Bridge in 2000.

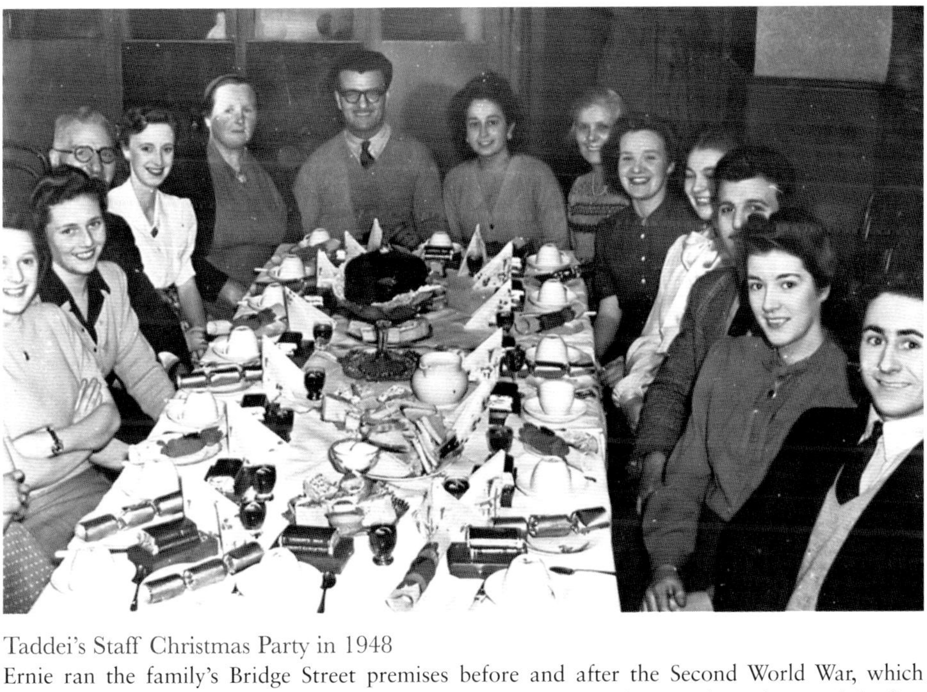

Taddei's Staff Christmas Party in 1948
Ernie ran the family's Bridge Street premises before and after the Second World War, which included an impressive set of billiards tables. This was later used as a café, with one of the first bingo halls in the Borders.

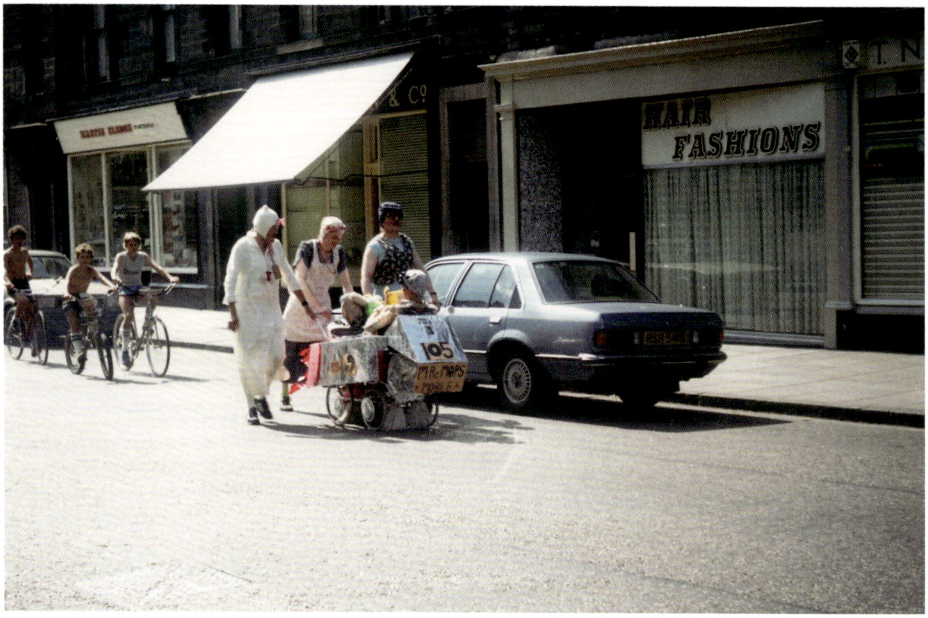

The Inaugural Hawick Summer Festival, 1984

A photo from the inaugural Hawick Summer Festival in 1984, more specifically of the Pram Race on North Bridge Street. In addition to the Common Riding, Hawick also plays host annually to the Reivers Festival, Vertish Hill Sports Day, Burnfoot Carnival and Christmas Parade.

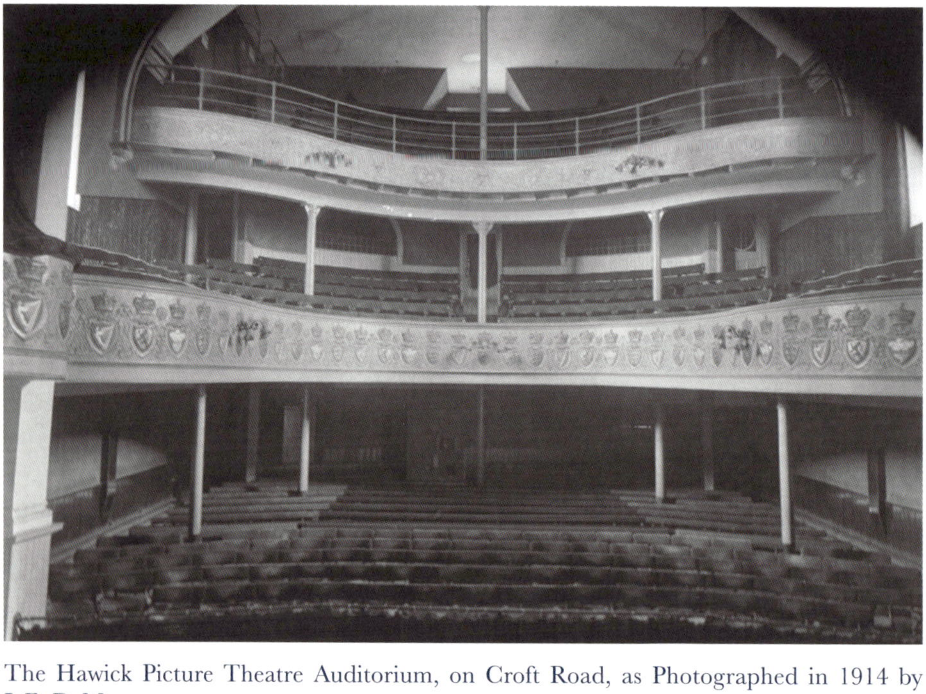

The Hawick Picture Theatre Auditorium, on Croft Road, as Photographed in 1914 by J. E. D. Murray

Converted from an old Temperance Hall in 1901, the 'Wee Thea' once hosted suffragette Emmeline Pankhurst. It was sadly destroyed by fire in 1955 and replaced by the Salvation Army Citadel.

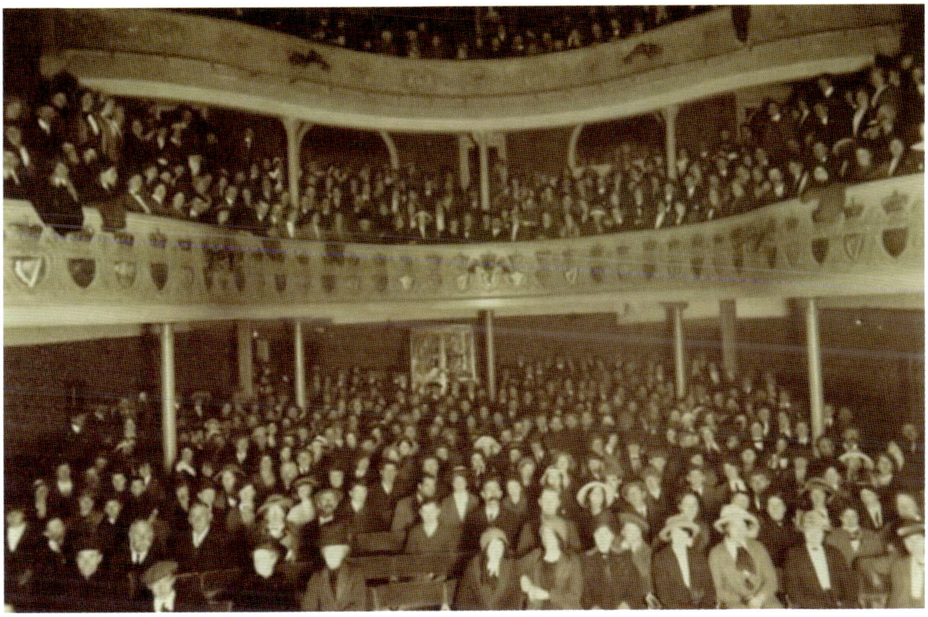

A Packed Auditorium at the 'Wee Thea', Also in 1914
By the outbreak of the First World War, its weel-kent slogan was 'we place the world before you'. The interior had plush red seats and gilt plaster crowns.

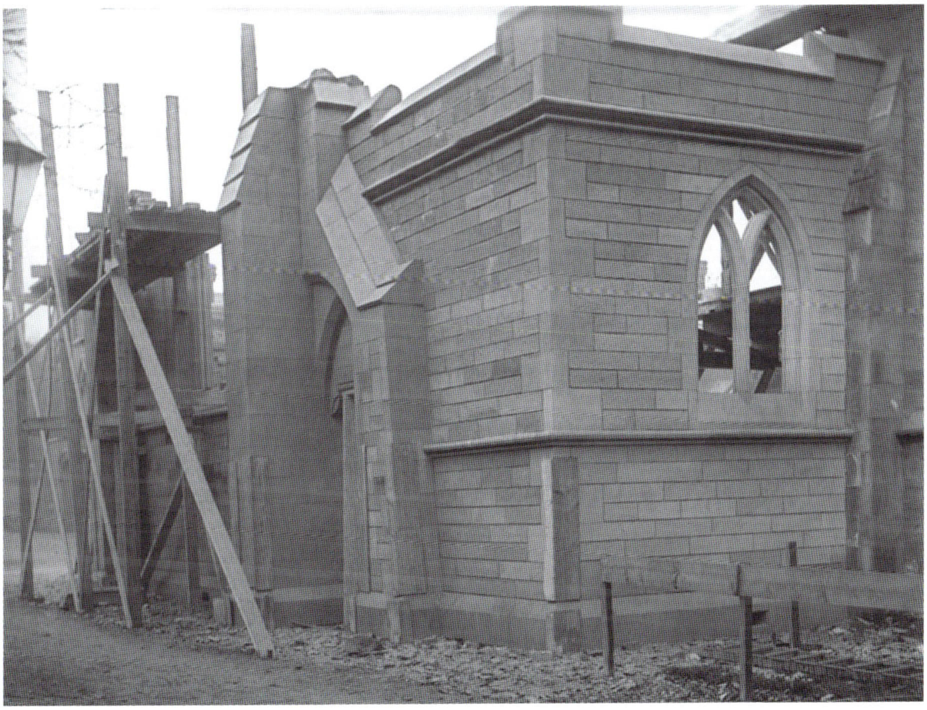

Wilton Parish Church, Dickson Street, Undergoes Some Alterations in 1908
The current building was erected in 1859, though the Auld Kirk (off Princes Street) remained in use for functions until 1861. A portion of the seventeenth-century graveyard remains there on open ground.

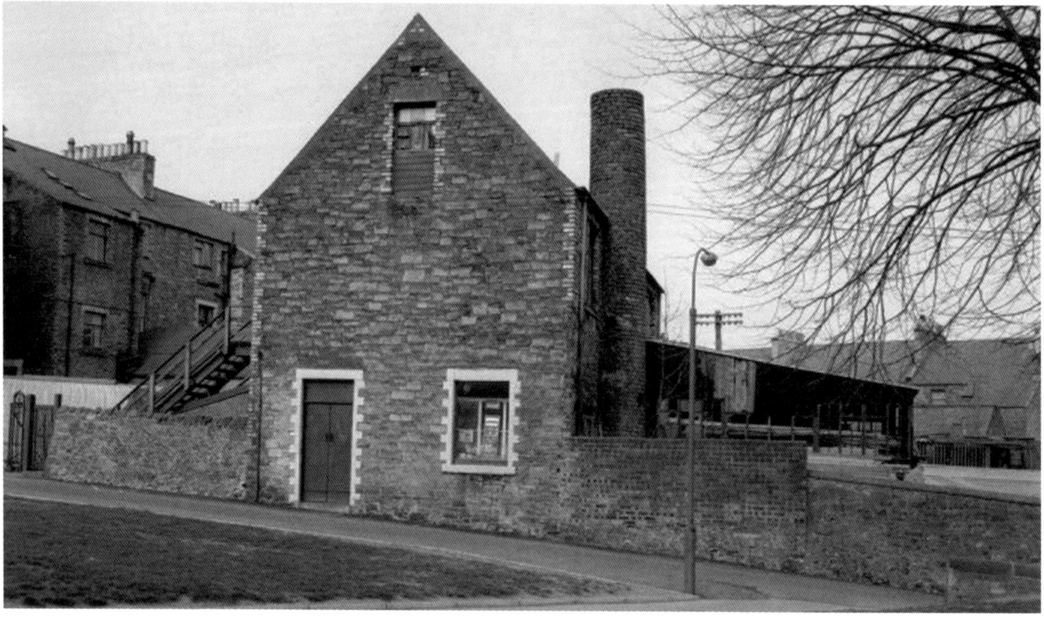

Armstrong's the Joiners on Wilton Lane in 1974
Owned by William Armstrong, the carpentry workshop was later demolished to make way for private housing. This area was once known as Kirkyard Entry, due to its proximity to Auld Wilton Kirk.

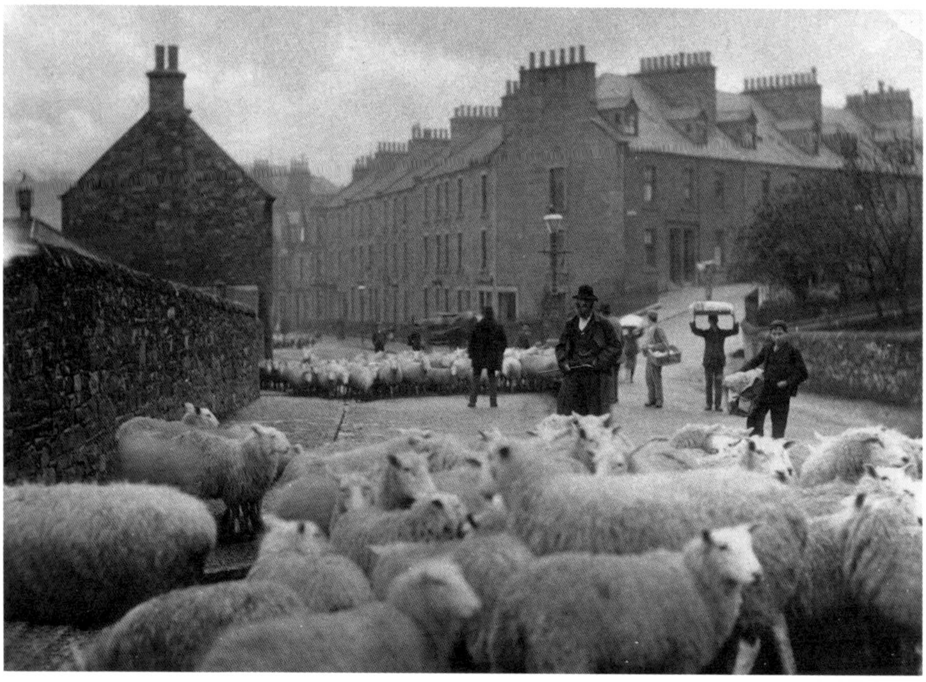

Sheep from Gatehousecote Farm Being Driven to Hawick Railway Station, in 1896
Gatehousecote, first farmed in the late-fifteenth century, lies between Abbotrule and Hallrule Mill, on the Foderlee Burn.

Right: The Former Kirklands Hotel, Located off West Stewart Place
Viewforth villa was built for hatter George Porteous. It became a temperance hotel prior to the Second World War, and continued as a hotel until being sold to the current owners in 2007.

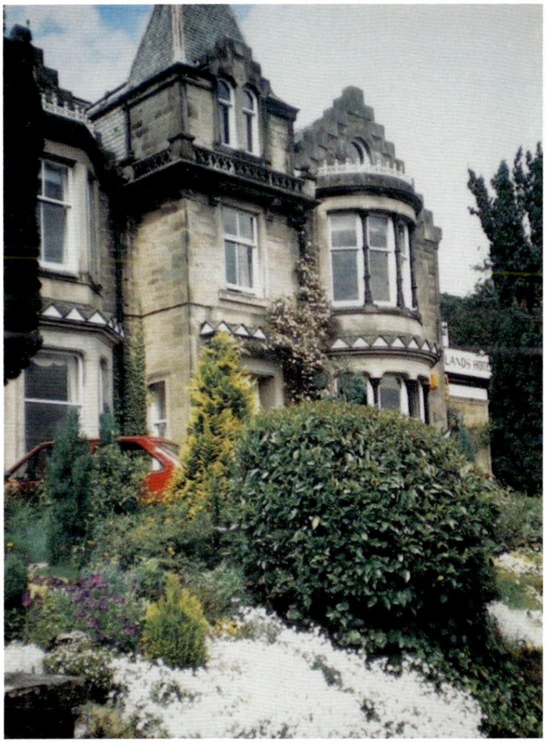

Below: An Aerial Photograph of Sillerbit Ha', Taken 18 July 1933
This mansion house was built in 1863 and demolished in 1946. The Town Council built over the land to solve Hawick's post war housing shortage; an abundance of 'prefabs' were laid out and subsequently replaced by modern housing in the 1960s and 1970s.

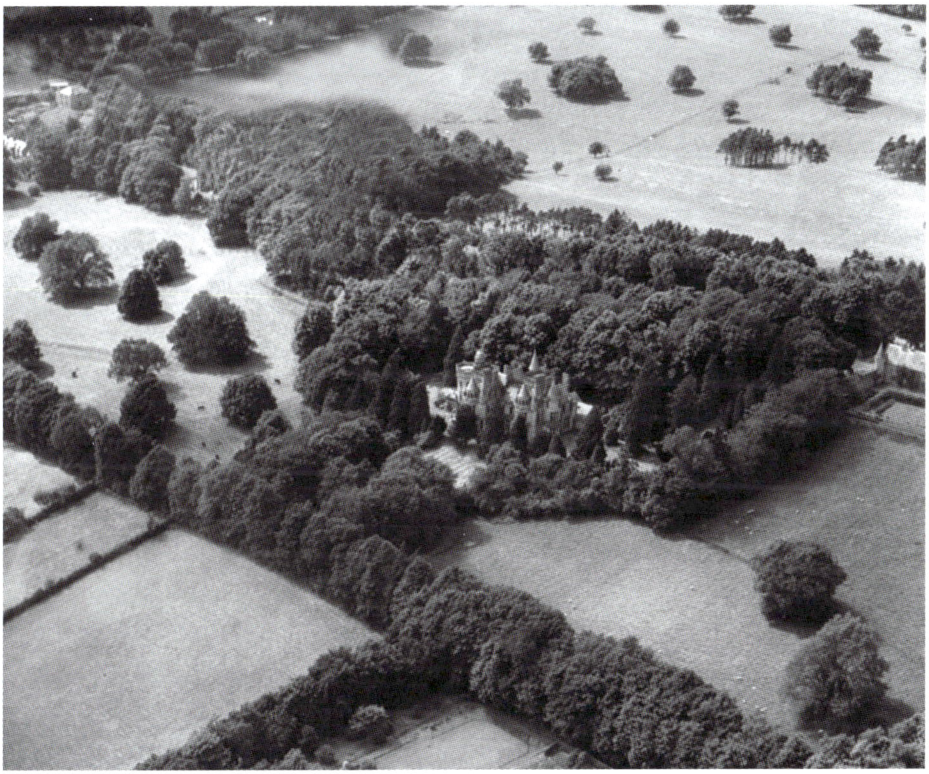

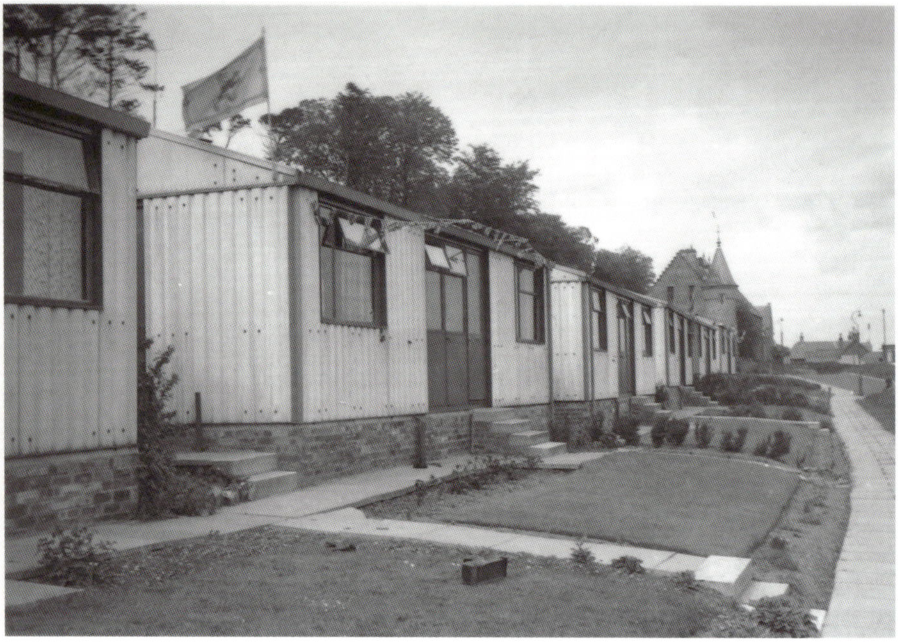

A Row of 'Prefabs' at Silverbuthall in the 1950s
The first ninety were erected between 1945 and 1947, with more built in the following years. They consisted of a mixture of Arcon and Uni-Seco types.

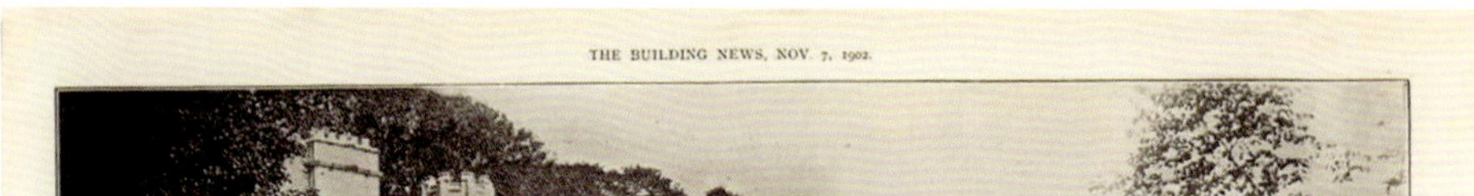

The Newly Altered Stirches House in 1902
The original tower was built in 1503 by the Chisholm family, overlooking the surrounding valley and burn. Rebuilt three times over the centuries, the Augustinian Order of Sisters took possession of the house in 1926 and opened a convent and geriatric home.

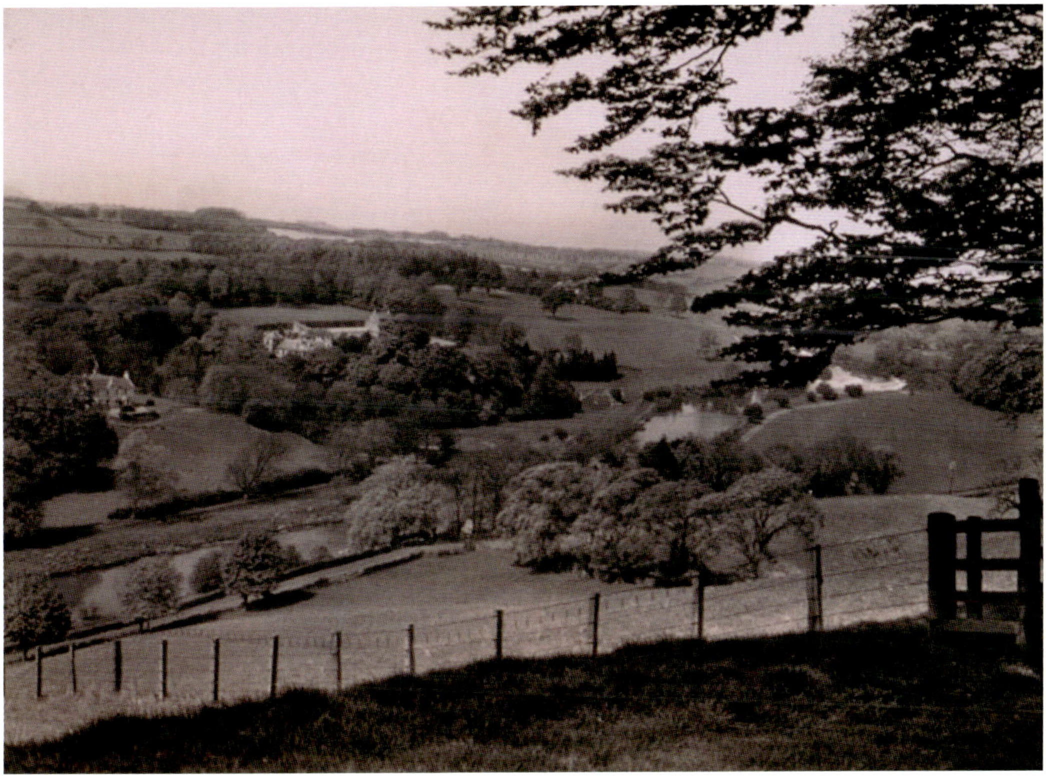

Looking Towards Burnfoot, 1936

This photograph looks across to the bare hills of Burnfoot in 1936, once home to the Hawick and District Joint Fever Hospital. Opened in 1902 at a cost of £6,000, the hospital later became an annexe to Burnfoot Primary School and a social work outreach centre.

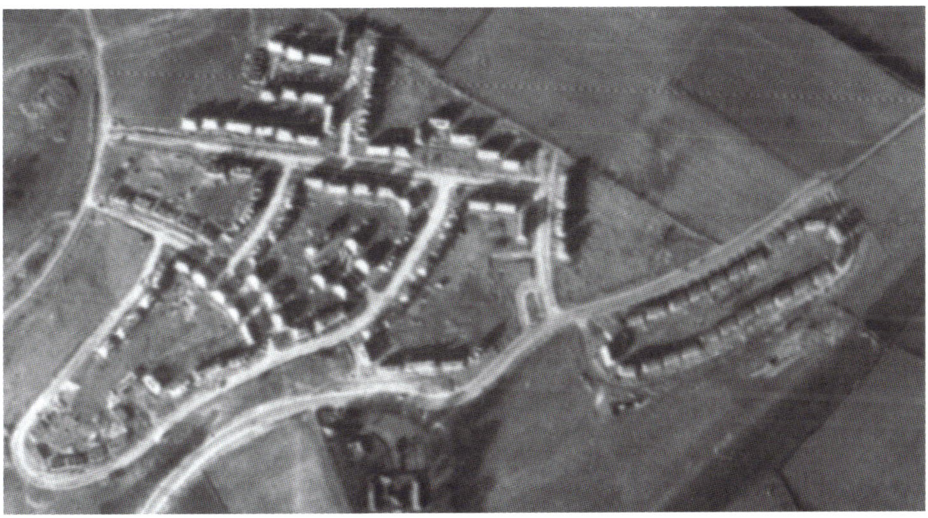

An Aerial Photograph of Burnfoot under Construction in March 1950

Burnfit is the largest housing estate in the Borders, built on former farmland in the 1950s. It has its own distinct identity, school, community hub (opening 2015) and shops.

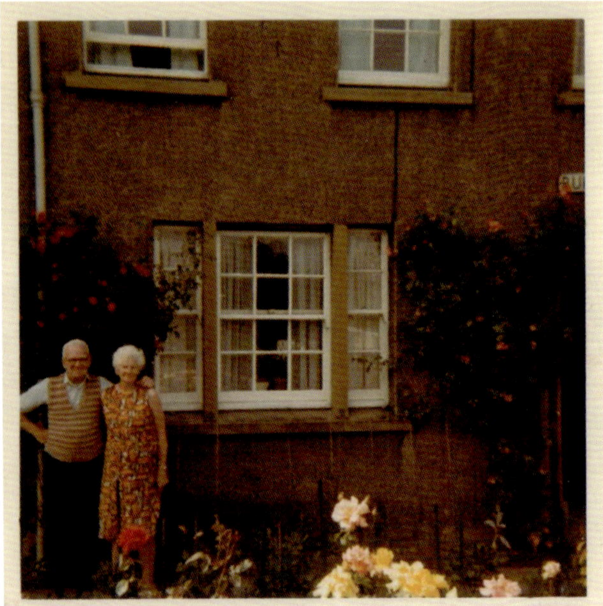

97 Burnfoot Road, 1970s
Neil and Eliza Redpath stand outside their home at 97 Burnfoot Road, in the 1970s. Burnfoot Road, previously a country lane, was re-aligned in 1949. Adjacent to here is Saint Stephen's Church, known as the Abundant Life Church since September 1981.

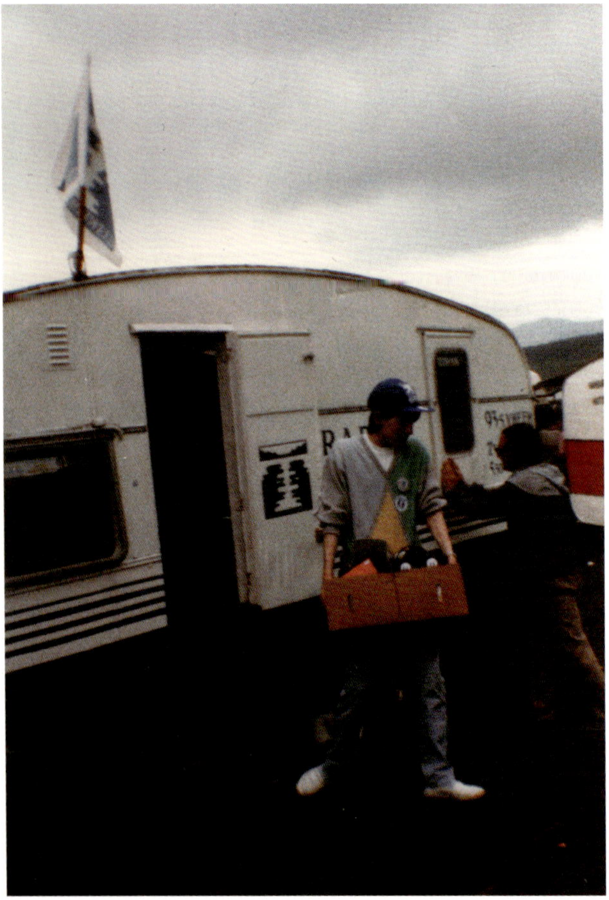

1989 Burnfoot Carnival
The BBC Radio Tweed team at the 1989 Burnfoot Carnival, which nowadays is held in the grounds of the local school. Burnfoot Community Carnival was started in 1969 by the local Residents Association.

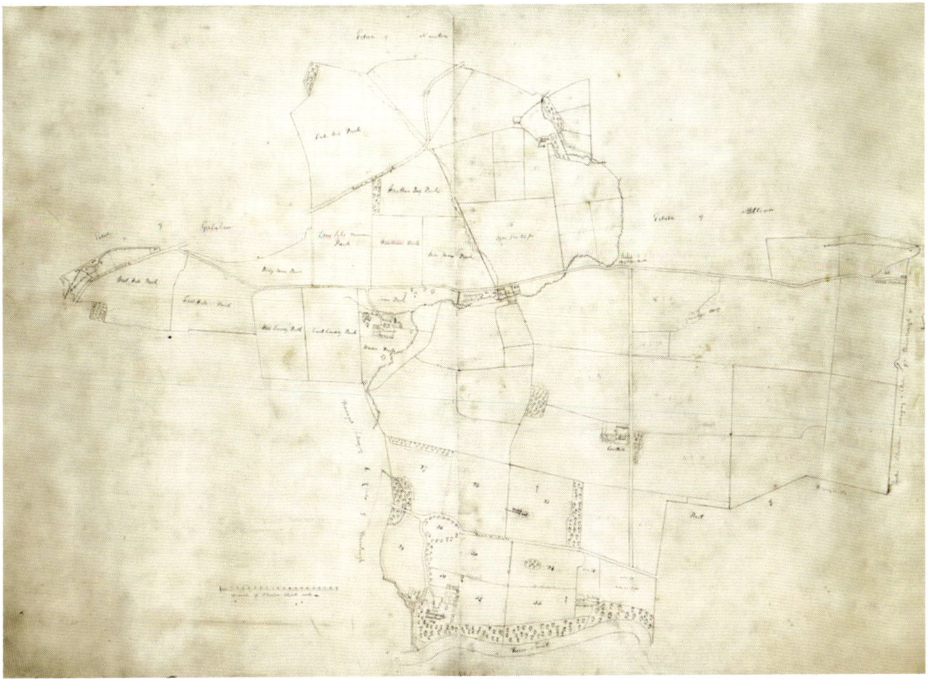

A Detailed Map of Courthill Farm and Its Surrounding Lands
The Usher family has farmed Courthill for more than six generations. The farm was established in 1794. On the summit of the nearby hill lie the remains of a fort and cart tracks, both now mutilated by years of quarrying and farming.

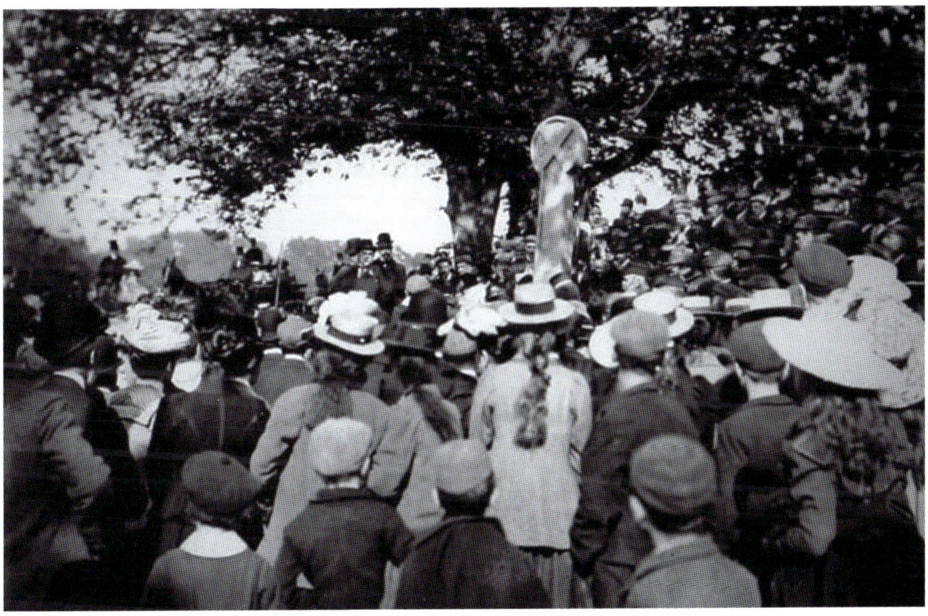

The Unveiling Ceremony of the Lest We Forget Monument at Hornshole in 1901
Erected as a tribute to the bravery of Hawick's youth during the Hornshole Skirmish of 1514, it was replaced at the cost of £3,000 in time for the recent quincentenary celebrations.

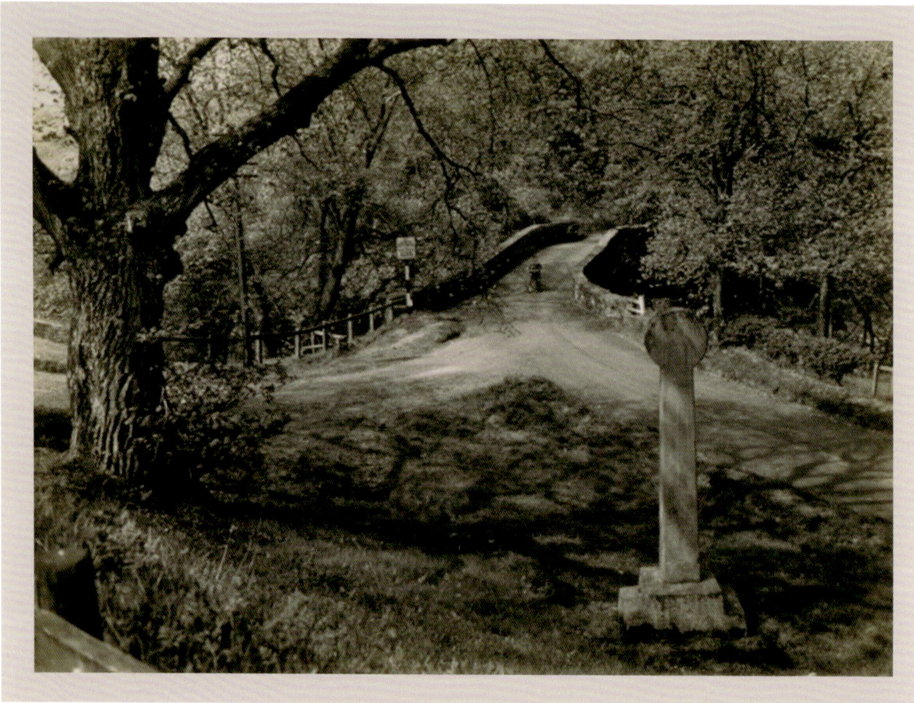

A Snapshot of the Lest We Forget Monument in 1936

Built on a small piece of land gifted by Captain Palmer-Douglas of Cavers, it was paid for with money left over from subscriptions to the 'Return to Hawick' painting.

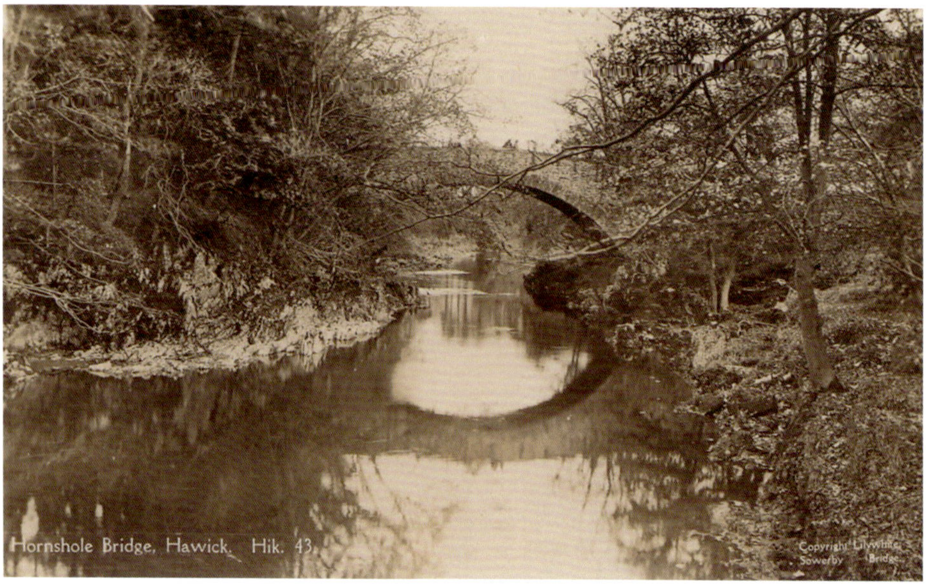

Hornshole Brig Was Built in 1772

Construction was overseen by Adam Scott and John Pott, although Scott retired when framework used to build the arch collapsed and injured him. Pott died soon after, as the result of the injuries that he sustained in the course of construction.

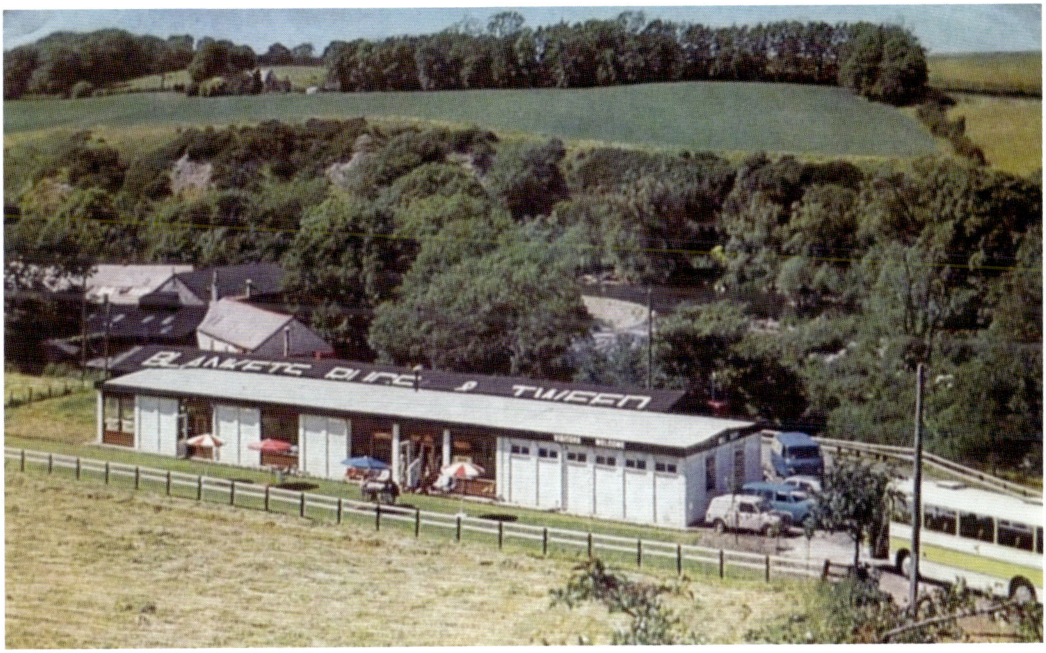

A Coach Party Visits Trow Mill in the 1960s

Begun as a corn grinding mill in the 1740s, the business focused on wool from 1886, producing famous scotch blankets. Though the millennium marked the beginning of a decline in the mill's fortunes, it has since been closed for a number of years.

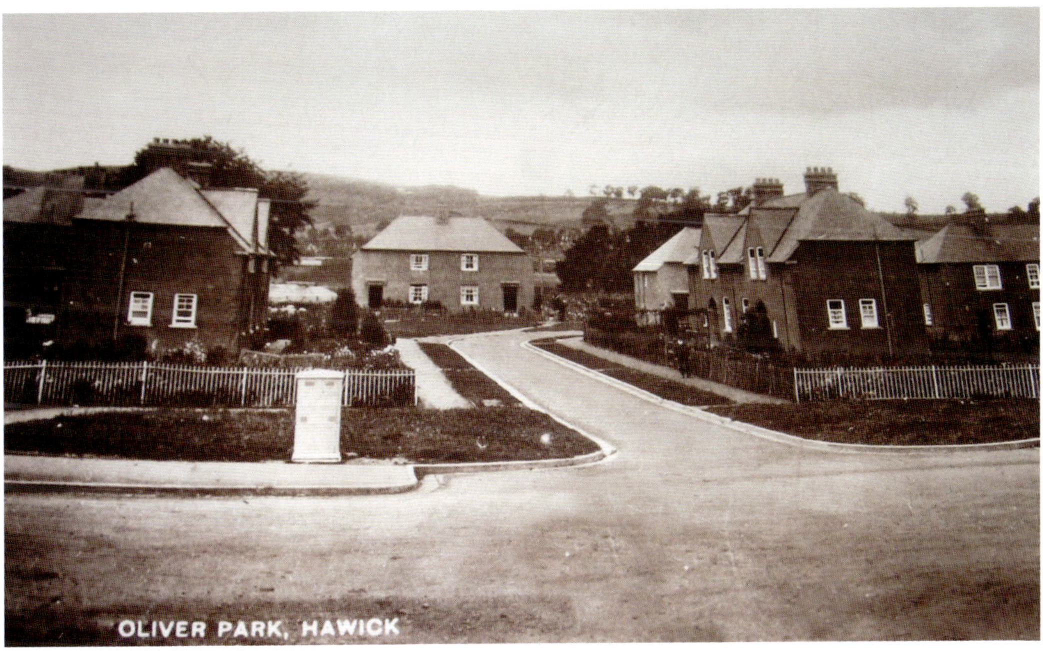

The Newly Built Housing Estate at Oliver Park Captured in 1925

Built in 1922, it was the first public housing scheme of its kind in Hawick. The street is named after auctioneer Andrew Rutherford Oliver, of nearby Thornwood House.

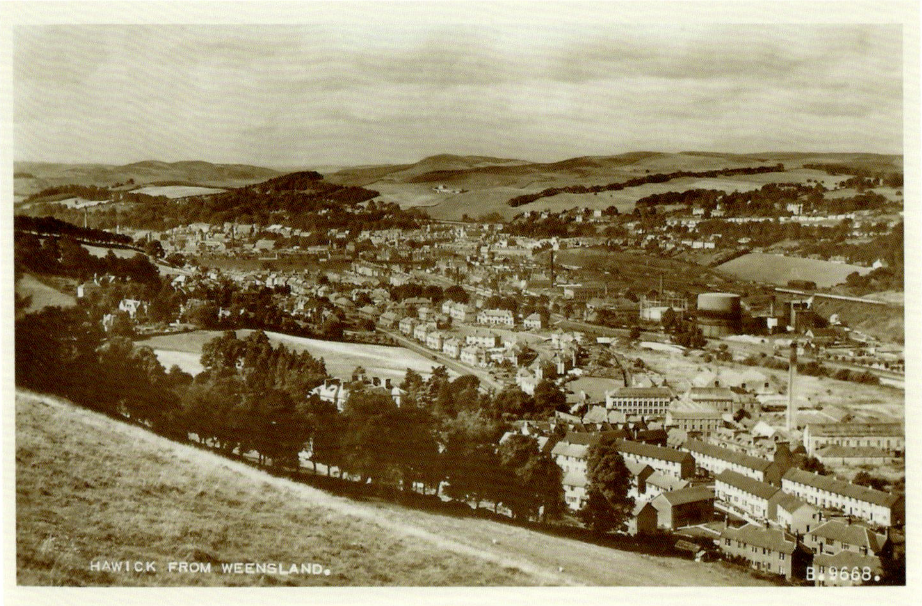

Hawick from Weensland in 1949

This area was once a small village, supported by a corn mill and several woollen mills, the most famous of which was Weensland Spinning Company. A large fire gutted the complex in 1999 and all but a few buildings were demolished.

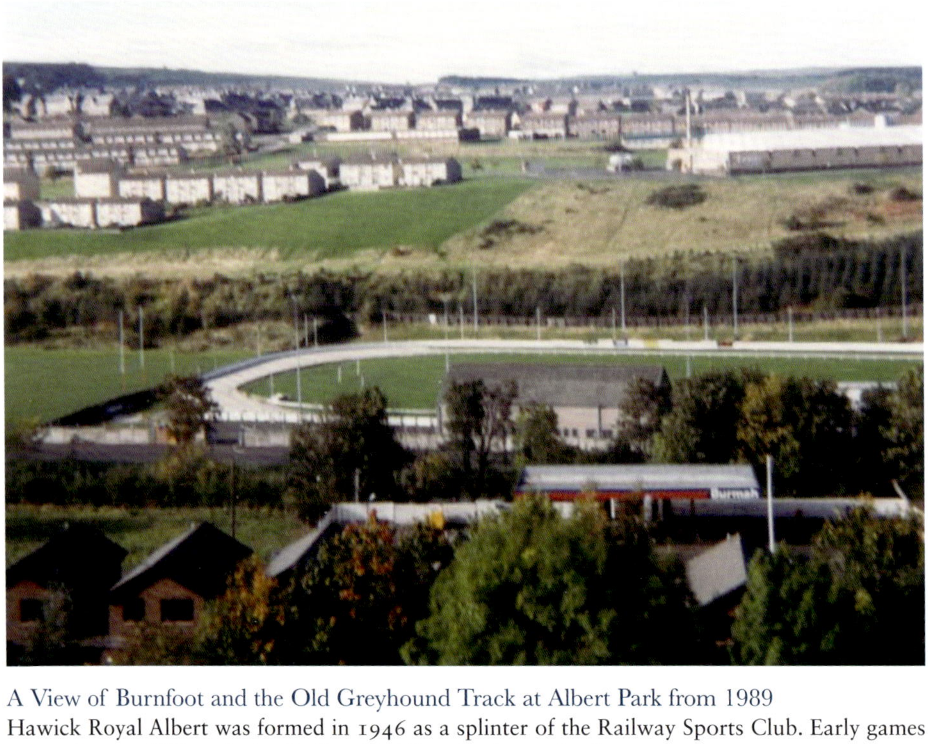

A View of Burnfoot and the Old Greyhound Track at Albert Park from 1989

Hawick Royal Albert was formed in 1946 as a splinter of the Railway Sports Club. Early games were played at Wilton Lodge Park, with Albert Park opening in 1963.

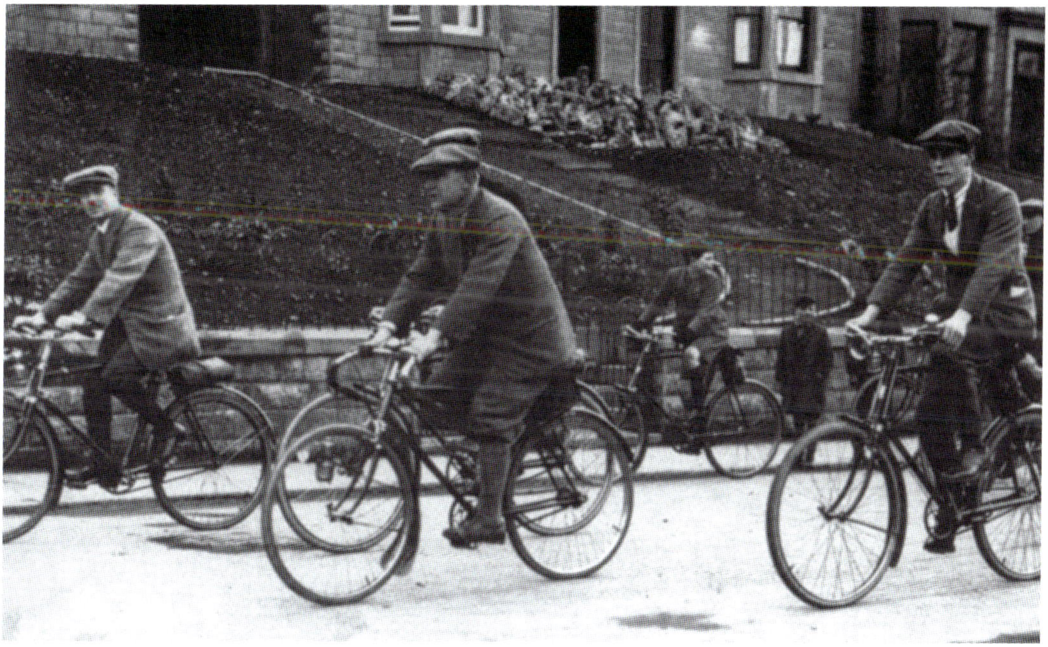

Hawick Cycling Club on Weensland Road in 1901

Formed in 1881 as the 'Hawick Bicycle Club', the organisation folded in 1911, reforming under new rules in 1925. Its most famous member is arguably Ken Laidlaw, who competed in the Tour De France.

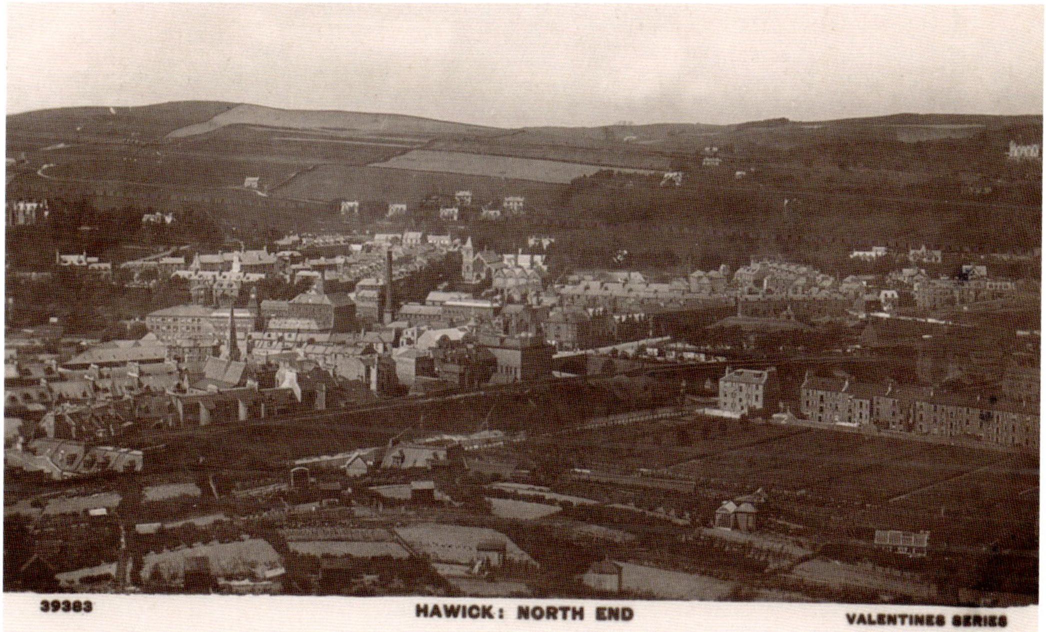

Hawick's North End as Viewed in 1910

To the right lies Oliver & Sons auction mart. The company moved here from Loch Park in 1883 and is credited with originating the livestock auction mart system in Britain. The site closed in 1992 and was developed into a supermarket.

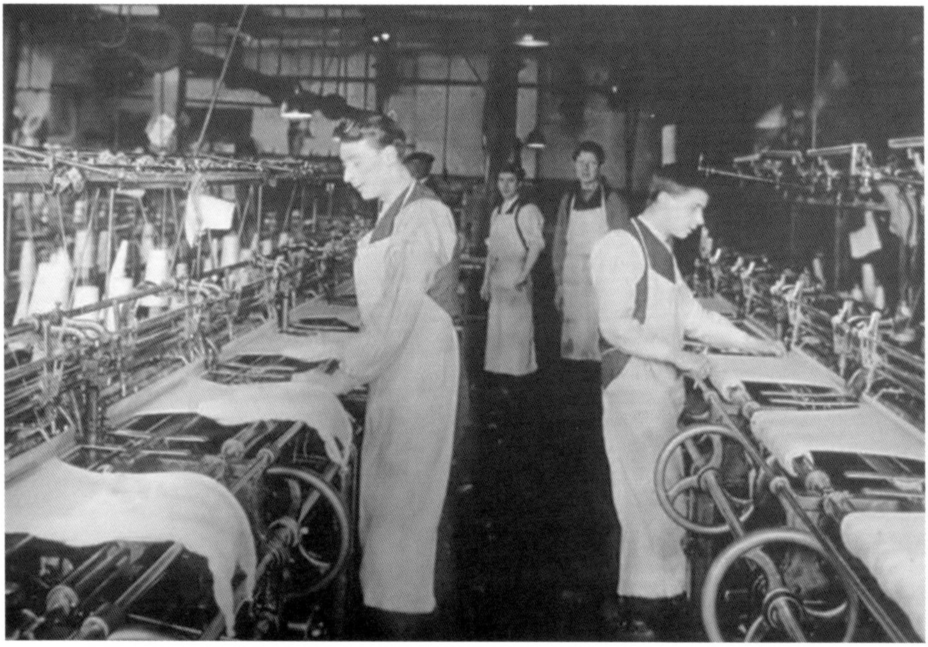

Hawick Hosiery Company's Trinity Mill, Late 1930s
Hard at work in Hawick Hosiery Company's Trinity Mill, during the 1930s. Sited on Duke Street, rather than Trinity Street as one would suppose, a woollen mill was first established here in 1874.

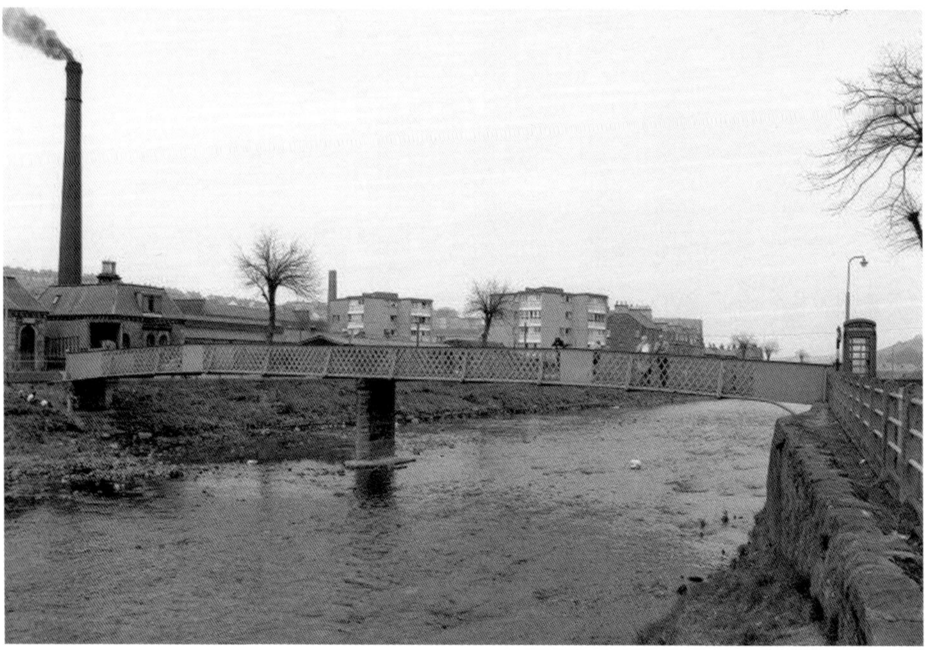

Trinity Footbridge and the Mid-Rise Flats of Mansfield in 1974
The Trinity area takes its name as a onetime holding of the 'House of the Holy Trinity'. In the fourteenth century, the mother church, comprising a hospital and a friary, was established at Soutra Aisle, forty miles north of Hawick.

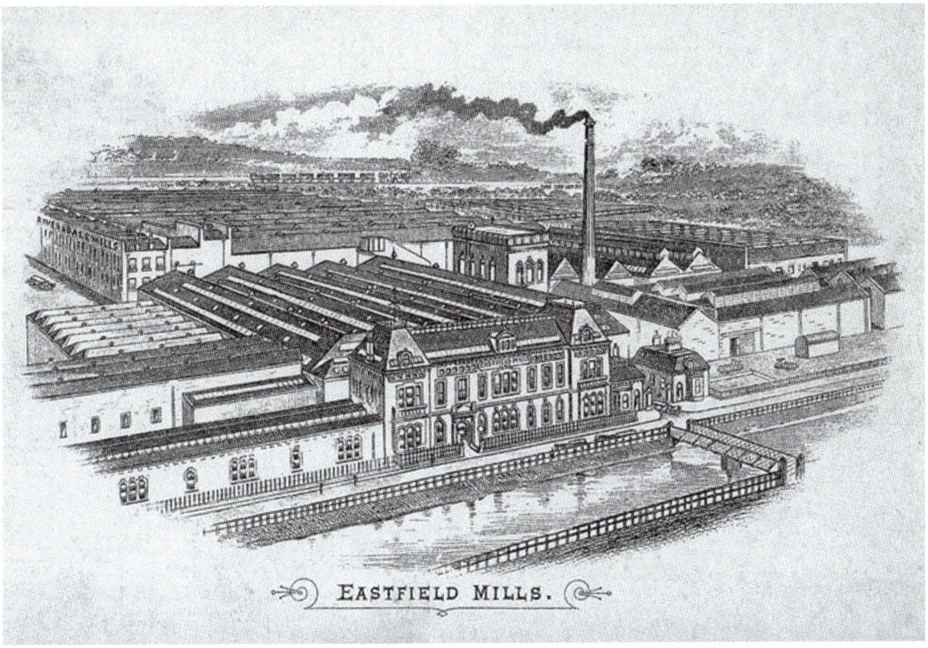

Eastfield Mill, Late Nineteenth Century
A nineteenth-century sketch of Eastfield Mill at Mansfield. Built in 1882 for tweed manufacturers Blenkhorn, Richardson and Co., the main building was 120 feet long. A decline in the industry led to its closure in 1974. Since 1981 it has been home to Johnston's of Elgin.

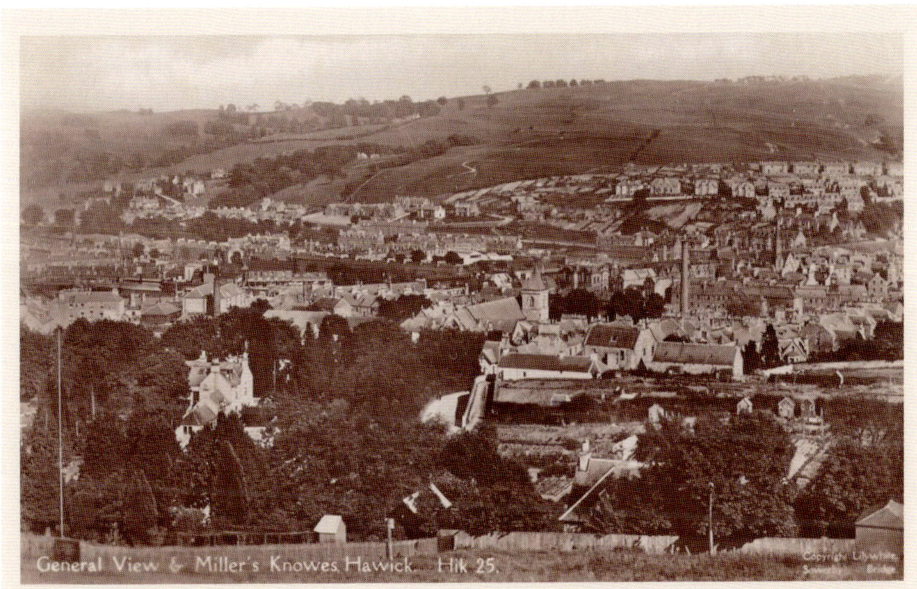

A View Across Hawick from the Early 1920s
In the background you can see the winding Douglas Road East, built in 1906 and named after Baillie James Douglas (1826-85). Housing was first erected here in 1922, by the Scottish Veterans' Garden City Association.

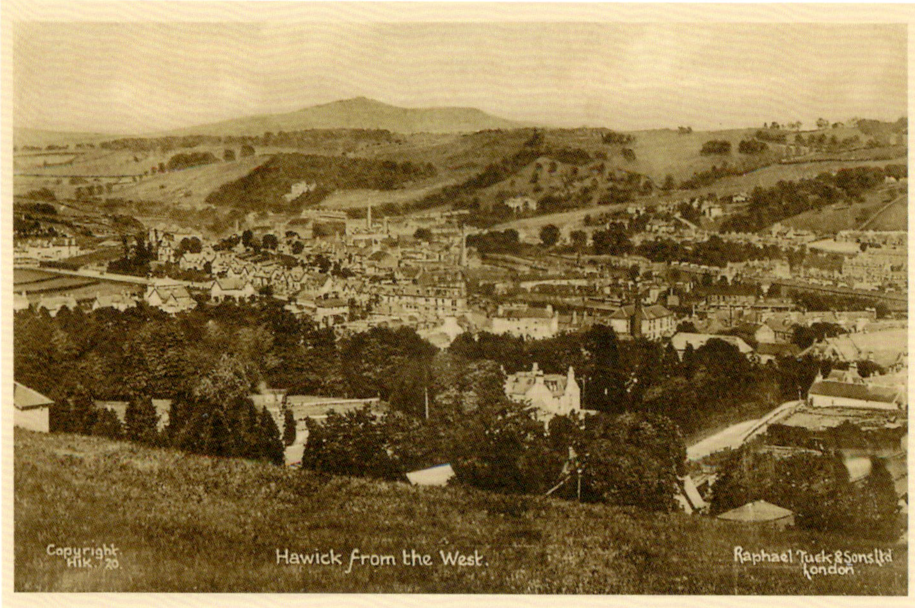

Hawick, 1930s

A general view of Hawick from the 1930s, with the curve of Wilton Hill featuring prominently in the centre of the photograph. Wilton Hill Terrace was built in 1879. Known originally just as Hill Terrace, it was renamed in 1882. The bungalows of Wilton Glebe were built in 1955, on land once belonging to Wilton Parish Church.

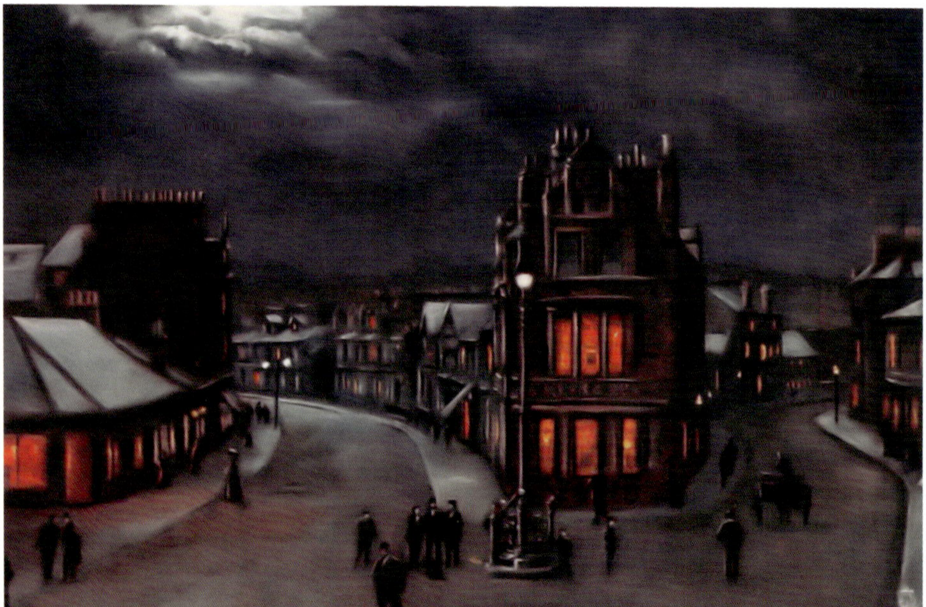

An Unusual Pre-1914 View of Bridge Street and Bourtree Place at Night

Bourtree Place was named around 1842, after the 'bour trees' (an Old Scots word for the Elder), a species planted to mark the eastern boundary of Hawick.

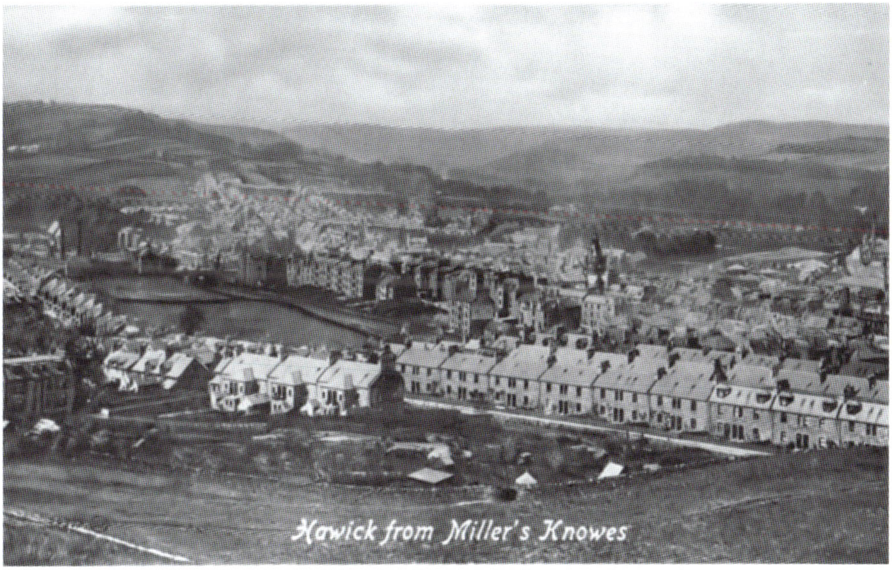

Miller's Knowes, 1903

A view of Hawick from the Miller's Knowes in 1903. This hilly area takes its name from the owners of the nearby Corn Mill, who were granted extensive grazing rights and corn fields above the Wellogate. It became a public park in 1892 and was gifted to the town in 1930.

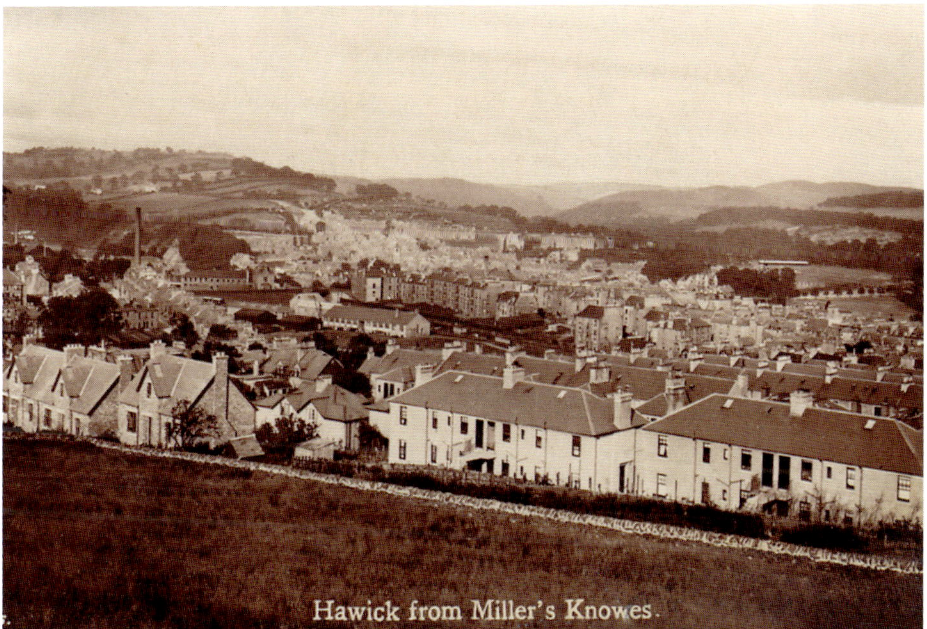

Miller's Knowes, over Half a Century Later

This photograph shows the same view but from a vantage point over half a century later. In the centre you can see that Loch Park has been developed. This was once home to a small pond, drained by the Burgh Council in 1835 to rid the area of its pestilential vapours, and grazing land.

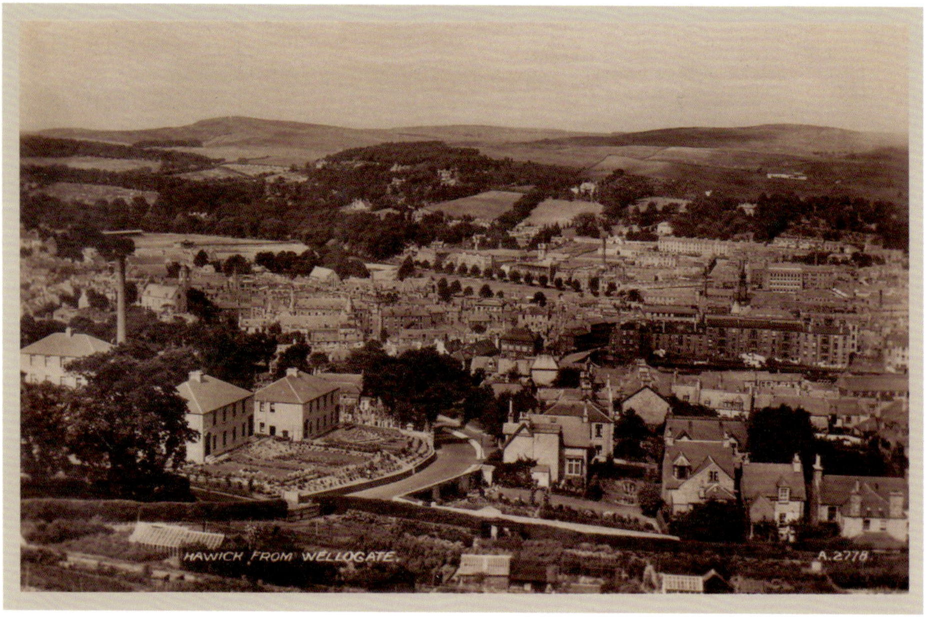

Hawick from the Wellogate, Late 1950s

A view of Hawick from the Wellogate in the late 1950s. The majority of housing here was built by Hawick Working Men's Building and Investment Co., formed in 1864 to build better houses for the working classes, and to encourage home ownership.

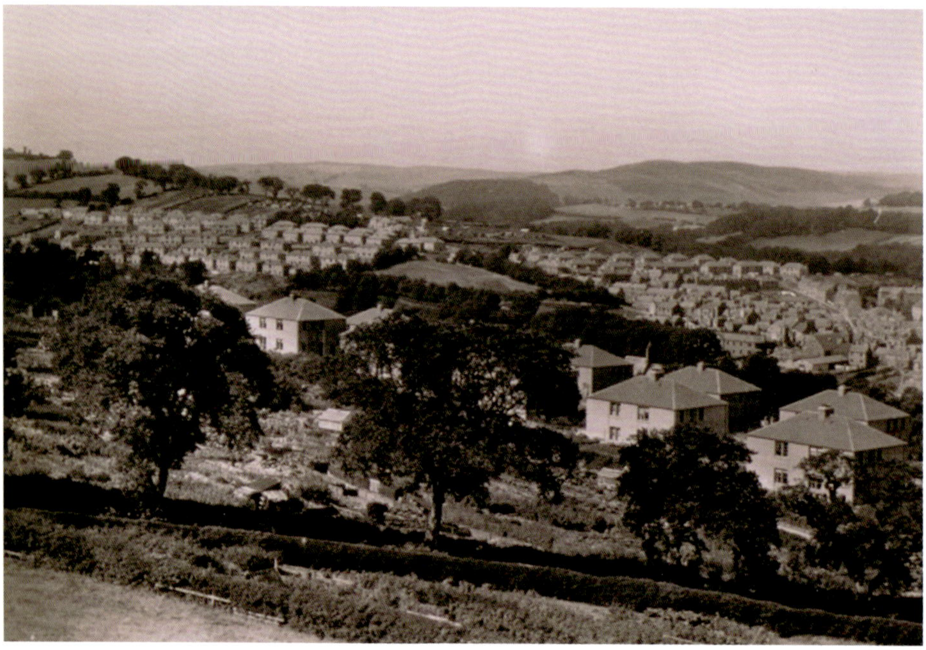

Fisher Avenue, 1935

A photograph looking onto the newly built Fisher Avenue in 1935, named after former Provost David Fisher. The nearby Wellogate Cemetery was opened in 1849, initially as an overflow for St Mary's. Most of the town's victims from the cholera epidemic that year are buried in the vacant middle area.

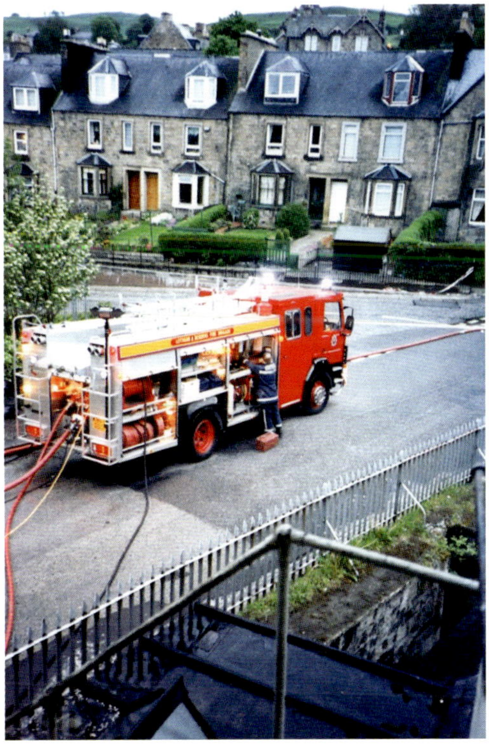

Firefighters Attending Hogg's Mill, 1995

Firefighters attend a blaze at Hogg's Mill in 1995. Built around 1860 and extended in 1887, the hosiery works became derelict during the 1980s. It was eventually demolished in 2000 and replaced with housing.

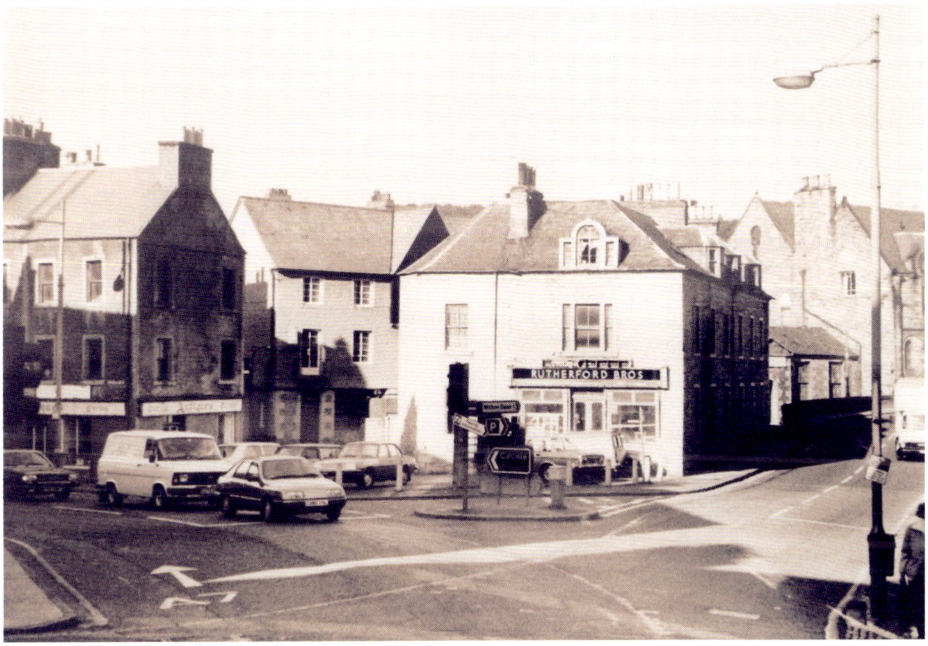

The Island Houses of Sandbed, 1987

The island houses of the Sandbed, demolished soon after this photo was taken in 1987 (Rutherford's Bicycle Shop facing the camera). The Sandbed was one of the first extensions beyond the medieval village of Hawick.

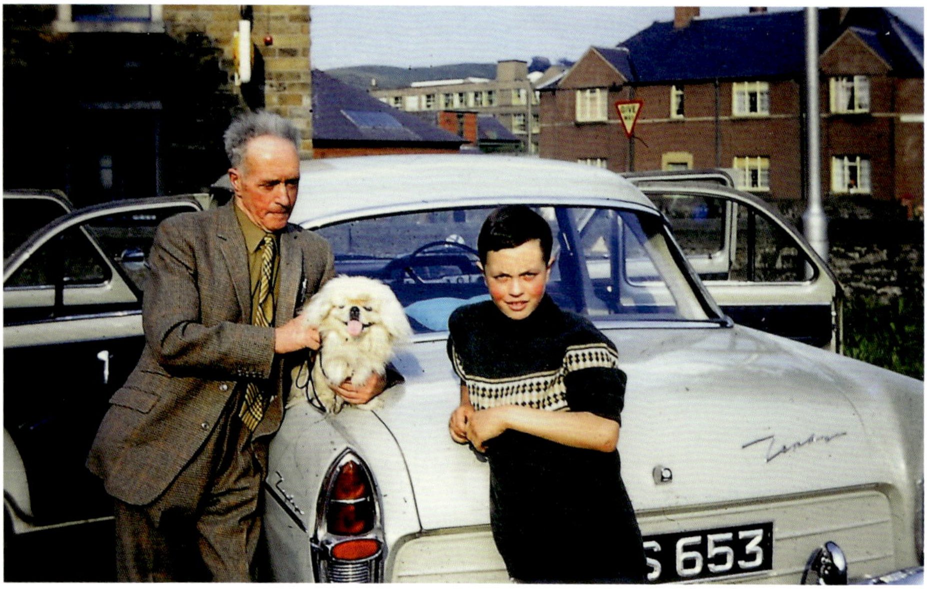

Common Haugh, 1967

A family photo, taken at the Common Haugh in 1967. Behind is the distinctive former Hawick Fire Station. After moving here from Slitrig Hall in 1913, it was not until 1963 that the local Fire Brigade went full-time following a series of serious fires. In March 1971, the crew moved to a modern facility at Howdenbank.

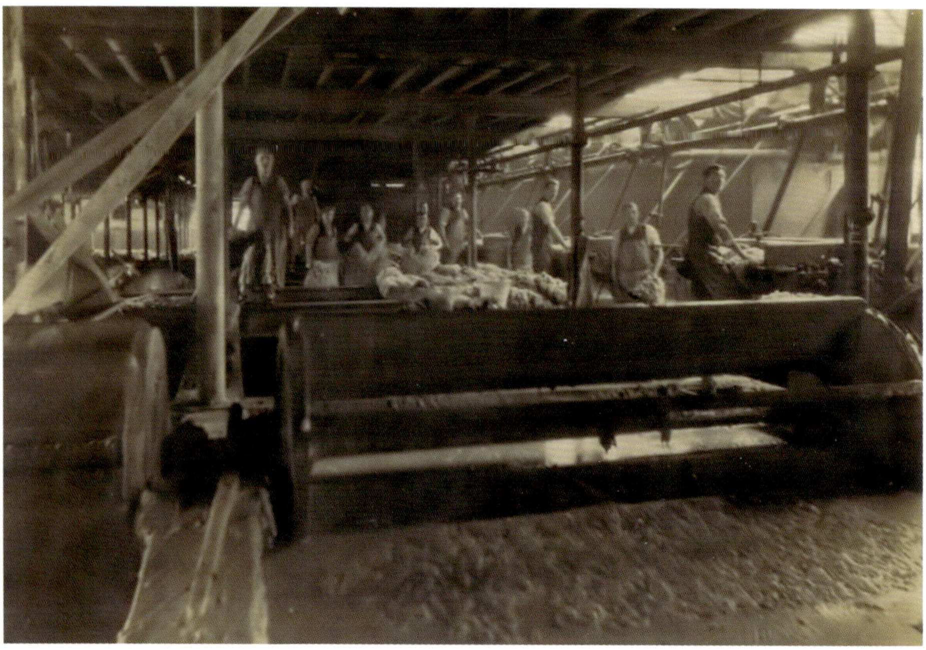

Workers at MacTaggart's Skinworks, *c.* 1930

Built as the main factory of Wilson, Scott & Co., the building later housed the 'skinyairds', which relocated from St. George's Lane. The company shut in the 1970s and the buildings were demolished by 1976.

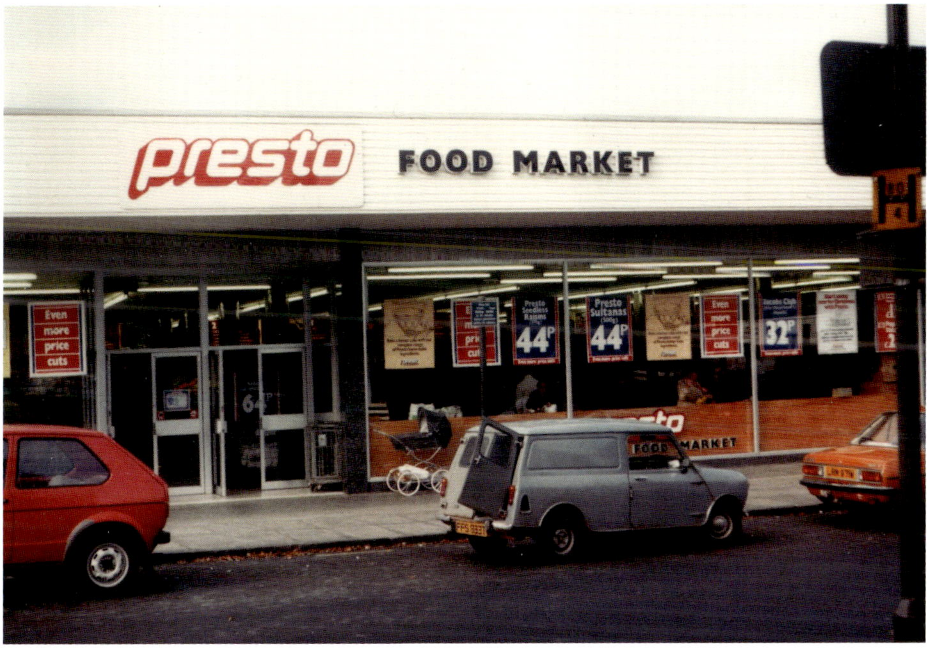

Presto Food Market, 1977

Presto food market, built on the site of the 'skinyairds' in 1977. It was the first large supermarket to be opened in Hawick and was a part of the Allied Suppliers business. In the late 1980s it was converted to a Safeway.

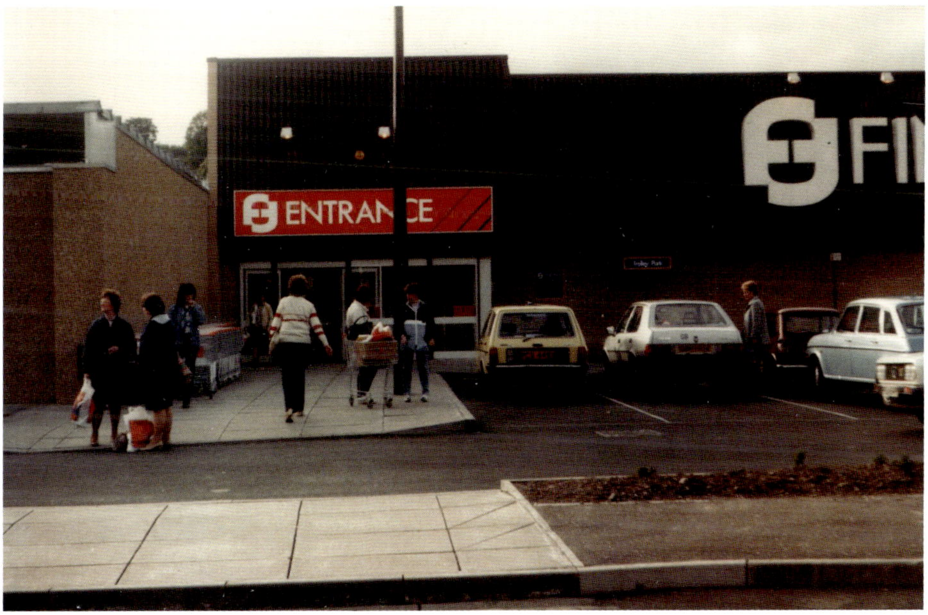

Finefare, 1980s

Finefare, captured in the early 1980s, is another supermarket that has since been consigned to history. It was famous for its yellow branded own-label range. Around 1986 this branch was sold to Somerfield, and is now B&M Bargains.

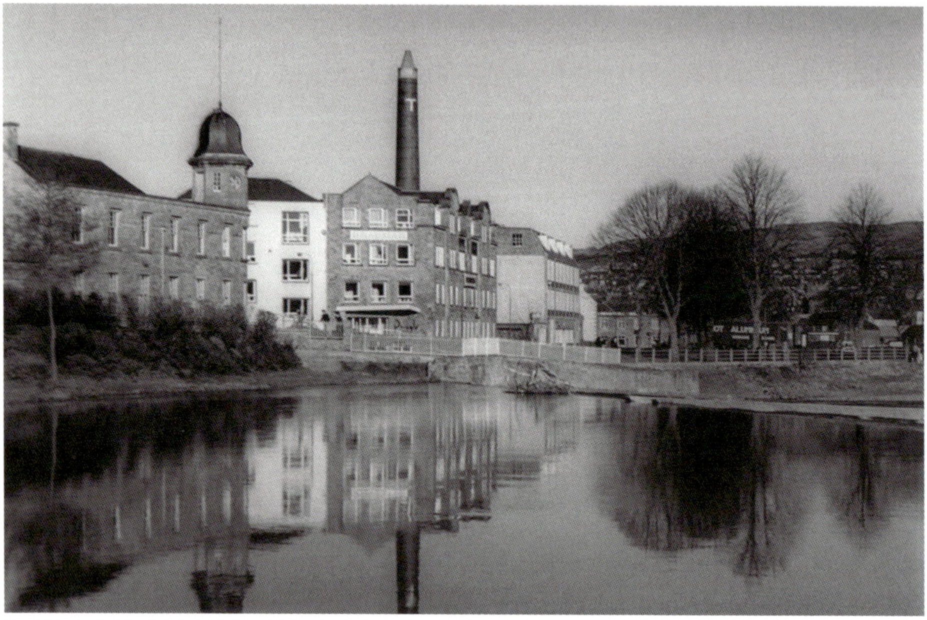

John Turnbull & Sons, Dyers and Finishers, Victoria Road, 1970

A photograph of the once bustling Victoria Road in 1970, featuring the prominent 70 feet tall chimney of Turnbull's. John Turnbull & Sons, dyers and finishers, was founded in 1819 at Nos 1–4 Slitrig Crescent. Most of the site was demolished in 1990, apart from the administration block.

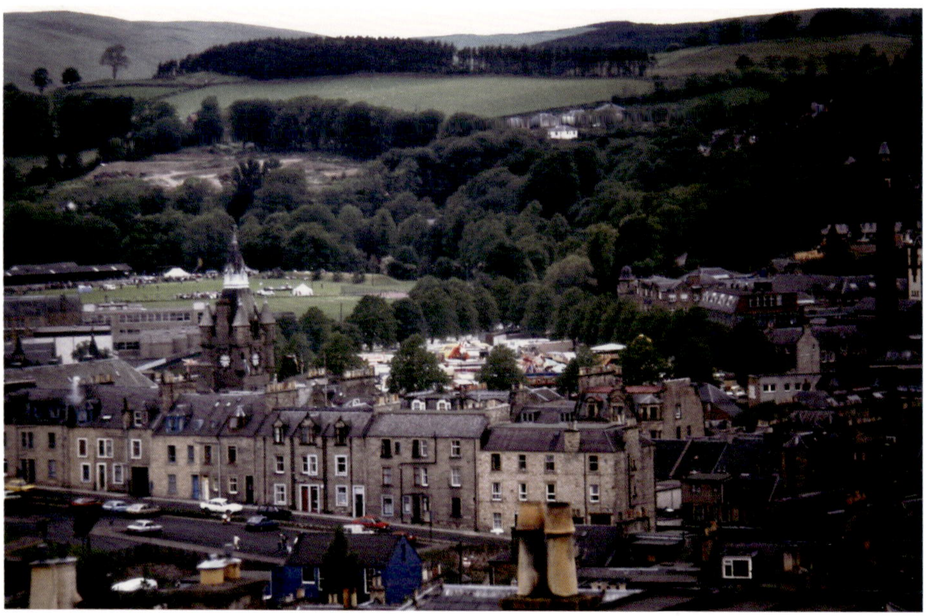

Hawick in the Late 1970s

Tucked behind the trees to the right is Howlands Mill, built by Greenwood, Watt & Co. in the 1880s. Empty through the 1990s, it was demolished in 2004 to make way for the new Community Hospital.

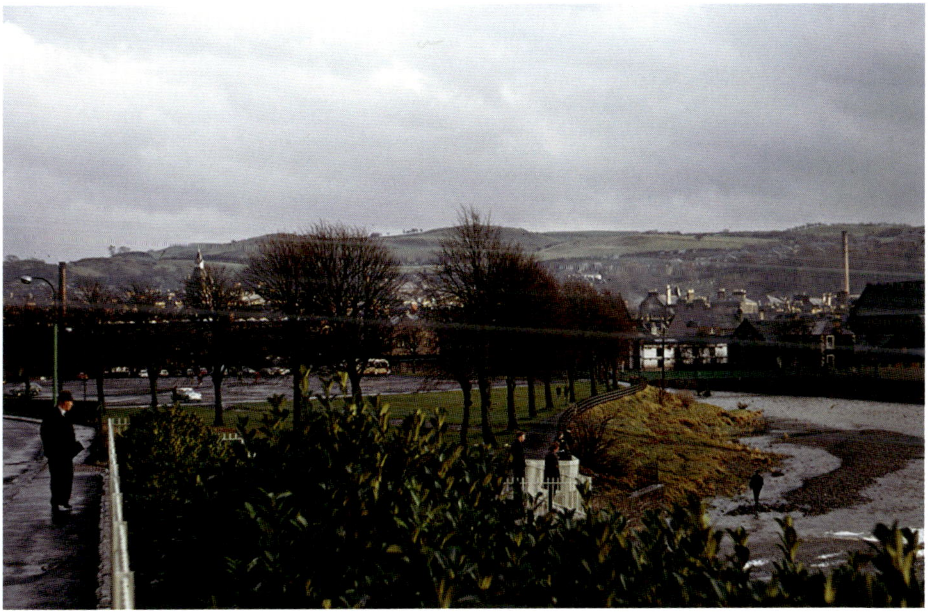

Hawick Common Haugh and the Teviot in 1970

A short-lived paraffin oil refinery was controversially located adjacent to the Haugh. Opened in 1866, it was closed just two years later when the owner was declared bankrupt.

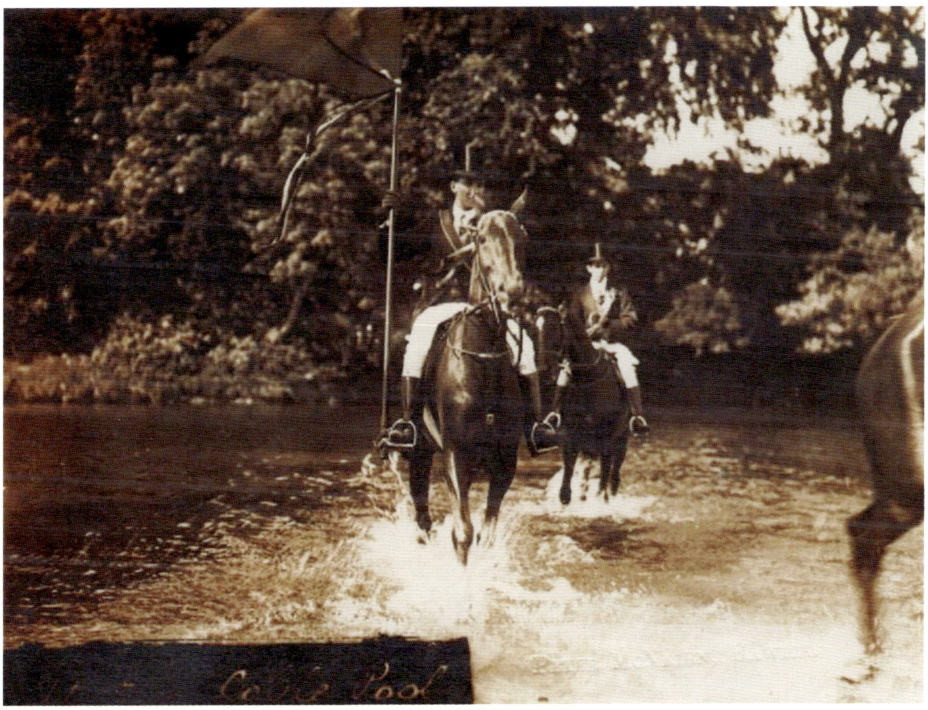

Cornet William Lockie Thorburn Dips the Banner Blue at the Coble Pool in 1911

This part of the Teviot, at the Cauld, is named after the small boats or 'cobles' used to ferry people over to the Langlands estate – long before the building of a road bridge.

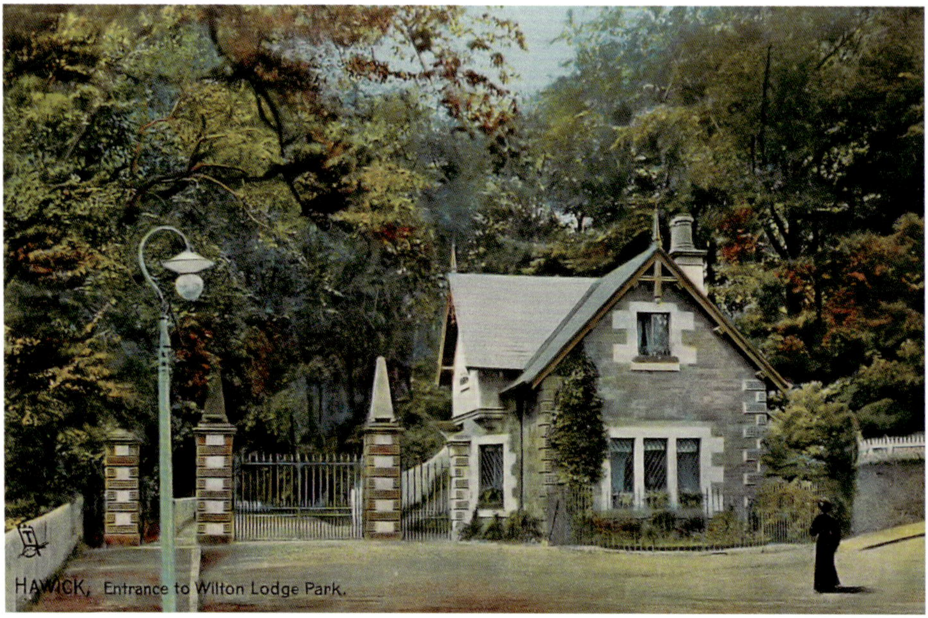

Wilton Lodge Gate House, 1907

This lodge was built some time before 1863 at the end of the Avenue – the estate road commissioned by then Wilton Lodge owner James Anderson – in 1810. A western extension was added around 1917.

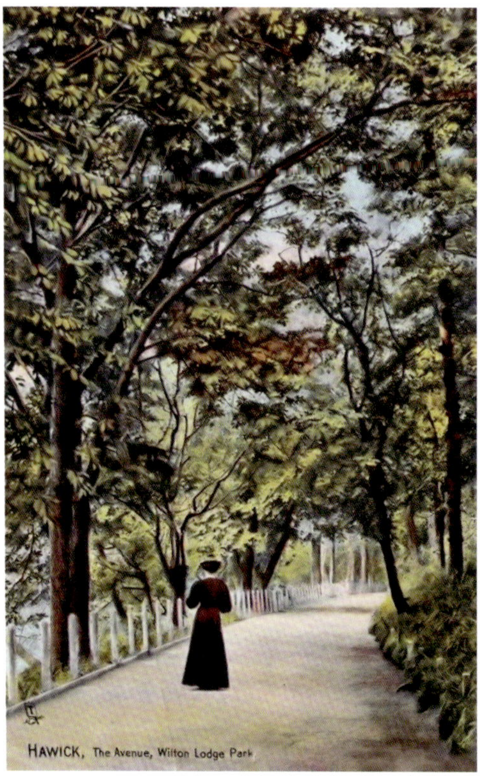

The Avenue, 1910

James Anderson was born in Perth and retired to Hawick in 1805, when he purchased Wilton Lodge from Lord Napier. He was a Lieutenant Colonel in the Roxburghshire Volunteers from around 1808 and appointed an Honorary Burgess in 1814.

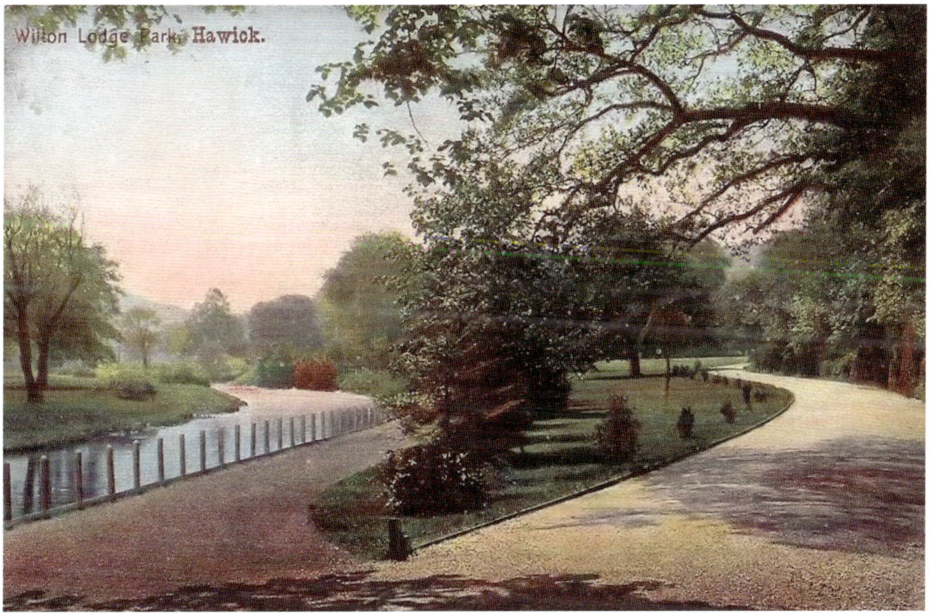

Wilton Lodge Park, 1905

This photo depicts the serene landscape of Wilton Lodge Park in 1905.The park was previously a privately held estate of the Langlands family. Hawick Town Council bought the land in 1889 and during the next decade it was laid out for public use.

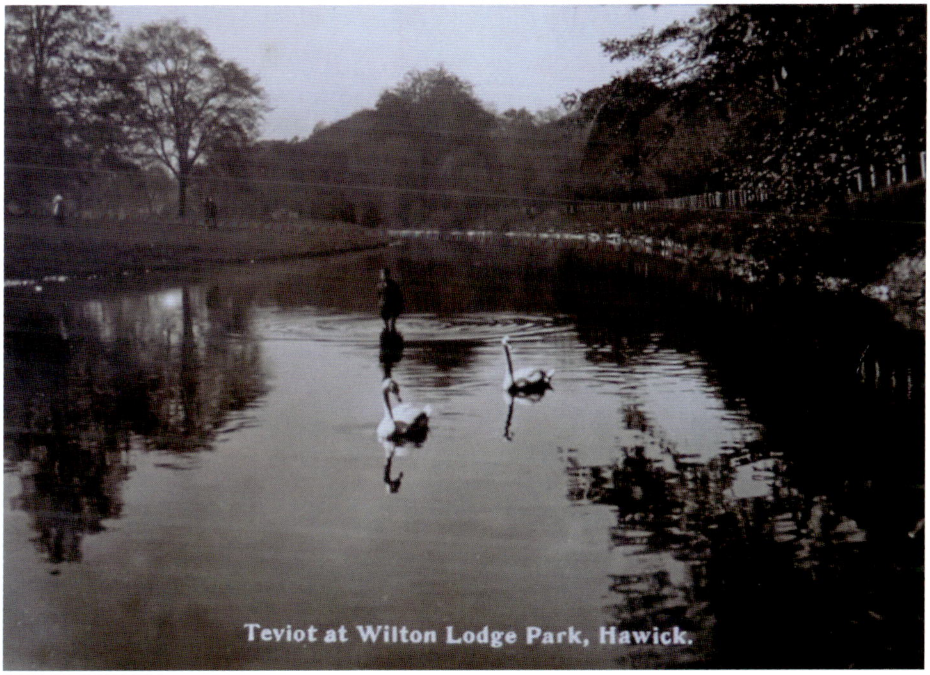

A Boy Plays in the Teviot near the Spetch', Early Last Century

At 37 miles long, the River Teviot is a tributary of the River Tweed. It originates in the hills, at Teviot Stone, where an inscribed boulder was erected by the Callants' Club in 1931.

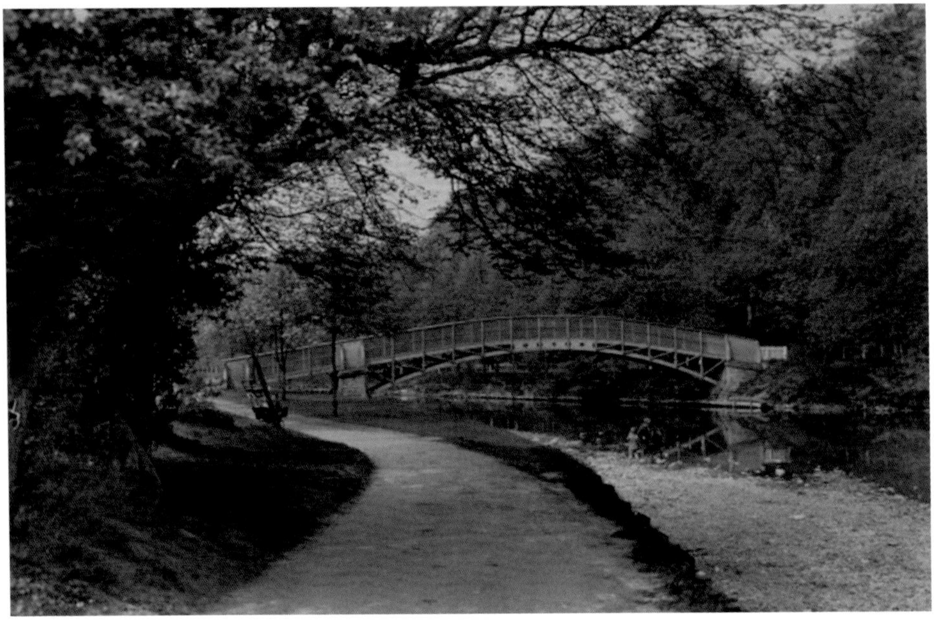

The Laurie Brig, Pictured in 1936

This picture shows the Laurie Brig as seen in 1936. It is named after Walter Laurie, who bequeathed money for its construction. The footbridge was built in 1924 and opened by HRH The Prince of Wales on 3 December that year.

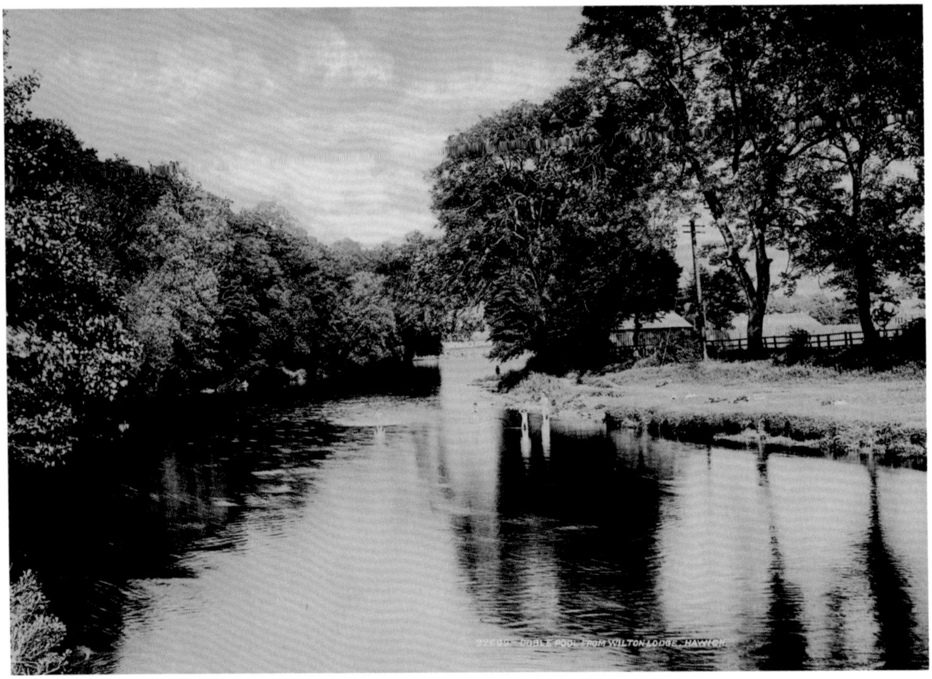

Midway Between the Spetch' and the Coble Pool, 1902

Sometimes humorously referred to as the Lido, this area of the park is probably named after the old Scots for a leather patch or a cobbler, rather than a surname.

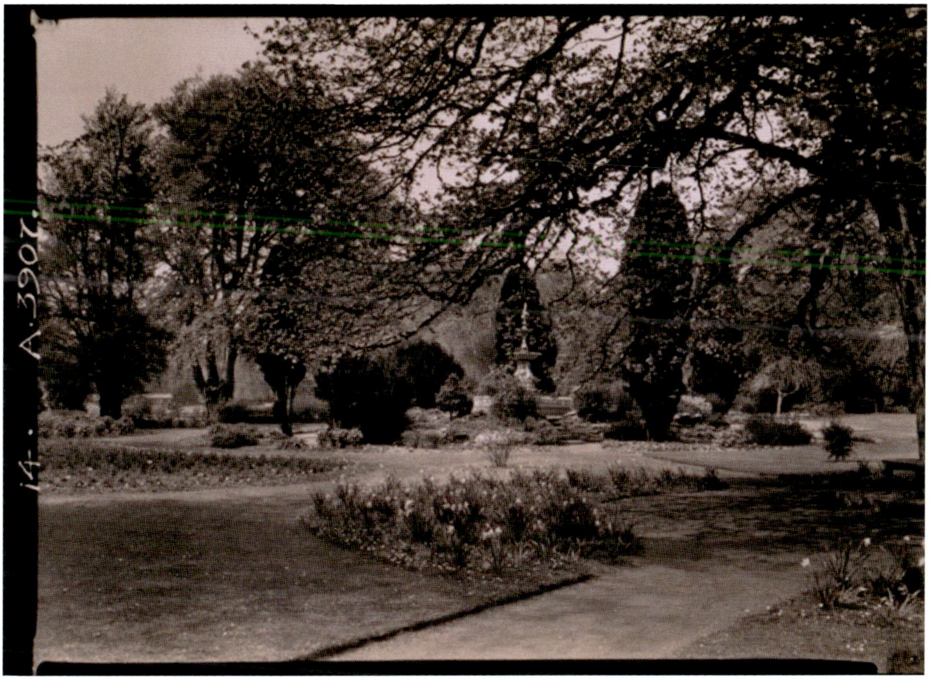

A View of the Gilbert Davidson Fountain, 1910

The fountain was unveiled in 1896, following the death of Mr Davidson, who bequeathed money for its erection. Made of cast iron from the Milton Works in Glasgow, it was unveiled the following year.

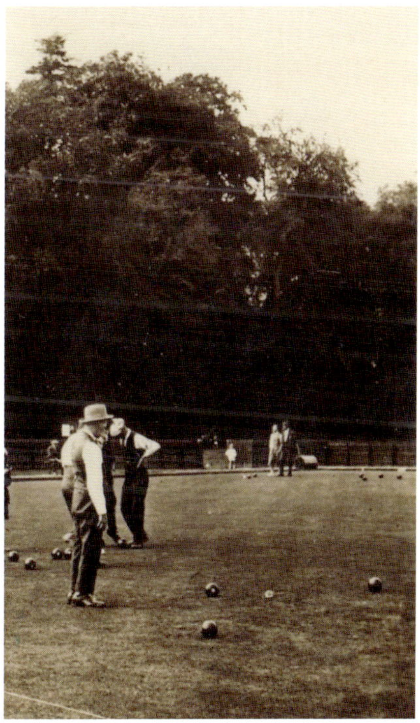

Enjoying a Game of Bowls at Wilton Lodge Park, *c*. 1955

Bowling was first introduced to Hawick around the turn of the nineteenth century. The first green was laid out where Pesco's factory on Buccleuch Street now stands, around 1820. Hawick Bowling Club, founded in 1854, is the oldest in the Borders.

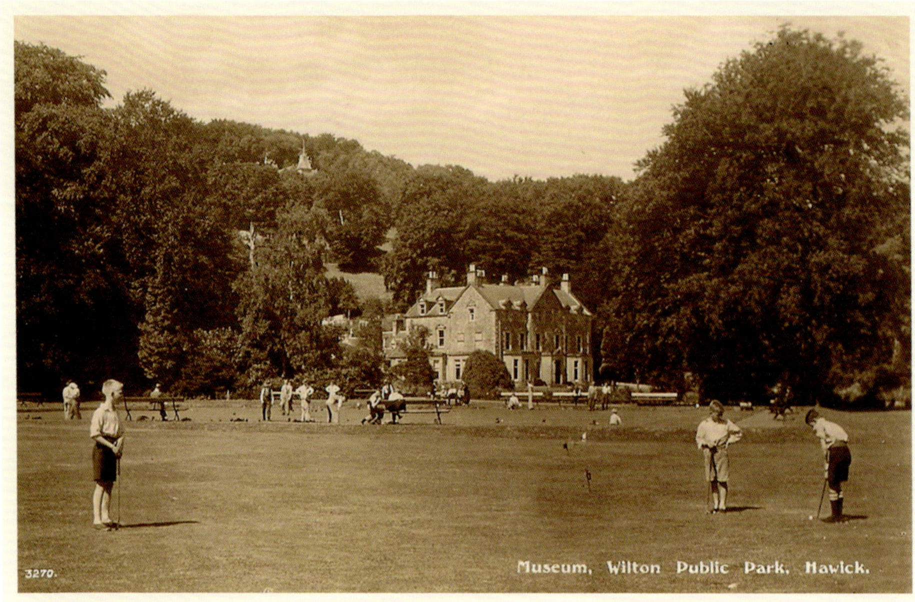

A Postcard from Edwards of Selkirk, 1950

This postcard from Edwards of Selkirk shows putting and bowls enthusiasts at Wilton Lodge Park in 1950. The Putting Green was installed sometime around 1889. Extensive renovations were carried out to the Museum in 1959, and in 1975, the Scott Gallery extension was added.

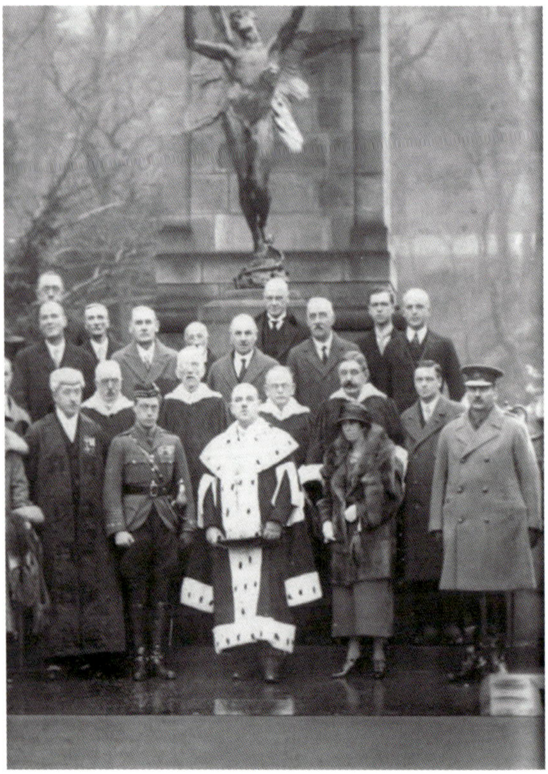

The Art Deco War Memorial

The art deco 'Glorious Dead' war memorial lists the names of men from the Hawick area who died during both World Wars. Designed by James B. Dunn, it was unveiled to a crowd of over four thousand people on Sunday 21 October 1921.

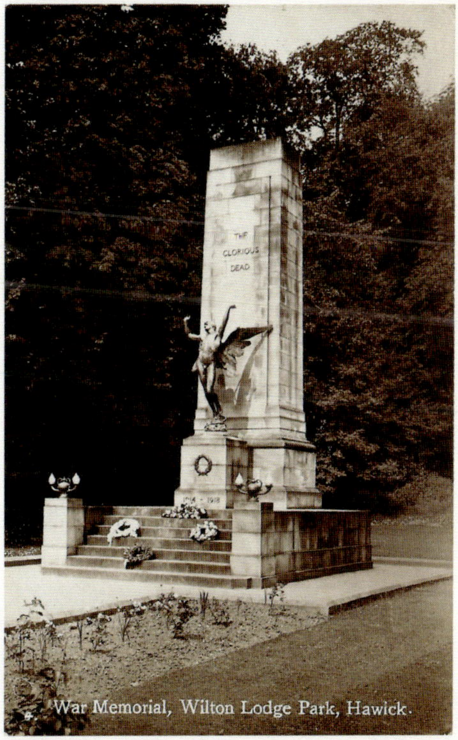

The War Memorial, 1933

The design caused great friction in the immediate post-war period, the naked bronze figure of youth causing most concern. Tower Knowe was initially the preferred site.

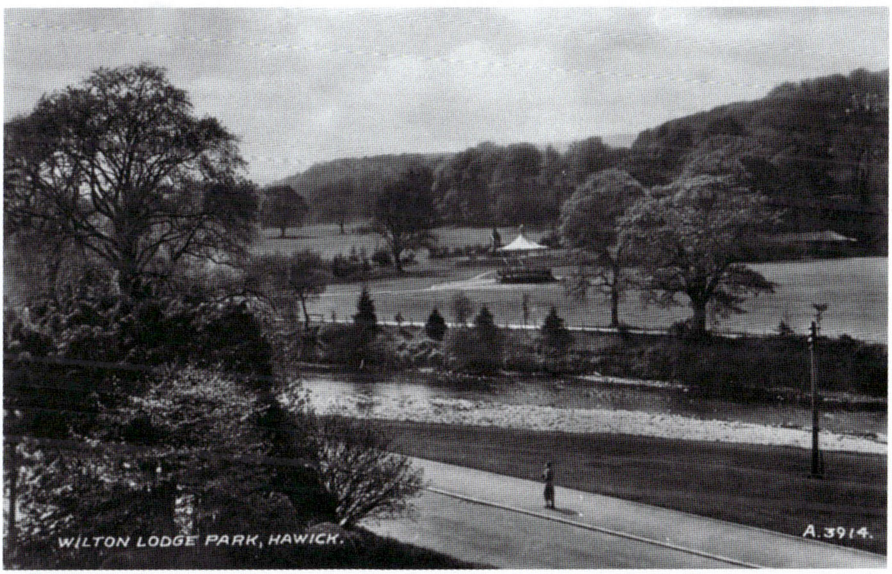

The Old Bandstand at Wilton Lodge Park, 1936

The base was turned into a paddling pool around 1970 and after only a few years became a flower bed. A new bandstand was unveiled in April 2015 and is named after the late Honorary Provost Zandra Elliot.

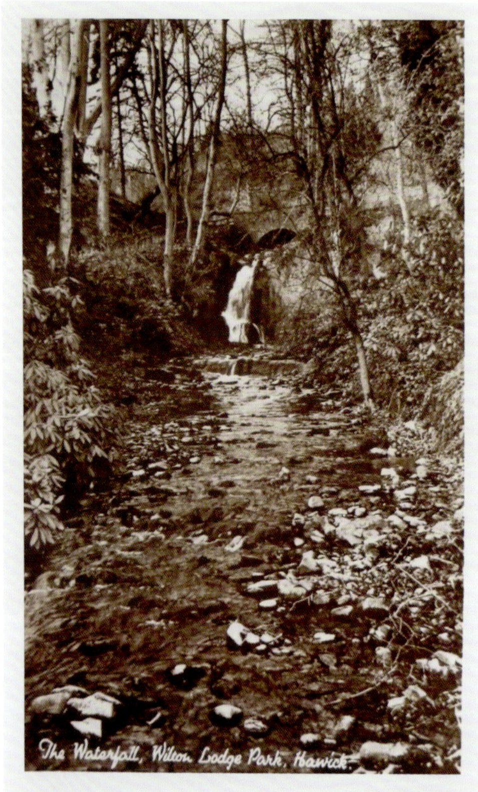

The Waterfall at Wilton Lodge Park, as Captured Early Last Century

The Cala Burn, a stream which runs through Wilton Dean, continues through the park with this picturesque waterfall behind the Museum, before joining the Teviot. In January 1940, the waterfall froze during an abnormally cold winter.

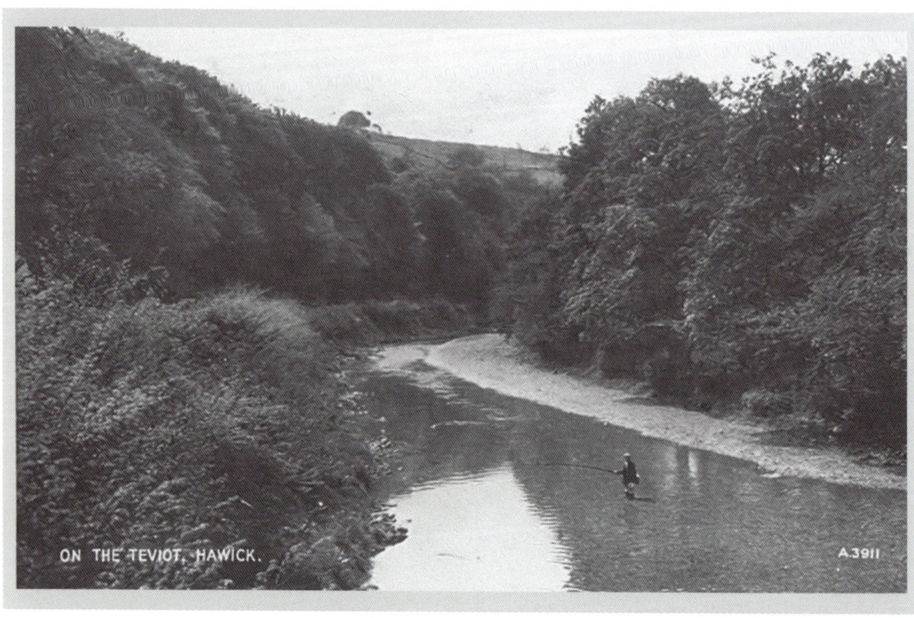

A Man Fishes on the Teviot at Wilton Lodge Park, 1936

Hawick Angling Club was formed in October 1911, after representation had been made to the Upper Teviotdale body, to administer licences and to help police local waters.

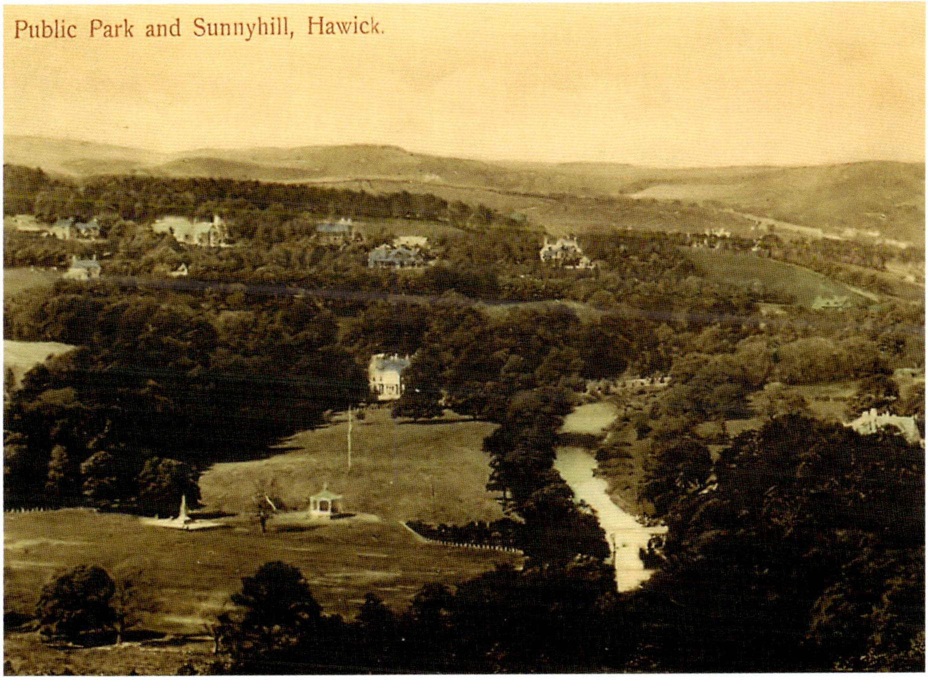

Wilton Lodge Park and Sunnyhill, from the Lumback Road, 1912
Named after its aspect with respect to the sun, this area was first feued under the supervision of John Guthrie in the nineteenth century. Ladylaw House was the first residence to be constructed here, sometime before 1846.

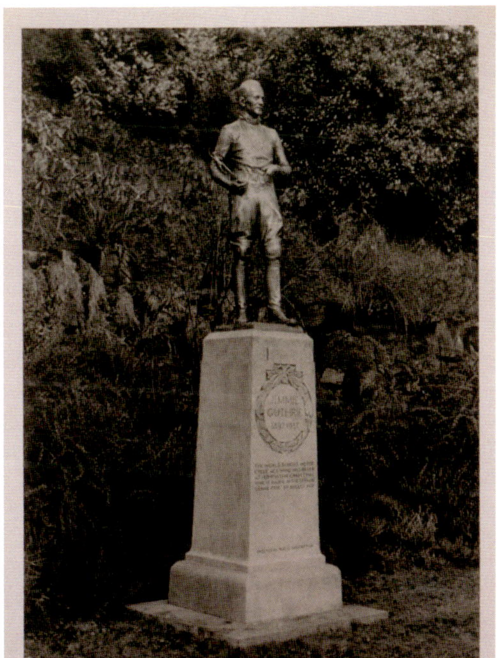

Bronze Statue of Andrew James 'Jimmie' Guthrie, 1939
A bronze statue of 'Jimmie' Guthrie, pictured soon after its unveiling in 1939. Erected by public subscription, the statue was sculpted by Thomas Clapperton. Jimmie was tragically killed in an accident at the 1937 European Grand Prix.

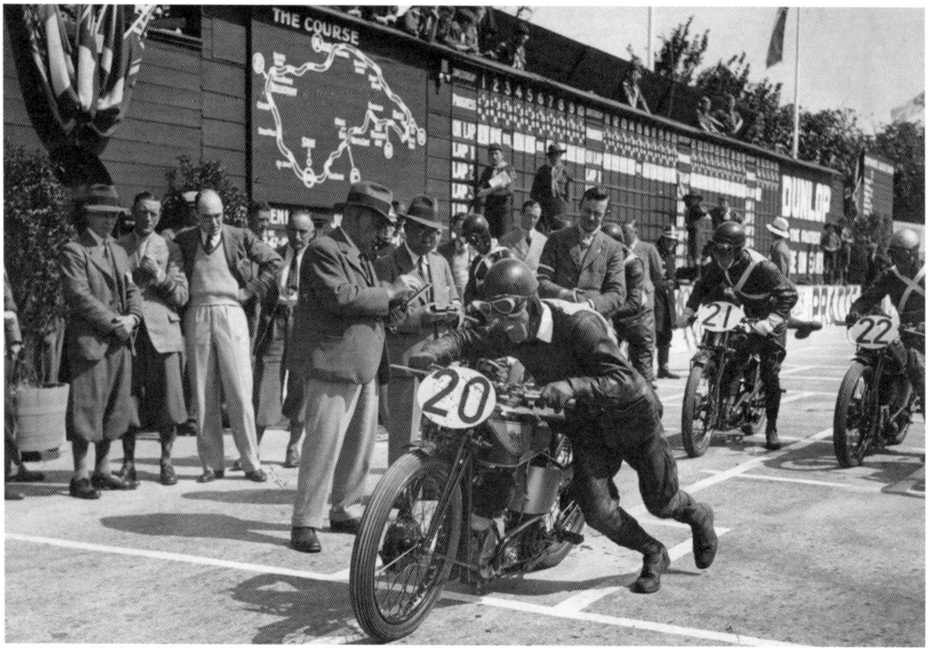

Jimmy Guthrie at the 1933 Isle of Man TT
Hawick motorcycling legend Jimmie Guthrie gives his works Norton Model 40 a push start at the 1933 Isle of Man TT. He went on to claim 3rd place in this event and six TT titles in all. It is a little known fact that Adolf Hitler was among his biggest fans.

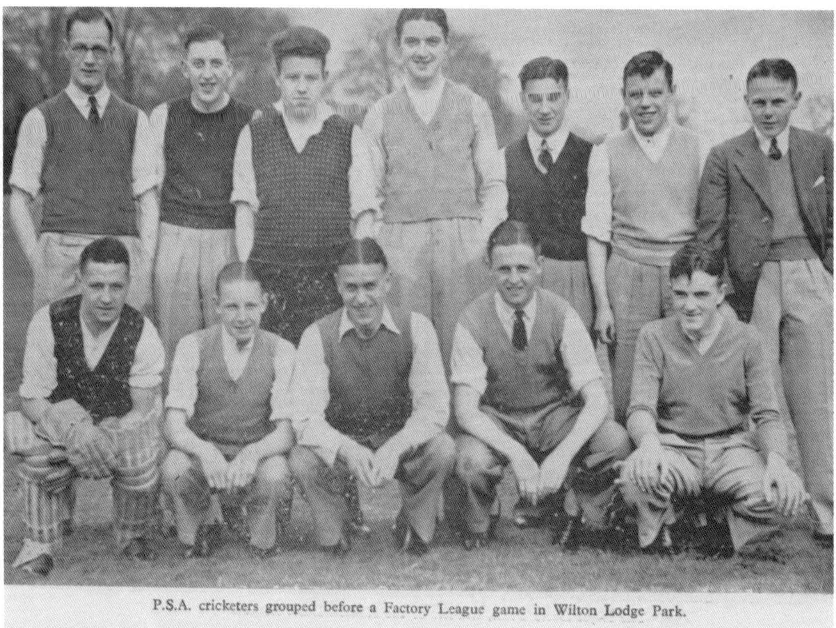

P.S.A. cricketers grouped before a Factory League game in Wilton Lodge Park.

P. S. A. Cricketers Grouped Before a Factory League Game at Wilton Lodge Park, 1939
The Pleasant Sunday Afternoon movement initially played at the English Cricket Field, now the site of Lyle & Scott's offices, before moving to the park.

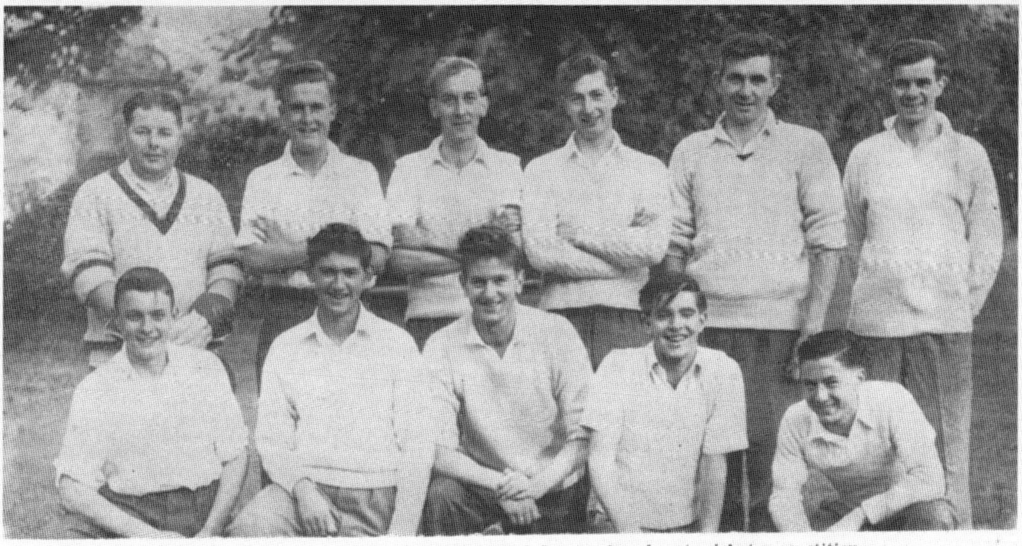

Hawick H.S. (F.P.) team, winners of the Park League knock-out cricket competition.

The High School's Former Pupils' Cricket Team
The High School's former pupils' cricket team, with Bill McLaren in the back row (second from right). This team was winner of the Park League knock-out cup, a purely amateur affair played between teams from the various factories, trades and organisations.

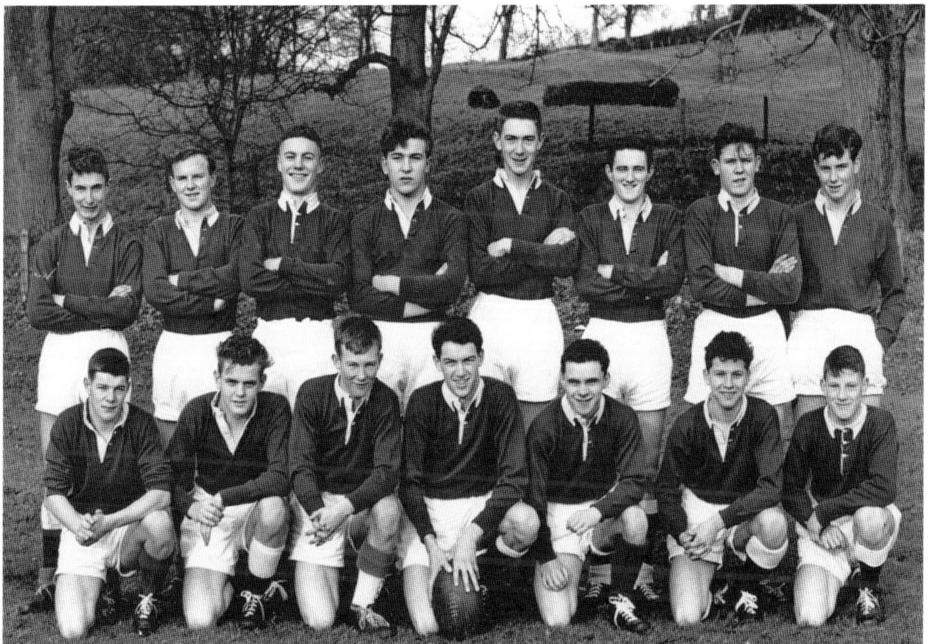

The High School's Rugby XV in February 1962
Hawick has a long affinity with the oval ball. In 1879 at nearby Buccleuch Park, the first floodlit game in Scottish sporting history took place in front of five thousand supporters when Hawick met Melrose in a close game (Melrose defeated Hawick by a goal to nil).

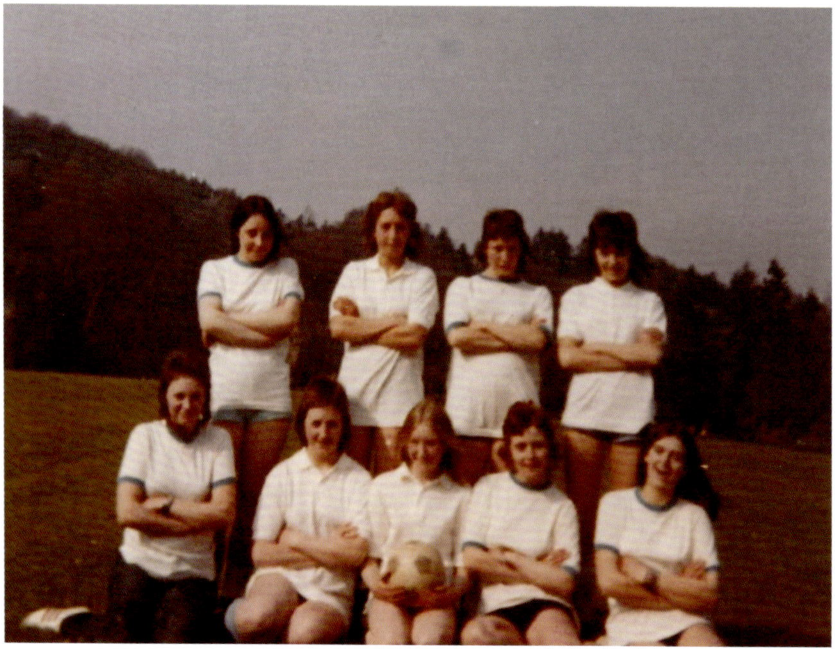

Hawick Women's Football Team, 1972

Other local sides still play at the park, including Hawick United (formed in 1927 and until 1931 members of the East of Scotland League), Hawick Legion (formed by members of the Royal British Legion in 1953) and Hawick Waverley (established in 1980).

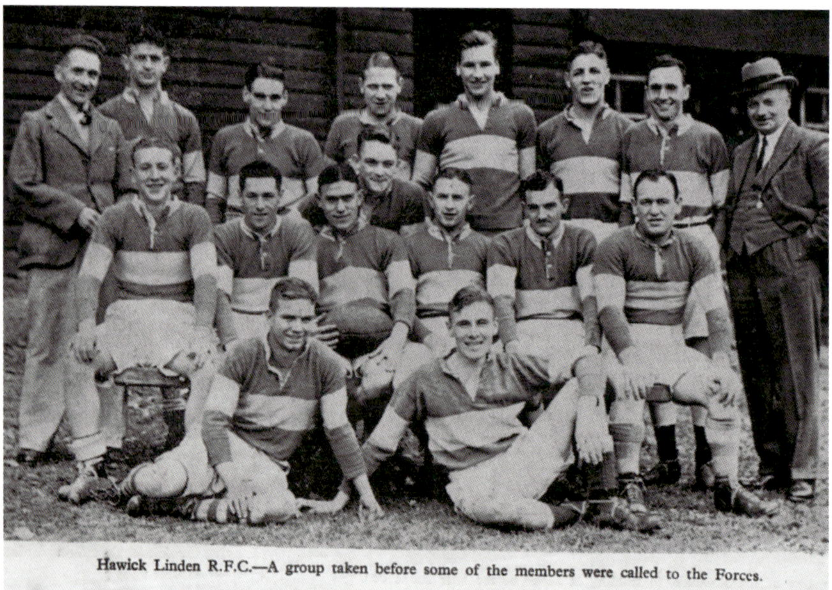

Hawick Linden R.F.C.—A group taken before some of the members were called to the Forces.

Hawick Linden's Squad, 1939

This portentous photo was taken before many of these young men were called into the forces to serve in the Second World War. Founded in the 1921/22 season, the club's name derives from the fact that many of the founders came from the Linden Terrace/Douglas Road area.

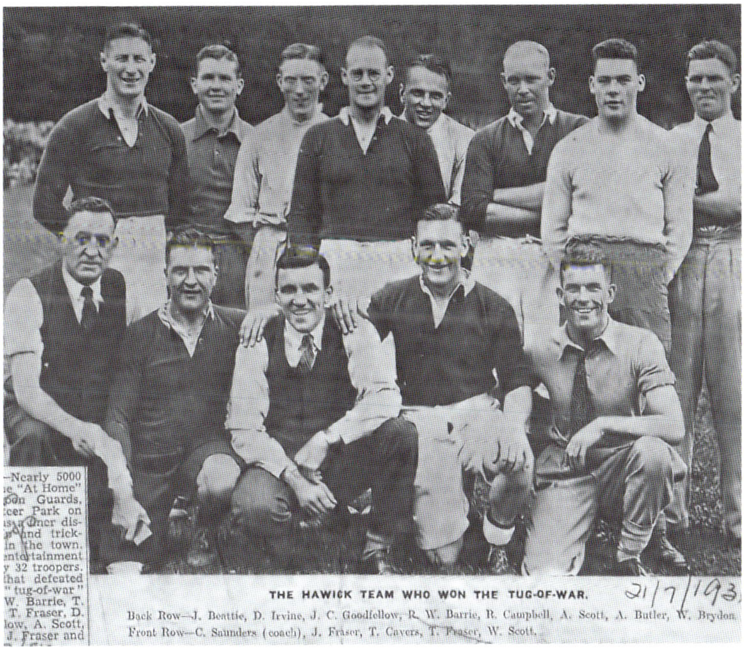

The Winning Tug-of-War Team at the Volunteer Park, 1936

In use for the Common Riding sports since 1893, the Volunteer Park was purchased by the Common Riding Committee from the Duke of Buccleuch in 1920. The Linden and the Trades have played here since 1963.

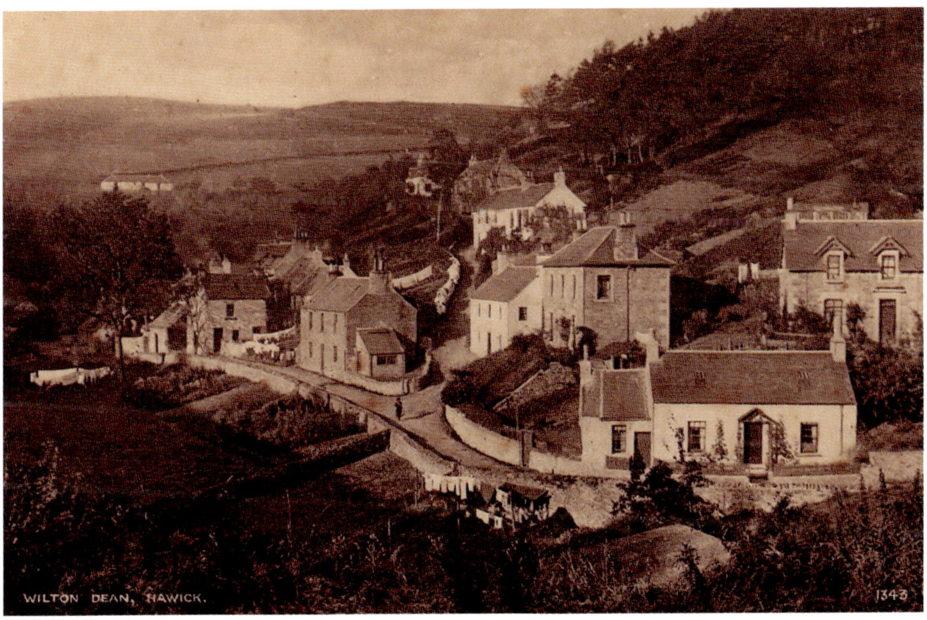

Wilton Dean, as It Looked in 1906

A settlement first appeared on the banks of the Cala Burn in the fifteenth century – the Dean constituting a separate village within Wilton Parish – though it was then known as Langlands Dean, after the estate in which it lay.

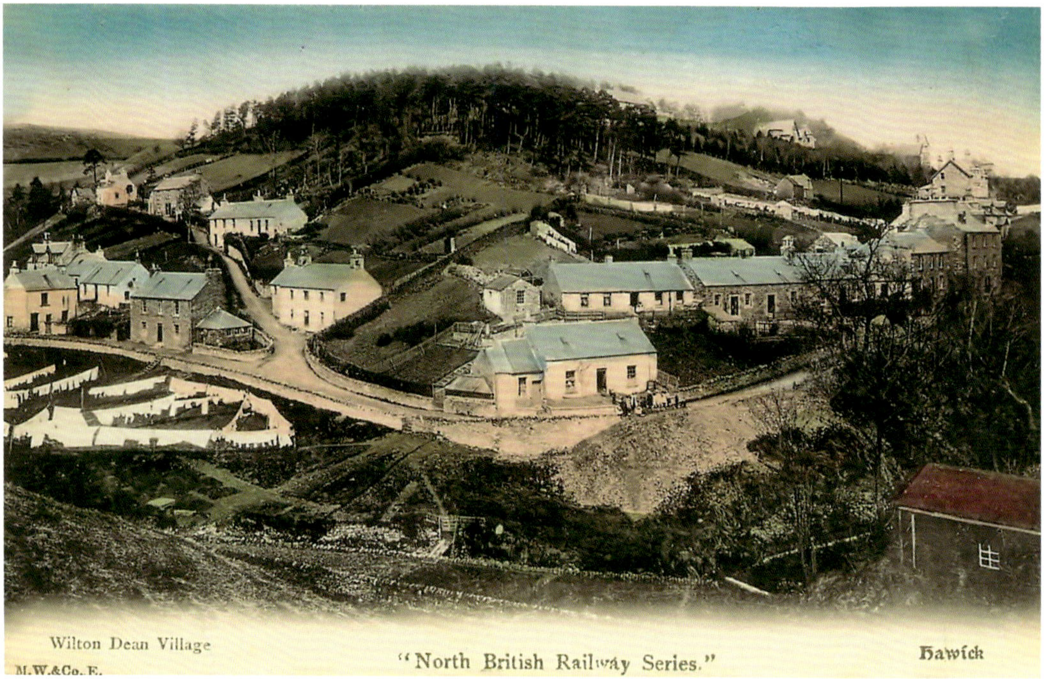

Wilton Dean, Pictured a Few Years Later

The Dean remained a rural village until the turn of the nineteenth century, when a stocking making business, the Dean Spinning Mill, was established. The buildings were demolished by the Laird of Langlands in 1860, whilst the old mill pond was drained to form a drying green.

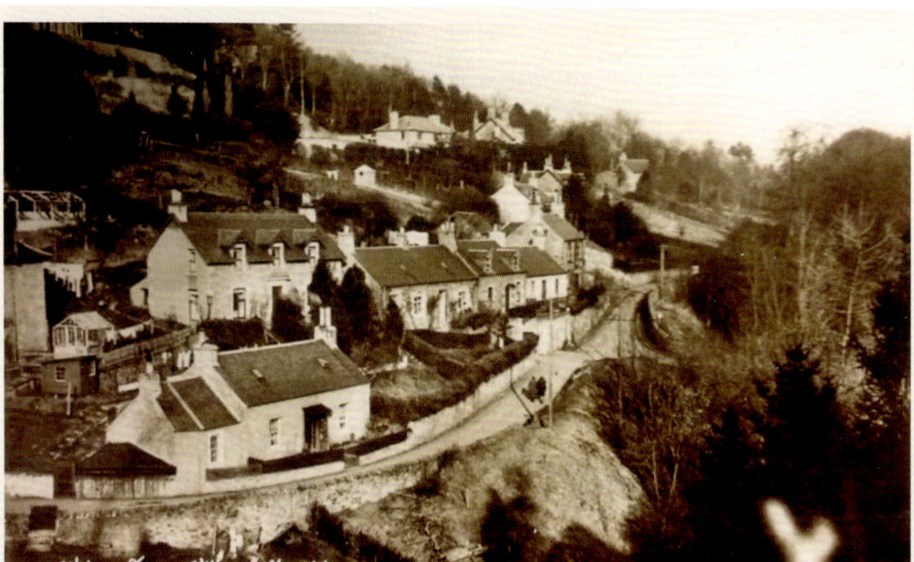

The Dean, Photographed in 1950

As the village's population fell, the nearby school closed its doors in 1937. The building was extensively refurbished in 2005 and now houses the Village Hall.

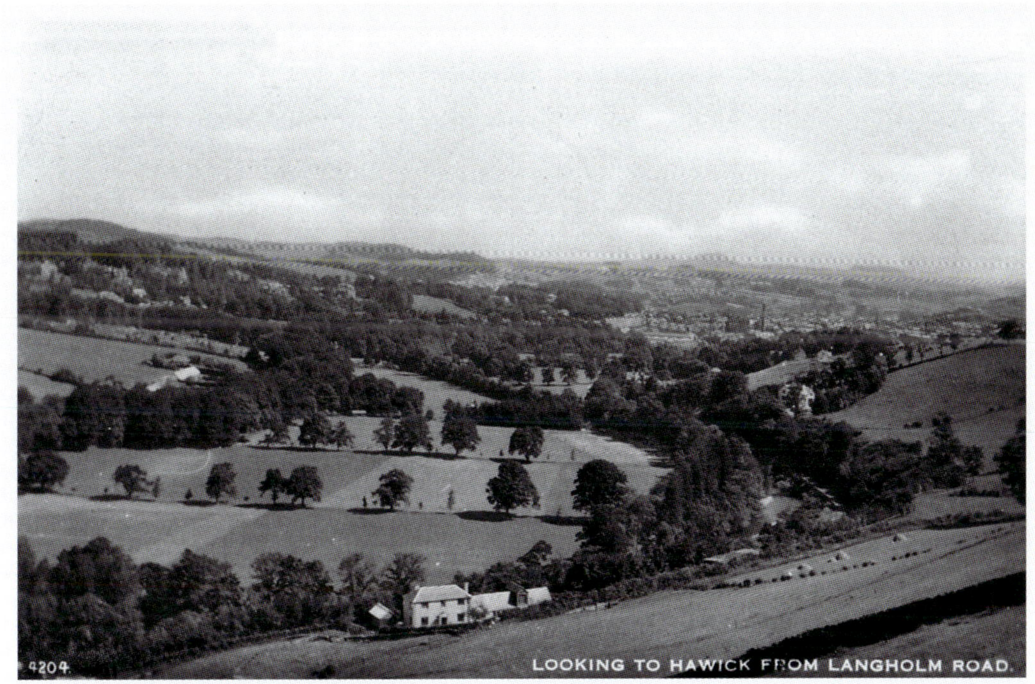

Hawick from above the Lumback Road in the Early 1900s
Housing was built off either side between 1970 and 1980, with further building in recent years. Trespassers were once prosecuted for evasion of the toll bar at Parkdaill.

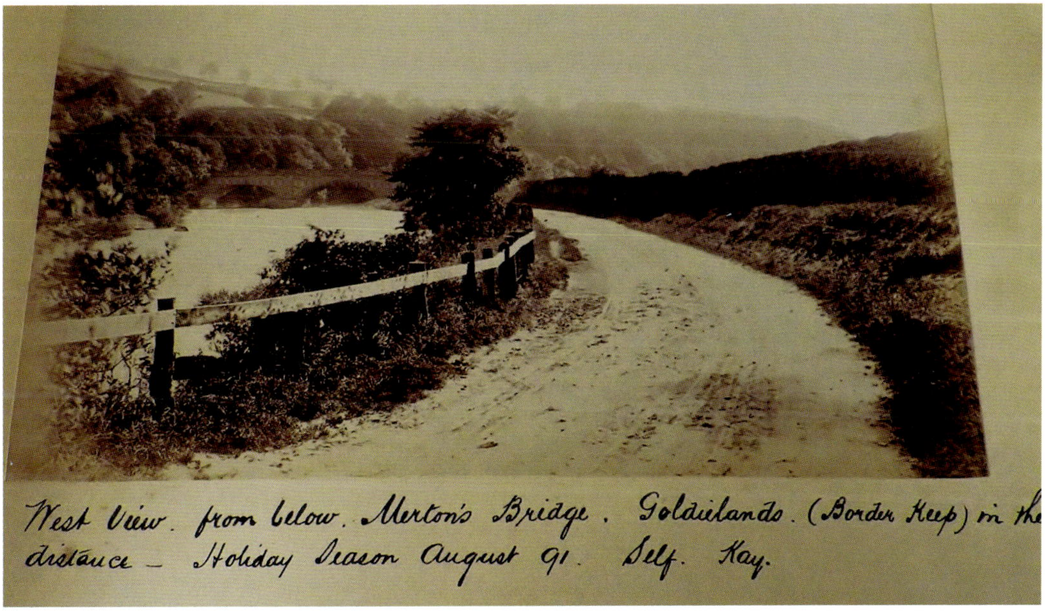

Looking Towards Martin's Bridge and Goldielands on What Is Now the A7, in August 1891
Martin's Brig was built on the site of an earlier ford in 1826 and carries the Roberton road to the Borthwick Valley. It was closed for strengthening works in 2013.

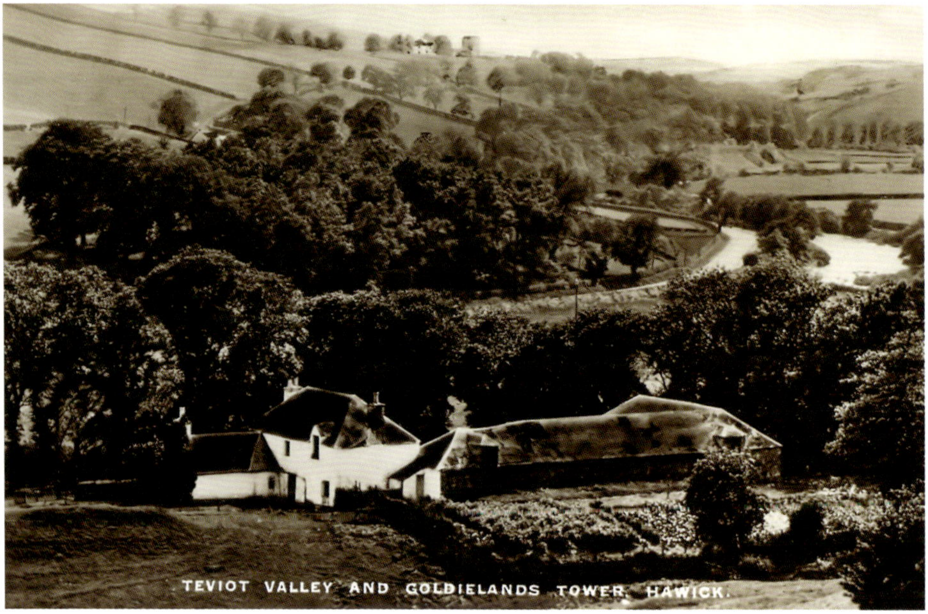

A View of the Teviot Valley, with Goldielands in the Distance, 1929

These lands were possessed by the Scotts of Buccleuch from 1446, when they exchanged half of Branxholme and neighbouring lands with John Inglis of Manor for some in Lanarkshire.

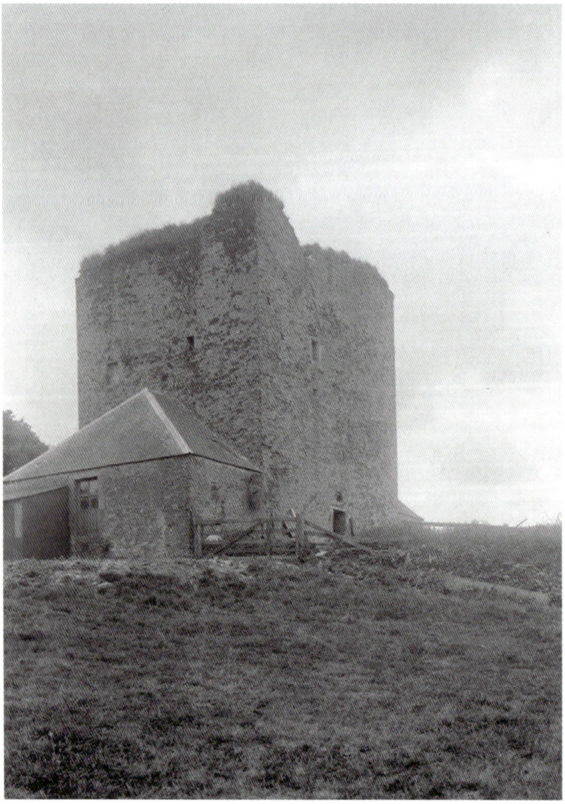

A Closer Look at Goldielands Tower, Captured in 1931

The building is a typical sixteenth-century peel tower, set in a prominent position overlooking the hamlet of Branxholme and its ford crossing. It is now a fairly well preserved ruin on the farm of the same name.

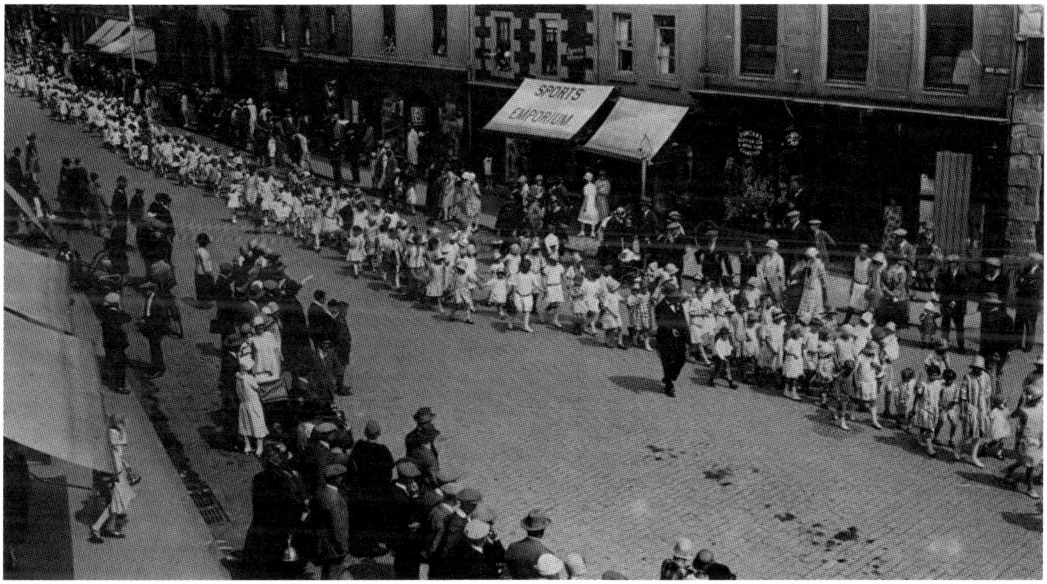

Children Make Their Way to the Vertish for the Annual Sports Day in 1938
Started in 1882 as a kite flying contest for boys under the age of sixteen, other games and races were soon added. A special event held for Queen Victoria's Diamond Jubilee in 1897 attracted a crowd of twelve thousand people.

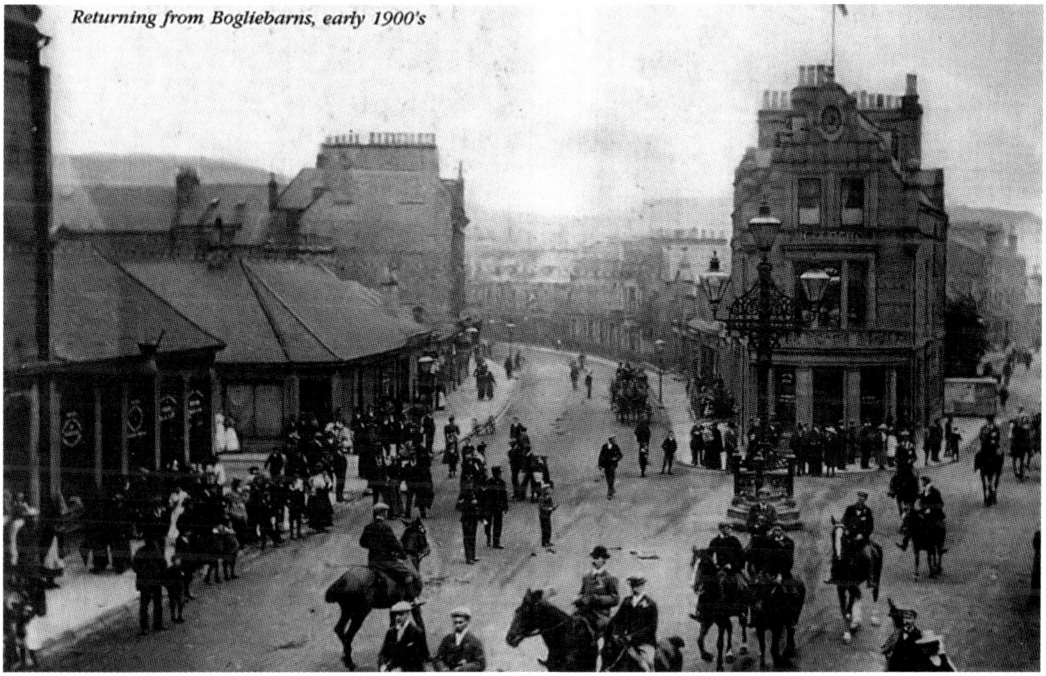

The Cavalcade Returns from Bogliebarns in the Early 1900s
Bogliebarns was a house that once stood on Weensland Road (demolished in 1902). The Cornet led a procession to here from the mid-nineteenth century until 1904. This was briefly revived between 1934 and 1936.

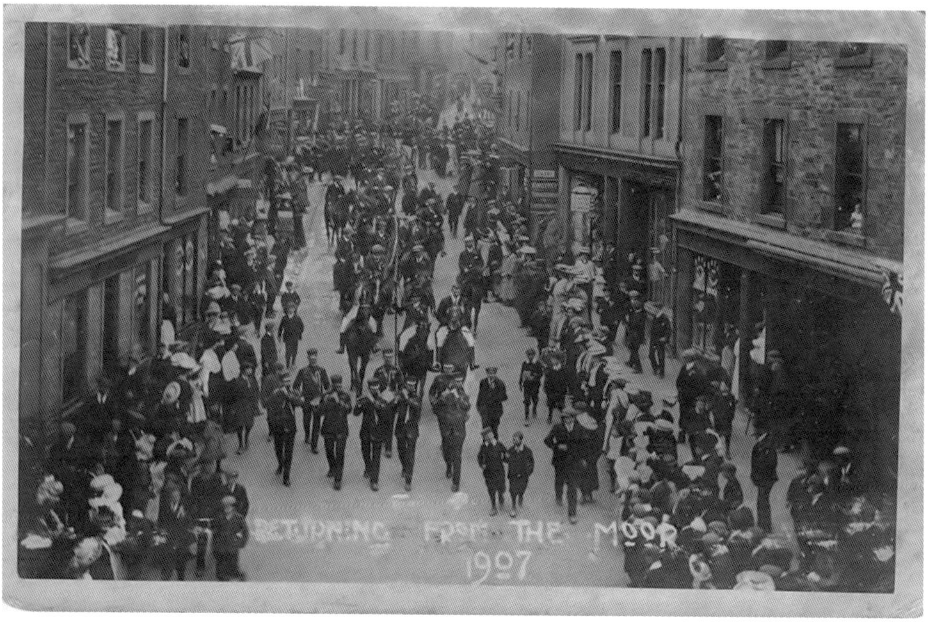

Cornet Thomas 'Tom' Jardine Leads the Cavalcade Back from the Mair, During the 1907 Common Riding
The Howegate's distinct curve follows a post-medieval route into Hawick. Its name derives from the Old English 'haugr' – meaning hill and 'geat' – or entrance, which corrupted over time.

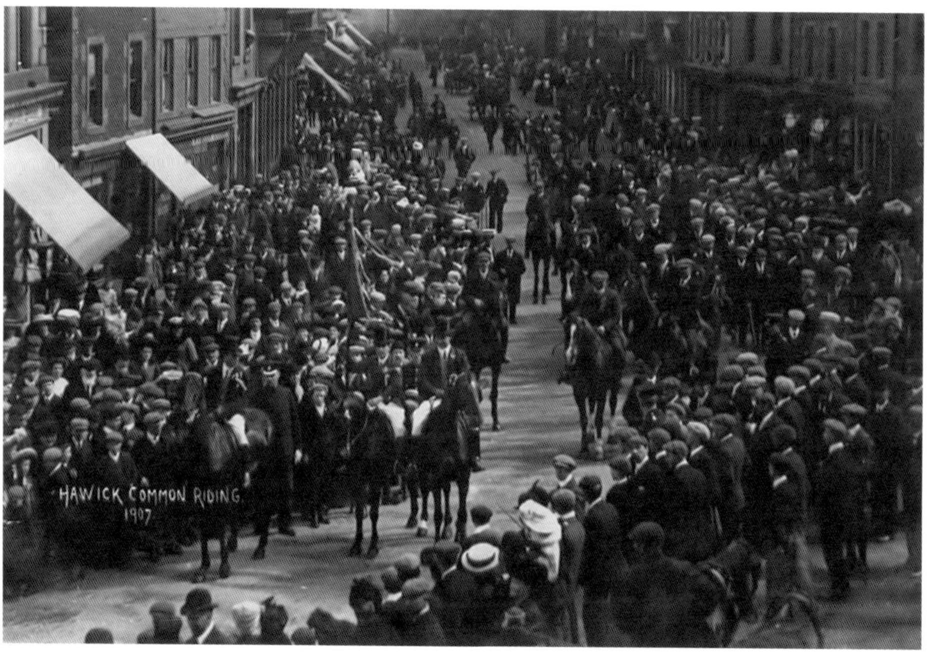

Another Snapshot of the 1907 Common Riding
That Common Riding of 1907 marked the sixth and final time that the actual father of the Cornet performed the role of Acting Father. The Caa' Knowe stakes were run for the first time at the Mair, and the Drums & Fifes first wore their new uniforms.

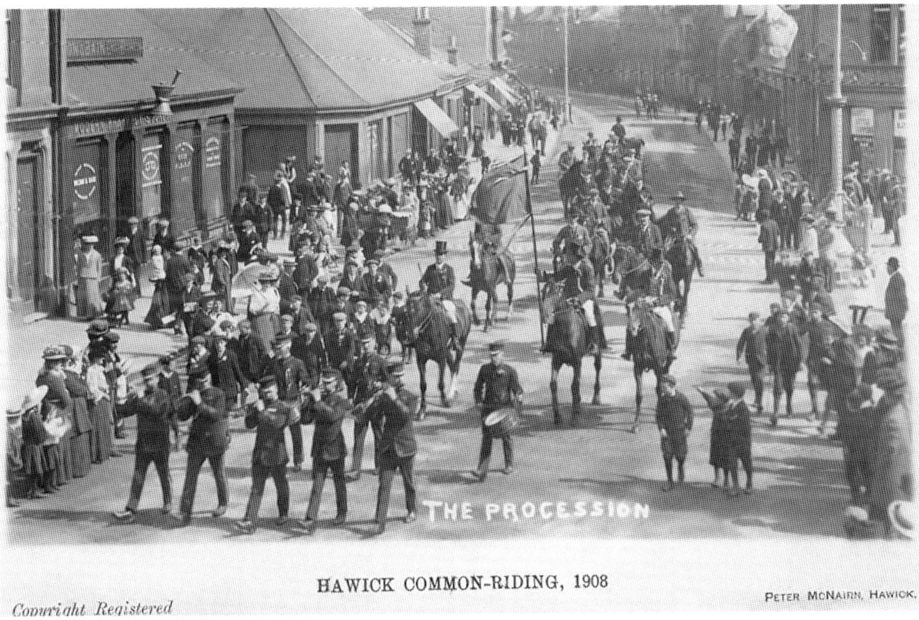

Cornet James Glendinning Leads the Procession past Central Square, 1908
The procession makes its way past a horseless Central Square, led by Cornet James Glendinning in 1908. He was a law clerk in Hawick and also served as Secretary of the Common Riding Committee and as Master of Ceremonies for the Common Riding.

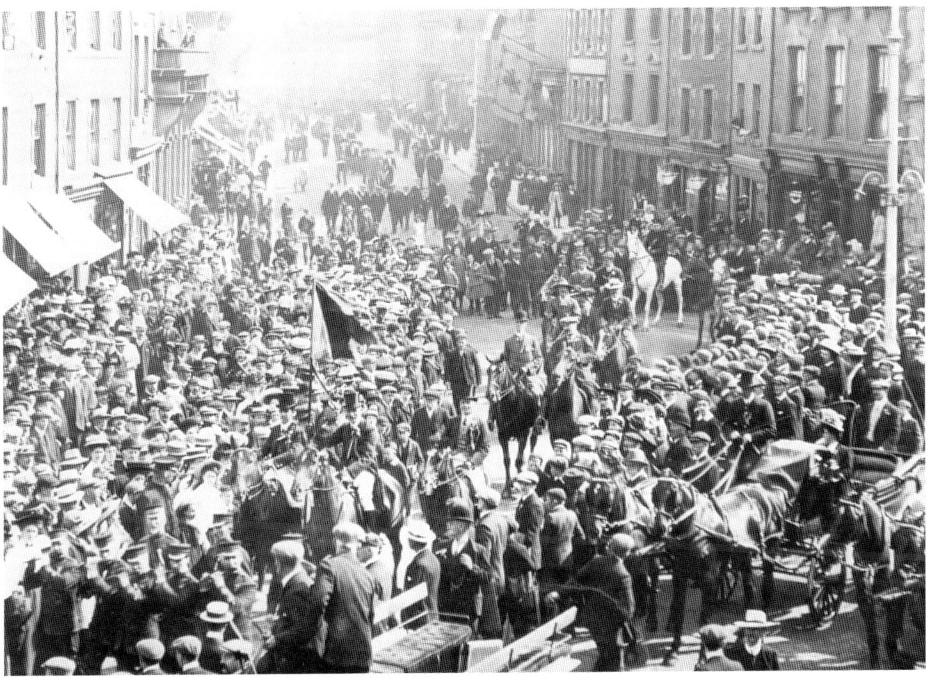

Crowds Gather at Tower Knowe in 1910 to See Cornet A. Douglas Haddon
He was the son of Walter Haddon, who was Acting Father to J. E. D. Murray in 1890. Walter served as secretary of Hawick Working Men's Building and Investment Co. for thirty years.

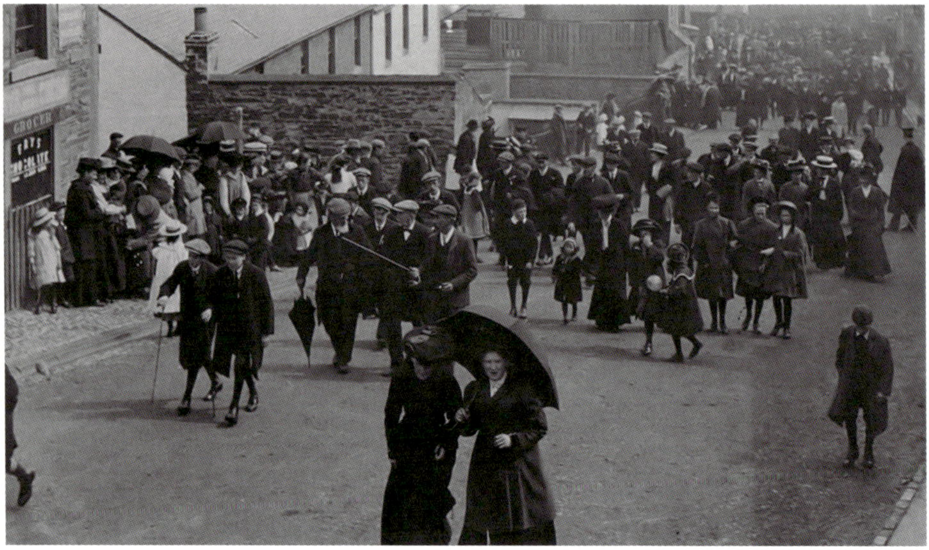

A Large Crowd of Teries Make Their Way to the Mair, During the 1910 Common Riding

The races are one of Hawick's biggest annual attractions. Saint Leonard's has been used exclusively for Common Riding races since 1855.

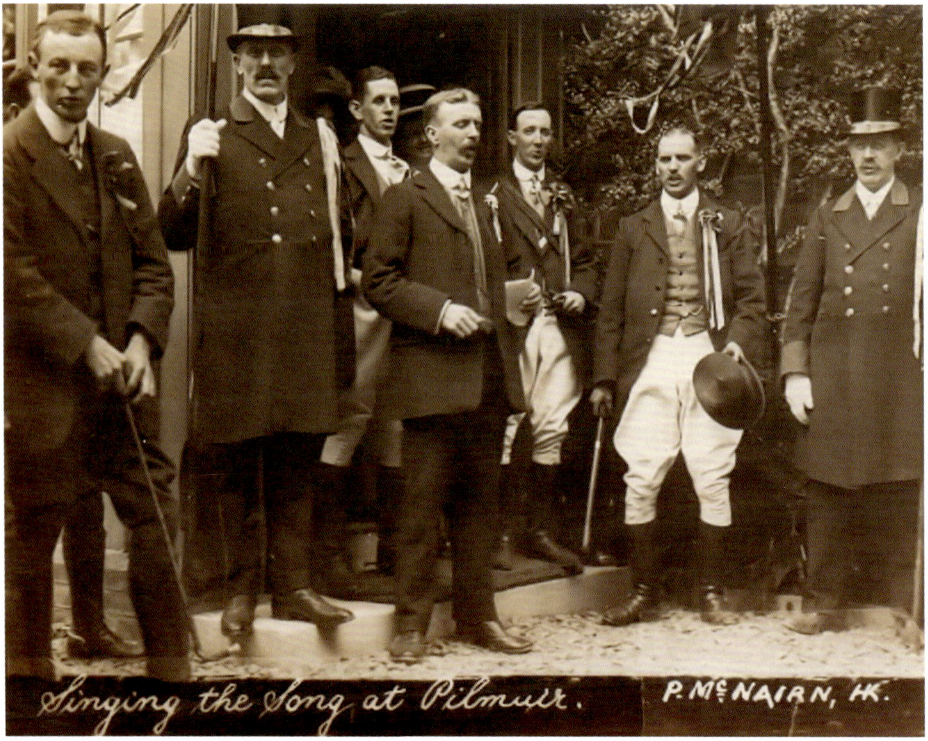

The Principals Sing Teribus at Pilmuir, During the 1911 Common Riding

Cornet William Lockie Thorburn was a hosiery manager, whilst his son Walter Lockie was also Cornet in 1937. Walter went on to be Right-Hand Man twice, the second time after the Second World War, in 1946.

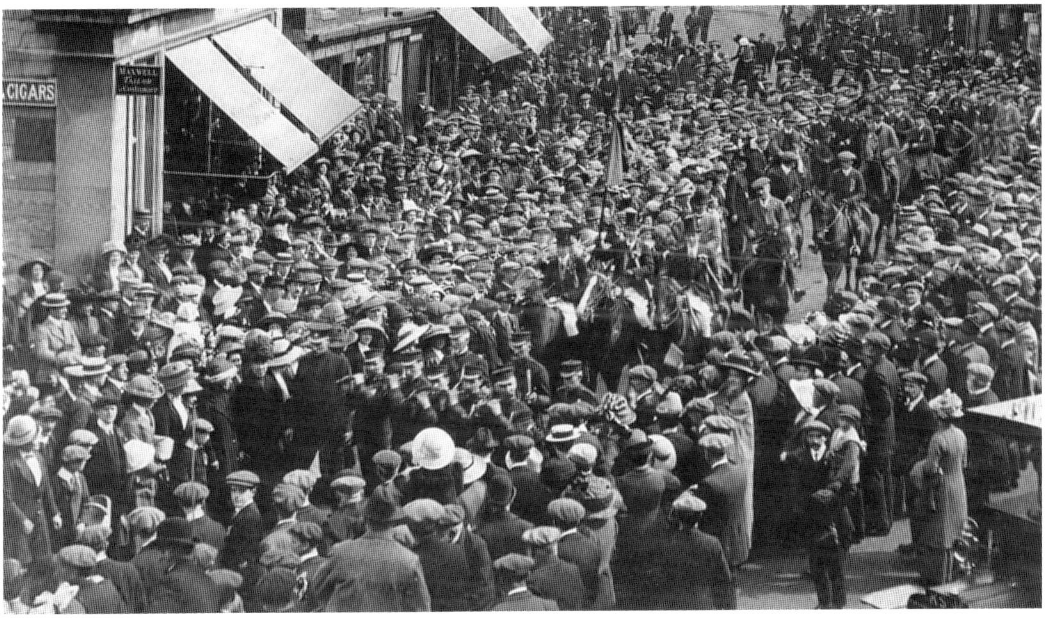

Crowds Flock to See Cornet John D. Bonsor, 1912
Note the old KS (Kelso) registration on the early motor car. John was a hosiery manufacturer who was also Acting Father in 1920.

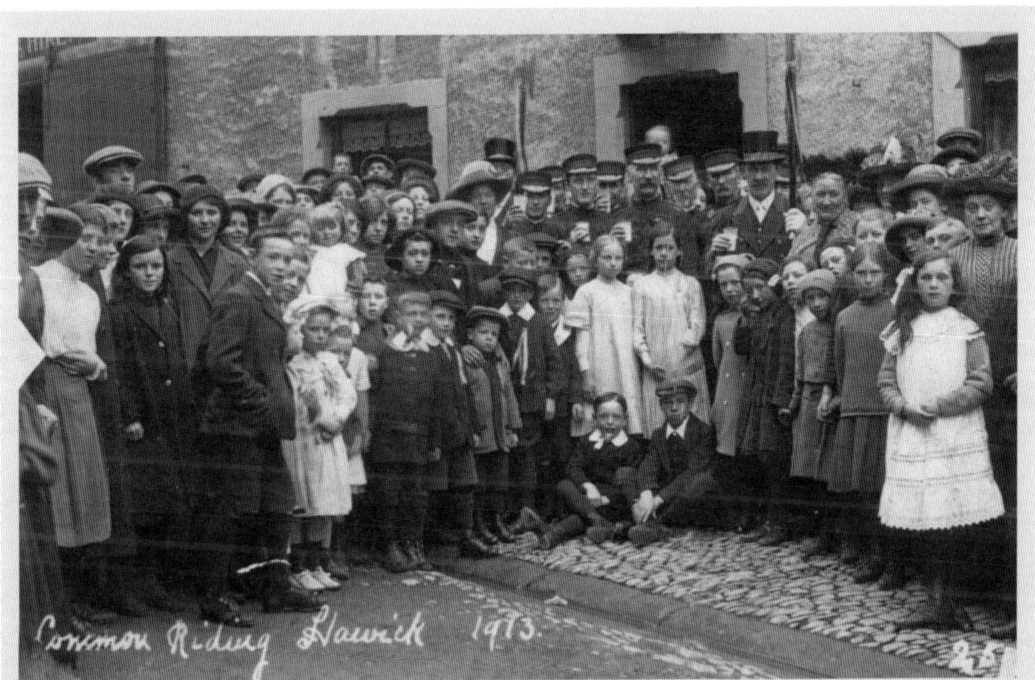

Stopping for a Wee Rum and Milk, Hawick's Traditional Common Riding Tipple, in 1913
That year's Cornet Robert Elder was a joiner by trade. He was sadly killed in France in October 1914 and is buried in the Houplines Cemetery.

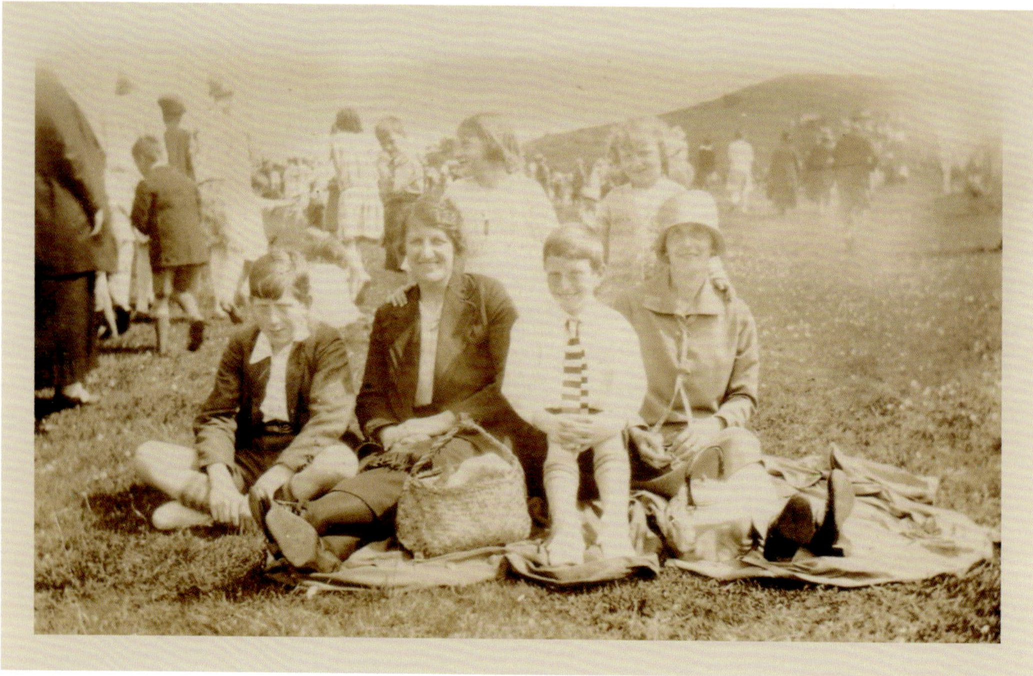

The Goodfellow Family Enjoying a Day at the Mair, During the 1927 Common Riding
That year's Cornet was James Esme Glenny, who lived at Deanfield and flew aeroplanes. The north side of Rosebank Road was built during the summer of that year.

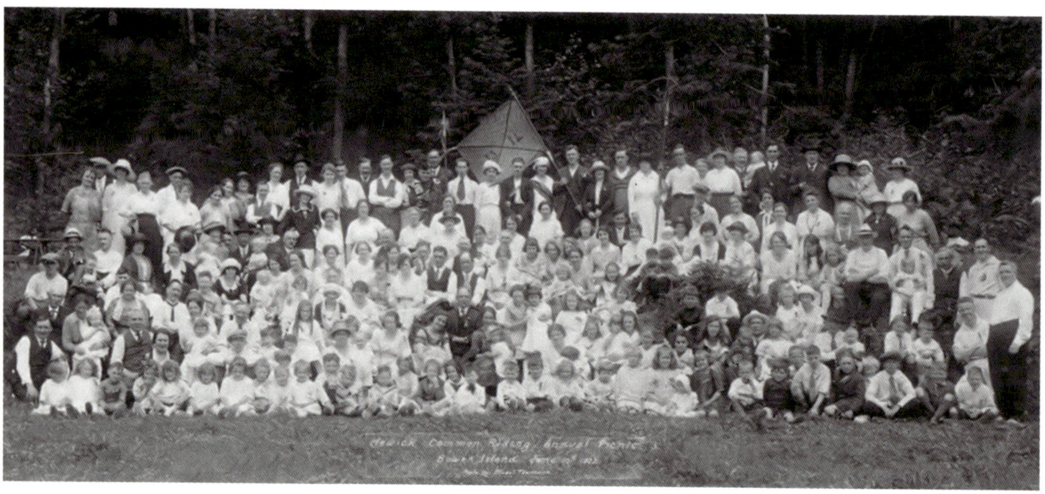

Exiled Teries Celebrate the Common Riding on Vancouver's Bowen Island, June 1922
A Hawick Callants' Club was formed in Vancouver in 1913, but went into abeyance following the Second World War. Plans are afoot to revive celebrations in Ontario in 2015.

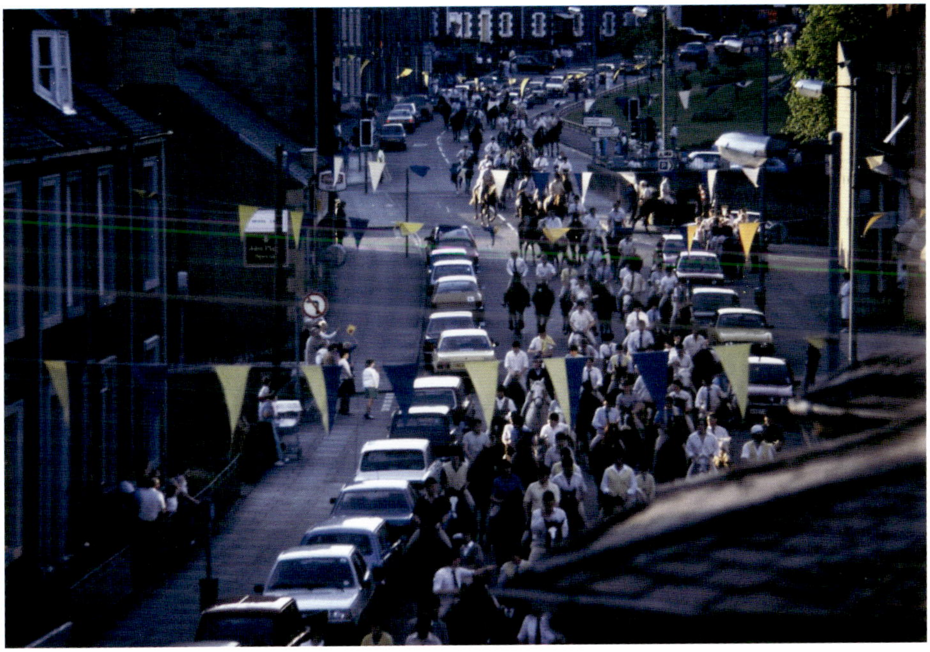

North Bridge Street During the 1985 Common Riding
A cracking shot of North Bridge Street during the 1985 Common Riding. The North Bridge has since closed to traffic and Dovemount Place is no longer a main thoroughfare. The road through Dovemount was built in 1832 to connect the east end of Hawick with Wilton.

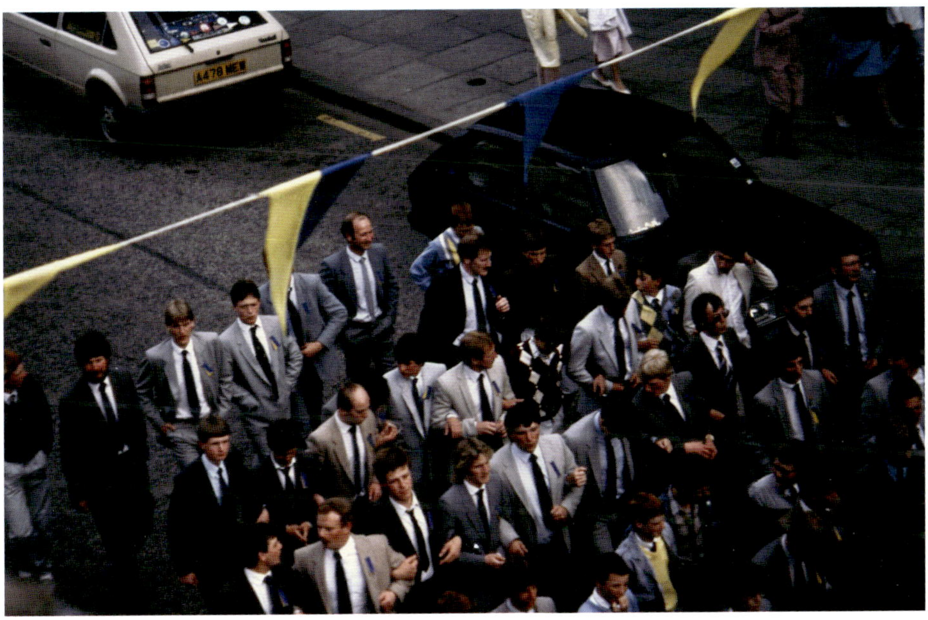

Another Photograph from the 1985 Common Riding, Taken on North Bridge Street
In the crowd is future 1993 Cornet Rory Culton (third row, fourth from right). The gold and blue bunting pays homage to colours of the Hexham Banner, captured by the youth of Hawick at the Battle of Hornshole.

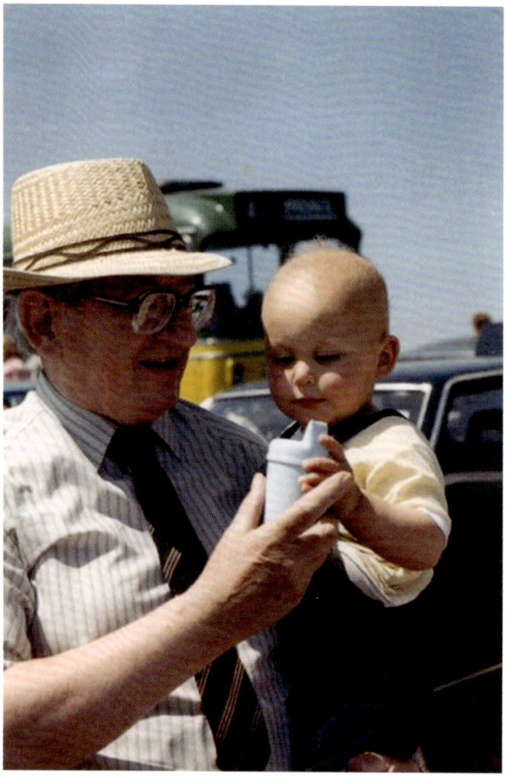

Jimmy Leithhead Holding the Author as a Bairn, up the Mair in the Late 1980s

Jimmy was Acting Father to John Hope in 1963. My family have lived in Hawick for generations and I was raised in Burnfoot.

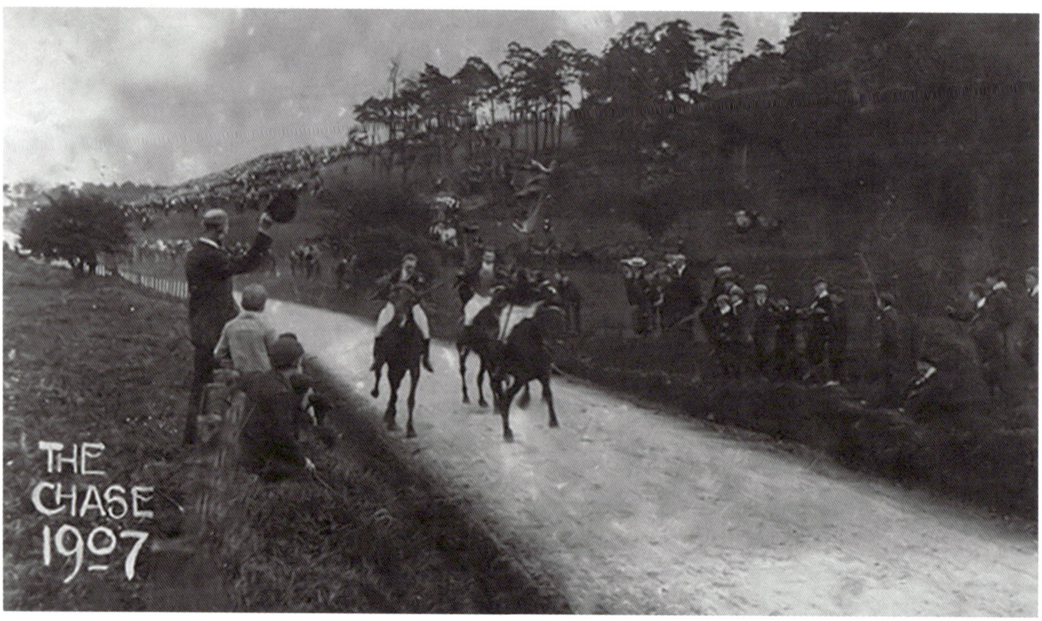

The Chase up the Nipknowes

One of the most thrilling Common Riding traditions, the chase up the Nipknowes, seen here in 1907. Similar events once took place at the Wellogate and the Loan, though the current location was moved from the latter due to a spate of serious injuries and fatalities.

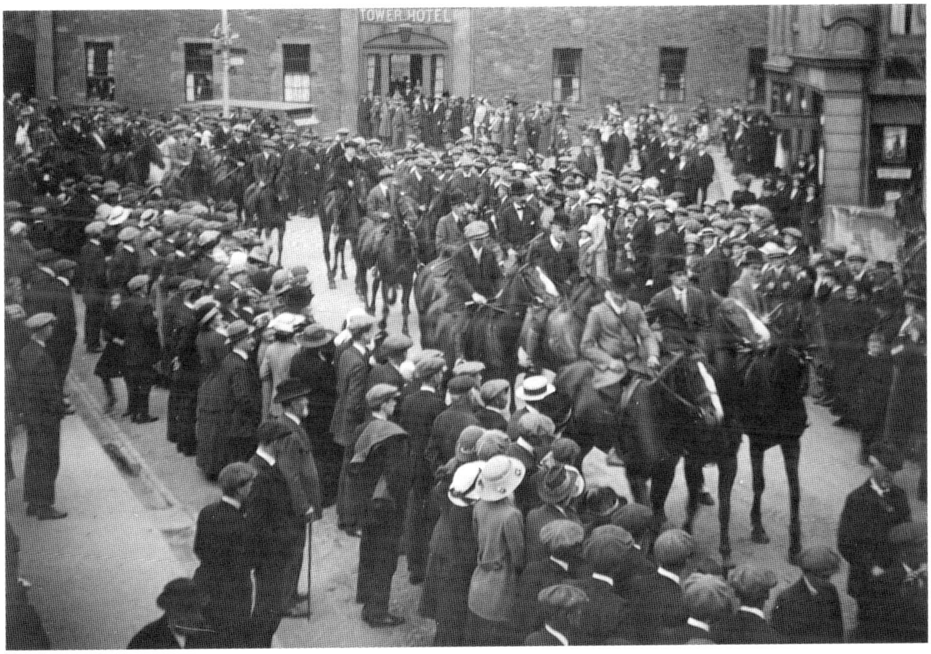

Cornet A. Douglas Haddon at Tower Knowe, 1910

Crowds gather at Tower Knowe in 1910, to see Cornet A. Douglas Haddon (1886-1952). Mr Haddon was a partner in the family law firm and was heavily involved with the Callants' Club, being President in 1928, and Treasurer and Secretary for about forty years.

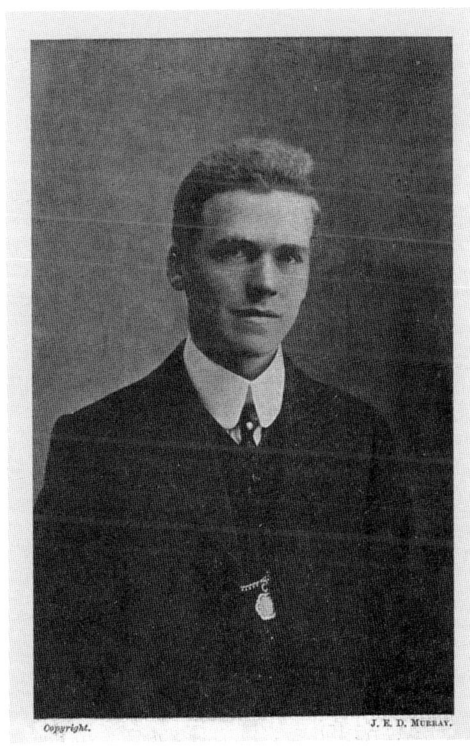

Spirit Merchant James W. S. Robertson Poses for an Official Cornet's Photograph in 1906

He was the first Cornet to be presented with an official racing crop on Common Riding Friday and the first to attend the annual Callants' Club dinner.

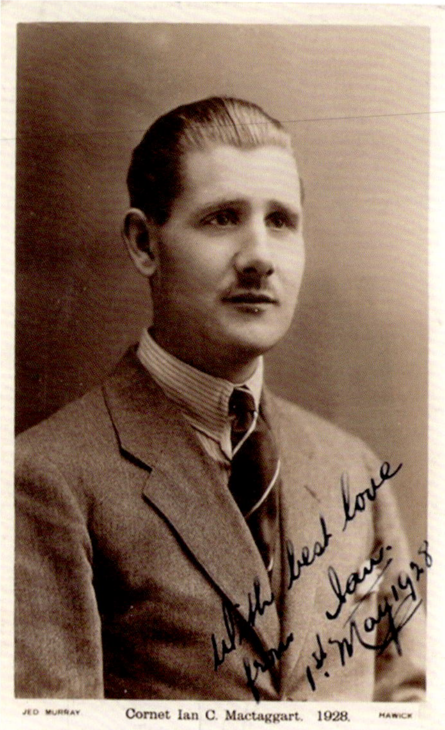

A Signed Official Photograph of 1928 Cornet Ian C. Mactaggart

His year as Cornet was recorded on a silent black-and-white film. He was Managing Director of Mactaggart wool merchants, selling the company in 1964.

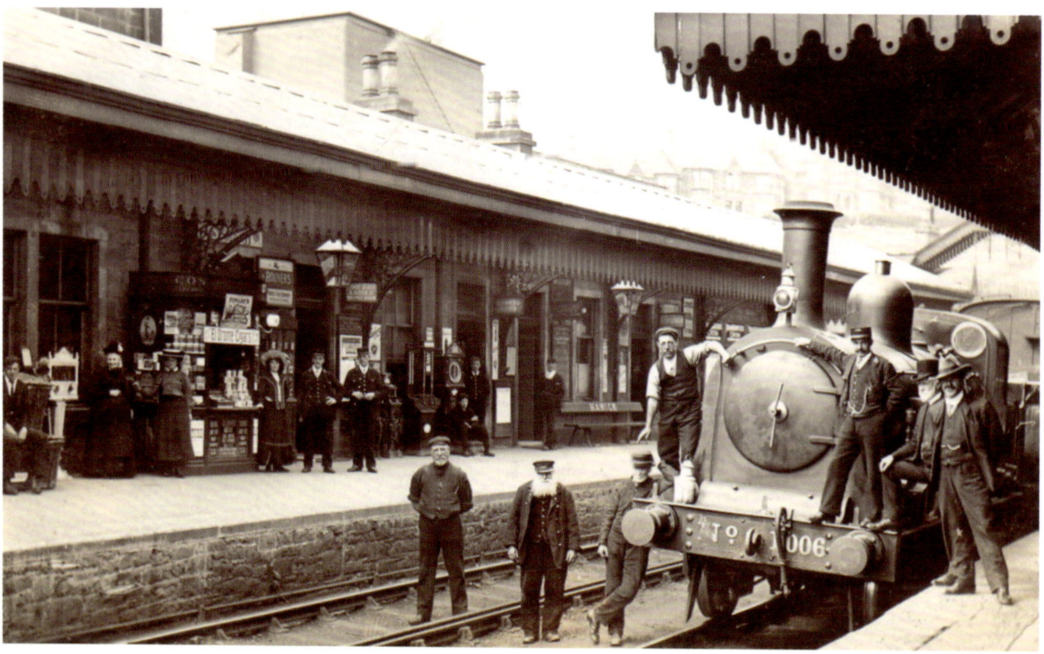

The Highly Decorative Platforms of Hawick Station, Seen Here in 1908

The gentleman standing to the left of the locomotive is William Fairholm (1866–1944). The large two-storey station building comprised a booking office, waiting rooms, toilets, offices and the stationmaster's quarters on the upper floor.

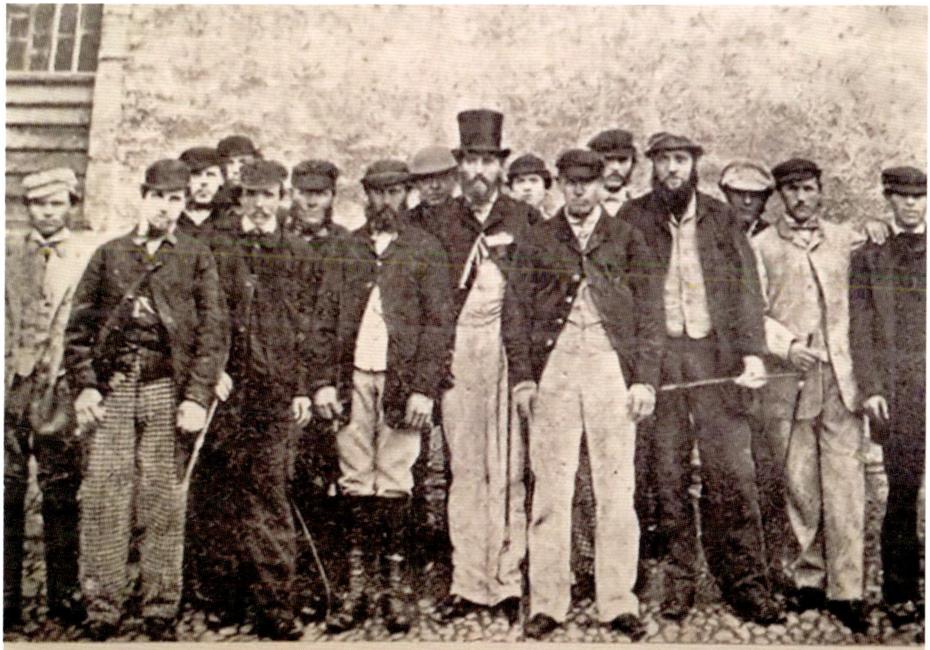

CORNET RICHARDSON AND HIS EQUESTRIAN SUPPORTERS, 1862.

Cornet James Richardson and His Supporters, 1862

Cornet James Richardson (top hat, centre) and his supporters in 1862 – the second earliest known photograph of the Common Riding. It is believed to have been taken on the Saturday, following a spell of drier weather.

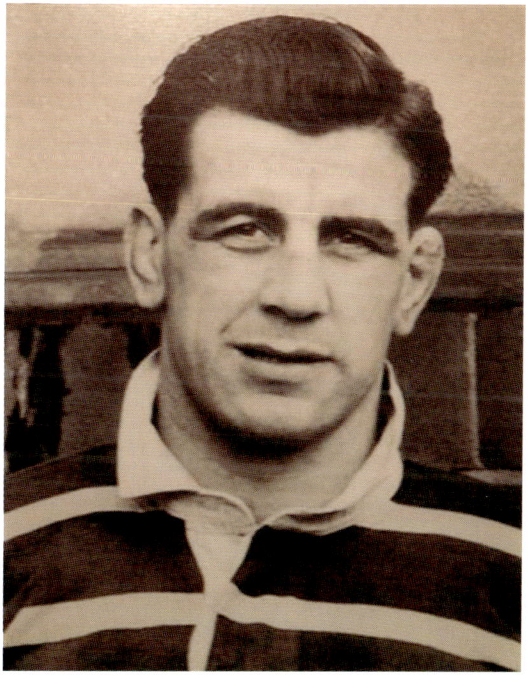

David Valentine

David Valentine was a Rugby Union internationalist and Rugby League World Cup winning captain, a dual-code player. In 2013 he was named the greatest Scottish Rugby League player of all time. The management of the SRL team annually award the Dave Valentine trophy to their player of the year.

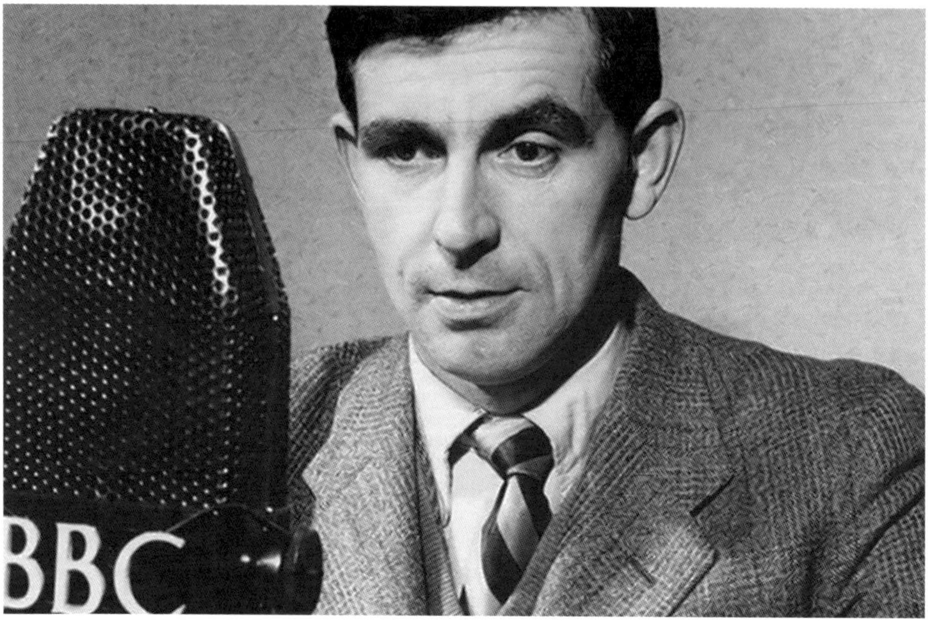

The 'Voice of Rugby'
Bill McLaren, popularly known as the 'Voice of Rugby', was a natural in front of the microphone. Here he is preparing for a broadcast with the BBC in 1955. Bill served with the Royal Artillery in Italy during the Second World War and was later a teacher, journalist and author. He played a Scotland trial in 1947 and was on the verge of a full international cap before contracting tuberculosis.

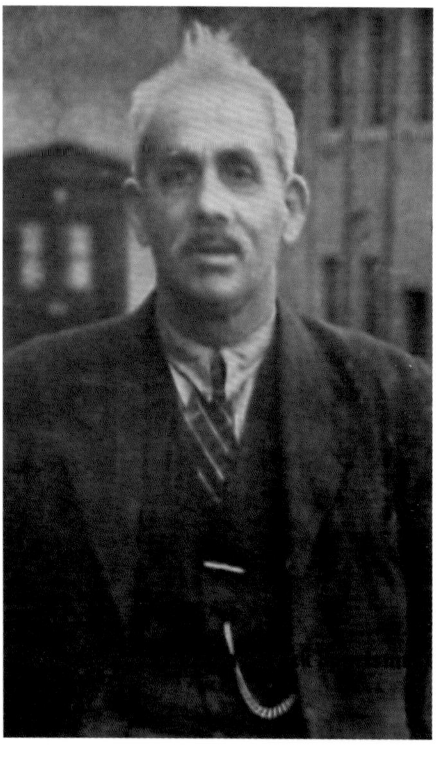

Hugh Rennie McGurk
This author's great-grandfather Hugh Rennie McGurk, who was a Cumberland Wrestling champion, quoiter and a weel-kent boxer. Hugh lived at Lynnwood all his adult life. One of his sons Llewellyn 'Lou' McGurk was among the last to leave the estate.

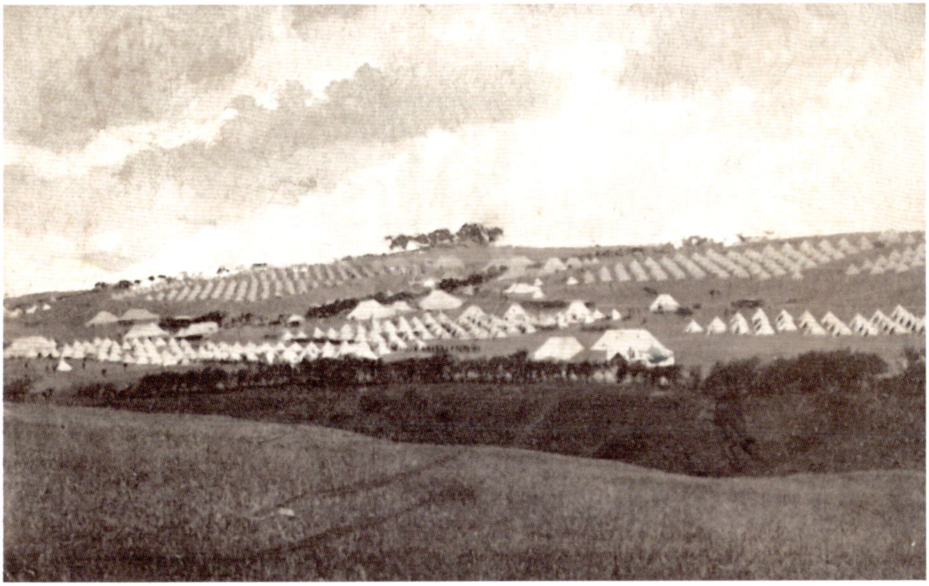

Stobs House, Late Nineteenth Century

The estate bridge to Stobs House, shortly before it was purchased by the War Office in 1903 to develop a training area for the British Army. The barony of 'Stobbs' was granted to Thomas Cranstoun by King David II of Scotland before 1370. It became a stronghold of the Eliott family during the time of the Border Reivers.

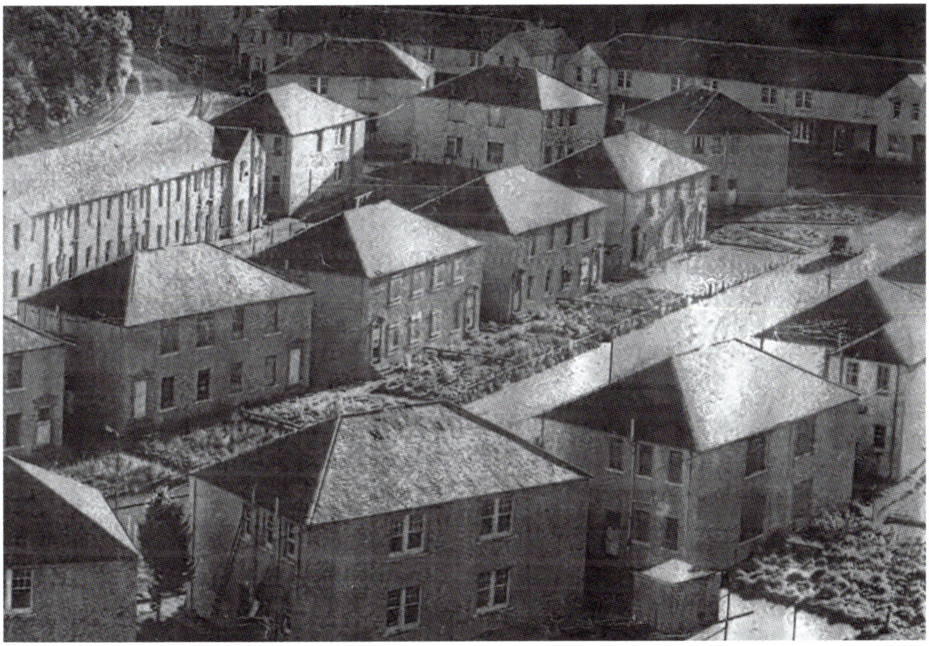

Lynnwood, a Place Dear to Many Teries

This housing estate was built in 1933 on land purchased from the Duke of Buccleuch two years earlier. Gradually falling into a state of disrepair, most homes were demolished in the early 1980s, being completely levelled in 1991 to make way for new housing.

Acknowledgements

The author is indebted to the following people for use of images and information in compiling this book: Douglas Scott (and his ongoing work 'A Hawick Word Book'), Alexander Cunningham, Cameron Reith, Iain H. Scott, Matthew Stoddon, Beverley Cornwell, Sam Cornwell, George Goodfellow, Iain MacIntosh, David Henderson, Derek Robertson, Eva James, John Baker, Mario Taddei, Steven Lothian, Lindsay Bridge, John McNairn, Bernadette McIntyre , Irene Hope, Stewart Donaldson, Jane Mitchell, Colin Fraser, Robert Middlemass and Jon Shek.

The author would also like to thank the following organisations for use of images and information: Project Hawick, Roy G. Perkins & Iain MacIntosh Collection, Scottish Cultural Resources Access Network, Turnbull Clan Association, Maxwell Ancestry, Scottish Screen Archive, J. Valentine & Sons Collection, Lyle & Scott Ltd, Hawick Museum Collection, Archaeology Data Service, Huddersfield Examiner, Ecclesfield School Virtual Community.